jim armstrong
danny franzreb
jd hooge
ty lettau
lifaros
keith peters
paul prudence
jared tarbell
brandon williams

fresh flash
new design ideas with Flash MX

credits

authors
jim armstrong
danny franzreb
jd hooge
ty lettau
lifaros
keith peters
paul prudence
jared tarbell
brandon williams

technical reviewers
marco baraldi
leon cych
steve mccormick
mike sloan
jared tarbell

indexer
simon collins

managing editor
ben huczek

commissioning editor
jim hannah

editors
jon bounds
alan mccann
ben renow-clarke
victoria blackburn

designer
katy freer

author agent
chris matterface

project manager
jennifer harvey

proof readers
kristian besley
cathy succamore

mega shouts out to ben and kristian for being wonderkids!

fresh flash
new design ideas with Flash MX

First printed August 2002

trademark acknowledgements
friends of ED has endeavored to provide trademark information about all the companies
and products mentioned in this book by the appropriate use of capitals. However,
friends of ED cannot guarantee the accuracy of this information.

Published by **friends of ED**
30 – 32 Lincoln Road, Olton, Birmingham, B27 6PA, UK.

Printed in USA.

ISBN 1-903450-99-3

contents

Jim Armstrong

Mr. Armstrong is a 3D animator specializing in Character Animation, Particle FX, and Digital Video. He is a four-time winner of a Creative Excellence Award at the International Web Page Awards, including 'Best Audio/Video', 'Best Personal Site' in 2000 and 'Best Personal Site' in 2001. He was a finalist in 'Best Use of Video' at the 1999 South by Southwest Interactive Festival and a finalist in the Video category at the NY 2002 Flash Film Festival.

Mr. Armstrong is a contributing writer to the 3D Cafe VIP Lounge and a moderator in the 3D Forum at Ultrashock.

Danny Franzreb

Danny is founder and art director of TAOBOT, an award-winning studio that specializes in interactive design and application development. Although studying economics and information technology, he has kept a vivid passion and drive for design. Being able to build what he designs and vice versa, exploration in both directions is what he enjoys most. Currently residing in Alsheim, Germany, Danny has become a frequent writer and speaker on the topic of Flash development, which gives him the possibility to meet inspiring people all over the world. In his spare time, he serves as a moderator for the Flashkit forums and explores new grounds with his personal website franzreb.com.

JD Hooge

After graduating from design school in 2000, I started the Fourm Design Studio with 3 close friends. After 2 years of focus and dedication to design and intraction, the co-founders of Fourm dispersed into different realms of the design field. Now I'm doing freelance work from my home-office, working on a few book projects (like this one), lots of side projects (gridplane.com, infourm.com, miniml.com) and cruising around in Craig's (miniml.com) '76 GMC Sprint.

Ty Lettau

Ty operates a site called soundofdesign.com which explores and experiments with the possibilities of interactive media. He also teaches design part-time at the Milwaukee Institute of Art and Design. Ty has been nominated for three Flash Film Festival Awards and has been featured in several web design magazines. Ty has recently created projects for VectorLounge (vectorlounge.com/04_amsterdam/jam/soundofdesign.html) and Born Magazine (bornmagazine.org/projects/core) as well as writing a chapter for friends of ED's Flash Math Creativity and contributing a photographic essay to the Backyard Project book

Lifaros

I'm an ActionScripter from Chile. There aren't many of us AS coders here, and there aren't many ActionScript jobs either, so I started searching for clients on the Internet instead, developing some applications, and participating on Flash forums. I have a lot of hobbies – sometimes I work as an electronics engineer on satellite communications and networking, sometimes I work as a painter and sculptor. As you can see, I love both art and math. Nowadays I work as a freelance ActionScripter for people from the USA and United Kingdom, and I also develop educational Flash math work for a company in Norway. Lifaros' own experimental flash gallery can be found at www.actionscript.cl

Keith Peters

I live in Lynn, Massachusetts with my wife Kazumi. I've been using flash off and on for nearly three years now, but far more heavily in the last year. My personal site, www.bit-101.com launched in August 2001, and I strive to keep up with the experiment-a-day schedule. It features fairly simple graphics, usually relying on math and scripting to build complex forms and movements.

Paul Prudence

The core of my time as an artist is spent making photons answer the call of simple mathematical equations and abstract forms recombine according to the movement of the mouse. Flash is a uniquely beautiful program that allows a perfect merge of both aesthetic concerns and math. It allows me to produce complex replicative forms with relative ease and system templates that can be tweaked often resulting in surprising new forms. In this sense structures and systems produced are often cultivated over period of succesive generations of code – splicing lines of code from here and there and grafting into new code sequences. I suppose about 10% of my experiments in Flash find their way onto my personal experimental space, transphormetic.com. When not lost in artistic adventure, I pay the rent and keep alive by working as a freelance creative developer/designer - examples of this kind of work can be found at slightspace.com. When working on client projects I am always looking for some artistic use of a commercial solution, the reverse is also true, some creative tinkering in flash can provide solutions for a lot of commercial projects.

Jared Tarbell

When I was 18, I decided to buy a computer instead of a car. That was back in 1991. I did this also in 1993, 1995, and again this year. To me, this is an absolutely brilliant thing to do - at least until cars can fly. Even before I owned a computer, in some form or another, I have been borrowing CPU time on other people's computers. I was initially motivated to use the computer through the text based adventure games my father would write while I was asleep. It became clear to me that a programmer truly could create something from nothing, and this idea intrigued me. I completed the ten year program at New Mexico State University and was rewarded a Bachelor of Science in Computer Science for my participation in their experiment. During this time I learned the value of abstracted programming and why I never want to program at a micro level.

Brandon Williams

Michael Brandon Williams is a freshman year Mathematics major at New York University. His mathematics focus has been real analysis, graph theory, combinatorics, and number theory. His computer science experience is based on programming design, object-oriented programming, and problem solving. In his spare time, he helps run the math forum at Were-Here (www.were-here.com) under the name of ahab, and works for Eyeland Studios (www.eyeland.com) as a games programmer.

The most exciting artwork in any medium is created by those pushing at its boundaries – but what happens when the goalposts are moved? What will the great Flash artists create with the new MX functionality?

With this book, we take a snapshot of exactly what designers are up to with their new toy. From the drawing API, to the fantastic sound and video support, these designers are dying to share their MX-citement and inspirations – and of course their code!

Since we're dealing with techniques and features new to Flash, each of the chapters in this book will teach new script and new techniques. Each new feature is explained, before the chapters dive off into a sea of iterations and design fantasy.

If you're looking to gain a sensitivity to MX, this is the place. All of the chapters have a wealth of script for you to investigate, changing values in some of these FLAs will radically alter the effects – cranking them up will really test the power of your CPU, and maybe your eyes and brain too!

The designers contributing to this book have created sites in previous versions of Flash that have astounded and stretched what people have thought possible with the tool. Now we present the chance to watch over their shoulders as they delve into the new super-powerful Flash MX!

You can download the source files from www.friendsofed.com/books/flash_mx_titles/fresh_flash/code.html

drawing api

keith peters

My whole life I've been into drawing. I have very early memories of family and friends telling me I should be an artist. In my younger days it was cartoon characters from MAD Magazine; in my teens it was realistic portraits of my favorite rock stars. I was never much into color, mostly using pencil or black ink. Although I never went into art as a career, I was always doodling an drawing, and in the mid-90s made a bit of money doing pen and ink illustration.

So it's not surprising that when I first got my hands on a computer in 1986 – a Commodore 128 – I was most awed by its ability to draw pictures. The Commodore's operating interface was itself a form of the BASIC programming language. I soon learned how to draw lines and turn them into basic shapes. I remember the two things that awed me the most on that computer: One was a map of the United States drawn in code. It was an array of coordinates and a FOR loop containing line drawing commands. The other one was a similar array that used the setPixel command to draw a bitmap of a human eye. This idea of using programming and numbers to draw cool pictures really stuck with me, and was the seed that later bloomed into the work I do on www.bit-101.com.

Over the years, I moved to a Commodore Amiga and eventually into the world of the PC. I made a few attempts at learning C and C++ and some other languages. During that time, I had two passions – computers and drawing. But for some reason, they never connected. They were two separate parts of my life. I played around with Paint Shop Pro and various 3D modeling programs, but the computer-art connection never clicked. Even when I first discovered Flash and started doing some web work with it, it was just another interesting application to learn and use and make money with.

Then one day I discovered ActionScript and my whole viewpoint shifted. I was transported back to the days of that Commodore 128 and the US map array. Again, the idea of creating art with numbers and math hit me. But now I had 100 times the computing power, a rich language like ActionScript *and* the ability to put my creations on the web where they could be seen around the world. Yes, I was hooked.

There were still some things in Flash 5 that I was disappointed with. One of the major ones was the ability to draw graphics on the fly. Any graphic element had to be pre-drawn and then attached or duplicated onto the screen. Of course, these limitations led to some amazingly creative workarounds. There is the 100x100 diagonal line movie clip trick, which I consider one of the most elegant things I've ever discovered in Flash. One time there was a little impromptu competition at www.were-here.com, to create an animation using only a 1x1 square pixel and 50 lines or less of code. Using ActionScript to stretch, rotate and color that pixel, some absolutely amazing movies were made. But even with all this creativity, there were still things you just couldn't accomplish.

Then came Flash MX and the new drawing API. The ability to create an empty movie clip on the fly! moveTo, lineTo, beginFill, beginGradientFill! When I saw these commands, I was in heaven!

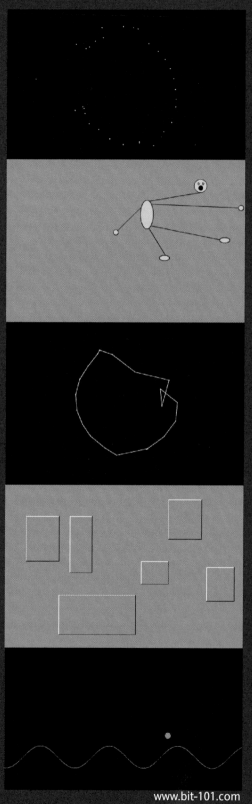

Altered vista

With all that in mind, I wanted to share some fun stuff with the drawing API. I figured that in order to show off the real differences between Flash 5 and Flash MX, I'd have to do something that would be virtually impossible in Flash 5. Note the use of the word "virtually". I've grown cautious of saying *anything* is impossible in *any* version of Flash! But with that disclaimer in mind, one thing you couldn't do easily in Flash 5 was filling a shape. Yes, I got pretty adept at scaling my 100x100 diagonal lines to make various dynamic shapes, but since each line was a separate movie clip, I never figured out how to fill the interior of that shape with a color. But now, it's a snap.

We're going to make a series of undulating movie clips that vary in shape, position and color, to create a virtual landscape.

First let's just get the hang of some of the new tools and make a wavy line.

The commands we'll be initially using are `moveTo(x, y)` and `lineTo(x, y)`. You can think of the line drawing tools as having a virtual pencil. Both of these commands move the pencil to a certain point on the stage, specified by the x and y arguments. `moveTo` is like lifting the pencil up and moving it, `lineTo` is like dragging the pencil from where it is to the new location, leaving a trail. If you don't specify an initial x, y, and use `lineTo` immediately, the line will be drawn from 0, 0. Also, after you draw a line, the pencil will stay where you left it, so if you then draw another line, it will be drawn from that point.

Now we could just issue these commands as is, and draw directly on the stage, or in `_root`. But since we will be making several shapes and positioning them, we'll draw each shape in its own movie clip. Here's another of my favorite features of MX: `createEmptyMovieClip`!

To create an empty movie clip, we merely need to give it a name and a depth. Add this to frame one of the main timeline.

```
createEmptyMovieClip("clip_mc", 0);
```

Now we have an empty movie clip named 'clip' on the stage. You should know that a new movie clip created this way will be located at 0, 0, or the upper left corner of the stage; you won't be able to see it though - there's nothing in it! Let's move it down to the middle of the stage so we can see it when we draw in it. We can keep it on the left edge though, since we'll be drawing left to right.

```
clip_mc._y = 200;
```

Next to define a line style, this is done, surprisingly enough, with the `lineStyle` command. This takes three arguments. The thickness of the line, the color, and its alpha or transparency. We'll make a one pixel black line, 100% opaque.

```
clip_mc.lineStyle(1, 0x000000, 100);
```

A quick note on colors. Any number beginning with 0x is a *hexadecimal* number (also called simply "hex"). Instead of going from 0 to 9, the digits in hex go from 0 to F, A-F standing for 10-15.

```
0   1   2   3   4   5   6   7   8   9   A    B    C    D    E    F
0   1   2   3   4   5   6   7   8   9   10   11   12   13   14   15
```

When you get into double digits, the left hand digit stands for "16's", just like in the decimal system it would stand for "10's". Therefore, in hex, 0x10 (remember the 0x prefix) is 16 decimal. 0xCA would be 218 decimal. (C=12. 12x16=208. A=10. 208+10=218)

Thus the numbers from 0-FF in hex are 0-255 in decimal. These are, coincidentally, the valid values for the color components red, green and blue. When you see a hex value as a color, with six digits after the 0X, the first two digits are the red values, the second two are green and last two are blue. Thus 0xFF0000 is red – it has a value of 255 for red, and 0 for green and blue. Note, that 0x000000 is simply 0, which is black. I usually simply use 0 if I am specifying black as a color.

Now we can start drawing. We don't need to do a `moveTo` since we'll start out at 0, 0 anyway. Remember, that's a 0, 0 as seen from the clip's coordinates, not the main stage. Since the clip is now at 0, 200, that's where the line will appear. We'll start out with a single horizontal line.

```
clip_mc.lineTo(550, 0);
```

You can go ahead and test what we've done so far and make sure it works for you.

Cool, but a single line doesn't give too much room for creativity. Let's break it up into a bunch of short lines. We'll replace the above line with a `for` loop to continuously increase the end point of the new line until it reaches the far end of the stage. Here's the whole thing:

```
createEmptyMovieClip("clip_mc", 0);
clip_mc._y = 200;
clip_mc.lineStyle(1, 0x000000, 100);
for (i=0; i<56; i++) {
    x = i*10;
    clip_mc.lineTo(x, y);
}
```

Here, the variable `i` will go from 0 to 55, giving us an `x` of 0 to 550. This doesn't look any different yet, but next we'll start messing around with the `y` values.

Here we'll just add in a `y` value somewhere between -10 and +10. This just makes a jagged line so we can see the individual segments – just so we know we're heading in the right direction.

```
for (i=0; i<56; i++) {
    x = i*10;
    y = Math.random()*20-10;
    clip_mc.lineTo(x, y);
}
```

Now let's make it a bit smoother. The best way to make a smooth wave is with the trigono-metric function, **sin**. Without getting into a big explanation of trig, this function is used like this:

```
variable = Math.sin(angle);
```

This will return a number from -1 to +1 as the angle goes around in a full circle.

The argument `angle` must be in radians, not degrees. One radian is about 59 degrees. You can convert them by using:

```
radians = degrees*PI/180;
degrees = radians*180/PI;
```

But for our purposes, we won't bother. We'll just use radians. A full circle is 2*PI radians, or about 6.28. So, as angle starts out at 0, `Math.sin(angle)` will return 0. As it gets to one quarter of the way through the circle, or about 1.57 radians, it will return 1. As it hits 3.14 radians, half way through the circle, it's back to 0, then goes through -1 then back to 0 again as it arrives at 6.28 and starts over.

Now we can easily multiply this return factor by any number we want to get a larger range. For example, if we multiply it by 20, we will get a wave going from -20 to 20. This multipli-cation factor will be the amplitude or height of the wave.

How fast we increase the angle will determine how fast it goes through the circle, and how quickly the resulting wave will go up and down. This is the wavelength.
So our `for` loop becomes this:

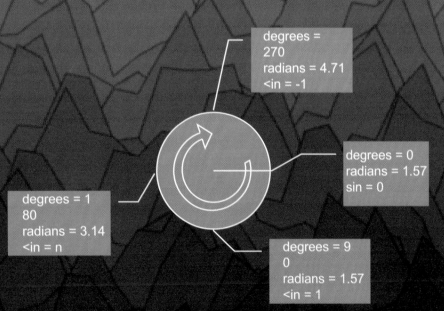

degrees =
270
radians = 4.71
<in = -1

degrees = 0
radians = 1.57
sin = 0

degrees = 1
80
radians = 3.14
<in = n

degrees = 9
0
radians = 1.57
<in = 1

5

```
for (i=0; i<56; i++) {
    x = i*10;
    y = Math.sin(angleX += .3)*20;
    clip_mc.lineTo(x, y);
}
```

There we have it, a nifty little sine wave snaking across the screen. The value of .3 is added to angleX on each frame. This moves the sin through -1 to 1, multiplied by 20 gives us a wave from –20 to 20. Go ahead and change the .3 to some different values, as well as the 20, and see what different waves you wind up with.

Now, let's close it up and color it in. The following lines, right at the end of the file, will turn the single line into a closed shape:

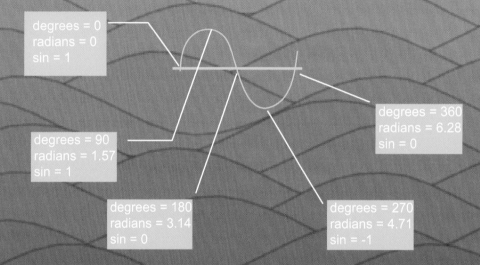

degrees = 0
radians = 0
sin = 1

degrees = 360
radians = 6.28
sin = 0

degrees = 90
radians = 1.57
sin = 1

degrees = 180
radians = 3.14
sin = 0

degrees = 270
radians = 4.71
sin = -1

```
clip_mc.lineTo(x, 50);
clip_mc.lineTo(0, 50);
clip_mc.lineTo(0, 0);
```

Now we color it in. This next bit is the part that was most impossible in Flash 5, but is only two lines of code in Flash MX! We simply tell Flash when to begin the fill, what color and alpha, and when to end the fill, using the two commands:

```
beginFill(color, alpha);
endFill();
```

The `beginFill` should go before you start drawing the lines — preferably right after you define your line style, and the end fill when you are done drawing lines. Color and alpha work the same way as with `lineStyle`. So let's fill it with a nice orange color. Here's our full code so far:

```
createEmptyMovieClip("clip_mc", 0);
clip_mc._y = 200;
clip_mc.lineStyle(1, 0x000000, 100);
clip_mc.beginFill(0xFF7700, 100);
for (i=0; i<56; i++) {
    x = i*10;
    y = Math.sin(angleX += .3)*20;
    clip_mc.lineTo(x, y);
}
clip_mc.lineTo(x, 50);
clip_mc.lineTo(0, 50);
clip_mc.lineTo(0, 0);
clip_mc.endFill();
```

OK, that about does it for making one shape, and that's about all we need to know about the drawing API for this file. All we're going to do now is make a whole bunch of these shapes and stack them up one behind the other.

First we turn the previous code into a function which we assign as an onEnterFrame handler to _root:

```
clipDepth = 0;
_root.onEnterFrame = drawShape;
function drawShape() {
    clip_mc = createEmptyMovieClip("clip"+clipDepth, 1000- clipDepth++);
    clipY = 400-clipDepth*10;
    if (clipY<=0) {
      delete _root.onEnterFrame;
    }
    clip_mc._y = clipY;
    clip_mc.lineStyle(1, 0x000000, 100);
    clip_mc.beginFill(0xFF7700, 100);
    angleX = 0;
    for (i=0; i<56; i++) {
      x = i*10;
      y = Math.sin(angleX += .3)*20;
      clip_mc.lineTo(x, y);
    }
    clip_mc.lineTo(x, 50);
    clip_mc.lineTo(0, 50);
    clip_mc.lineTo(0, 0);
    clip_mc.endFill();
}
```

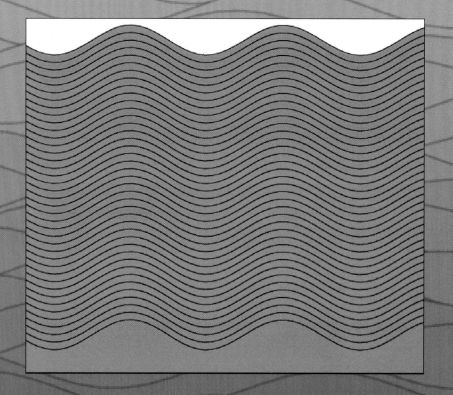

This might need a few points of explanation. First we assign the function `drawShape` as our `onEnterFrame` handler for `root`, so it is executed once each frame. Then in the function itself we create our empty movie clip and assign it to a temporary variable `clip_mc`. The movie clip itself will have a dynamically generated name, because each clip will need a different name. We do this by adding the variable `clipDepth` to the string `clip`. We then assign a depth to the clip of `1000- clipDepth`. This has each successive clip assigned a lower depth, which puts it behind the last one. Also note we automatically increment `clipDepth` at the end.

We then set a variable named `clipY`, which is used to set the clip's `_y` property. This will start out at 400 and subtract 10 each time the function is run. If it becomes zero or less, then we have reached the top of the screen, so we can delete the `onEnterFrame` handler and be done with it.

The last change is the line which sets `angleX` back to 0 for each new clip.

You can test that and see the landscape begin to take shape.

Landscape painting

We now have the basic structure of the file down. From here on in, we are just making it more interesting. First thing you notice is that the waves are all lined up perfectly in rows, which is pretty boring. That's because we reset `angleX` to zero on each loop. Well, heck, let's throw a wave in there too! In the same way we set a wave using `Math.sin` for the wave height, we can put a wave on the horizontal position of the wave by varying what `angleX` starts with. This is probably more easily seen than explained. We change the `angleX` definition to:

```
angleX = Math.sin(angleY+=.24)*3;
```

Hey! Now we're getting somewhere! Now, you might be asking where I got those numbers - .24 and 3. Again, those are the wavelength and amplitude of the side-to-side wave we just created. The number you add to `angleY` determines how fast the wave will go back and forth. The number you multiply the result by will determine how far back and forth it goes. The numbers I used were just ones I got after playing around with until it started to look right. Bear in mind that I may look like a genius because I'm explaining all this so matter-of-factly. You don't see the hours of trial and error that went into it! Anyway, the wave is easier to see in action. To make it a bit easier for you to play around with, I've replaced all the hard-coded values with variables:

```
ampX = 20;
wavelengthX = .3;
ampY = 3;
wavelengthY = .24;
clipDepth = 0;
_root.onEnterFrame = drawShape;
function drawShape() {
    clip_mc = createEmptyMovieClip("clip"+ clipDepth, 1000- clipDepth++);
    clipY = 400- clipDepth*10;
    if (clipY<0) {
      delete _root.onEnterFrame;
    }
    clip_mc._y = clipY;
    clip_mc.lineStyle(1, 0x000000, 100);
    clip_mc.beginFill(0xFF7700, 100);
    angleX = Math.sin(angleY += wavelengthY)*ampY;
    for (i=0; i<56; i++) {
      x = i*10;
      y = Math.sin(angleX += wavelengthX)*ampX;
      clip_mc.lineTo(x, y);
    }
    clip_mc.lineTo(x, 50);
    clip_mc.lineTo(0, 50);
    clip_mc.lineTo(0, 0);
    clip_mc.endFill ();
}
```

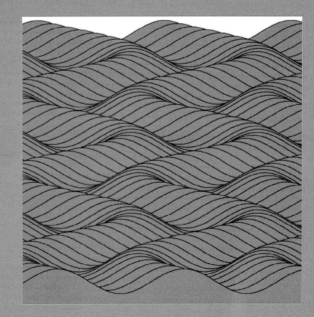

Now let's jack up the fascination factor by throwing another wave into the mix. This will go right alongside our angleX but will be a lower amplitude and higher wavelength. It will serve to make the existing wave a little "bumpy". We'll call this angleX1. We'll also need a amplitude, ampX1, and a wavelength, wavelengthX1. When we create our y value, we'll add both of these waves into it:

```
y = Math.sin(angleX += wavelengthX)*ampX + Math.sin(angleX1 += wavelengthX1)*ampX1;
```

Here's the final code:

```
ampX = 20;
wavelengthX = .3;
ampX1 = 3;
wavelengthX1 = 1.5;
ampY = 3;
wavelengthY = .24;
clipDepth = 0;
_root.onEnterFrame = drawShape;
function drawShape() {
  clip_mc = createEmptyMovieClip("clip"+ clipDepth, 1000- clipDepth++);
  clipY = 400-clipDepth*10;
  if (clipY<0) {
    delete _root.onEnterFrame;
  }
  clip_mc._y = clipY;
  clip_mc.lineStyle(1, 0x000000, 100);
  clip_mc.beginFill(0xFF7700, 100);
  angleX = Math.sin(angleY += wavelengthY)*ampY;
  for (i=0; i<56; i++) {
    x = i*10;
    y = Math.sin(angleX += wavelengthX)*ampX
    +Math.sin(angleX1 += wavelengthX1)*ampX1;
    clip_mc.lineTo(x, y);
  }
  clip_mc.lineTo(x, 50);
  clip_mc.lineTo(0, 50);
  clip_mc.lineTo(0, 0);
  clip_mc.endFill();
}
```

By playing around with that, you can add all sorts of textures to your evolving landscape. I should also mention that if you want to get a slightly higher resolution, you can change the line that says:

```
clipY = 400-clipDepth*10;
```

to:

```
clipY = 400-clipDepth*5;
```

This will put each successive clip a little closer to the last, and make more of them in total.

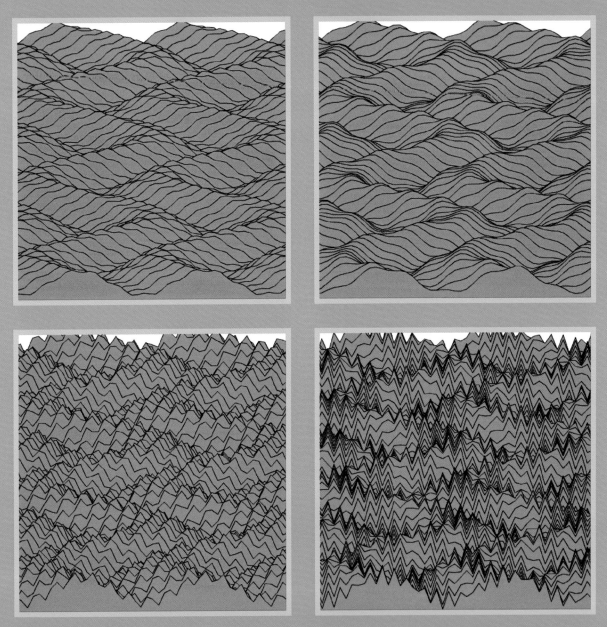

Now, if you've been following along exactly, typing each line exactly as written ... then I bet you are pretty sick of orange hills right about now. Let's throw in some color gradients. You may be aware of the `beginGradientFill` command in the drawing API of Flash MX, but we aren't even going to get into that just yet. We'll just use the color settings in `beginFill` but vary them for each new clip, the same way we are varying the angles.

First, we need to set up six values. These will be the beginning (bottom) and end (top) values for the red, green and blue components of our color fill. Each one of them can be anything from 0 to 255. These will be decided right up at the top of the file. Here's what I chose:

```
r1 = 160;
g1 = 128;
b1 = 32;
r2 = 0;
g2 = 255;
b2 = 96;
```

Right after that, we need to find the difference between the two and divide that by how many shapes we will actually draw. For what we've done so far, we wind up with 40 individual shapes (we start at `_y = 400` and subtract 10 until it's 0. 400/10=40).

```
rinc = (r2-r1)/40;
ginc = (g2-g1)/40;
binc = (b2-b1)/40;
```

This gives us the amount we have to increment each color value each frame/new shape, to go from the beginning color to the end. Remember if you change any of the factors that we used to calculate the 40 with, you'll have to change that number. For example, if you only subtracted 5 from `_y` each frame, you'd wind up with 80 shapes, so you'd use the 80 instead of 40.

Then, just before our `beginFill` line, we need to combine the three color components into a color that Flash can use. Here I'll show you one of my favorite neat little tricks for working with color. It involves bitwise shift operators (<<) and the bitwise OR operator (|)which is the vertical line, often called the "pipe" usually right on the same key as \ on most keyboards). If you want more info on how these work, check the ActionScript Dictionary. Basically, we are using some fancy, but very concise code to combine the three component colors into one large 24-bit number representing a color value. Here's the line:

```
shapeCol = r1 << 16 | g1 << 8 | b1;
```

Now we just use that variable, `shapeCol` in our `beginFill` command:

```
clip.beginFill(shapeCol, 100);
```

Here's what we have so far:

```
r1 = 160;
g1 = 128;
b1 = 32;
r2 = 0;
g2 = 255;
b2 = 96;
rinc = (r2-r1)/40;
ginc = (g2-g1)/40;
binc = (b2-b1)/40;
ampX = 20;
wavelengthX = .3;
ampX1 = 3;
wavelengthX1 = 1.5;
ampY = 3;
wavelengthY = .24;
clipDepth = 0;
_root.onEnterFrame = drawShape;
function drawShape() {
    clip_mc = createEmptyMovieClip("clip"+ clipDepth, 1000- clipDepth++);
    clipY = 400-clipDepth*10;
    if (clipY<0) {
      delete _root.onEnterFrame;
    }
    clip_mc._y = clipY;
    clip_mc.lineStyle(1, 0x000000, 100);
    shapeCol = r1 << 16 | g1 << 8 | b1;
    clip_mc.beginFill(shapeCol, 100);
    angleX = Math.sin(angleY += wavelengthY)*ampY;
    for (i=0; i<56; i++) {
      x = i*10;
      y = Math.sin(angleX += wavelengthX)*ampX
      +Math.sin(angleX1 += wavelengthX1)*ampX1;
      clip_mc.lineTo(x, y);
    }
    clip_mc.lineTo(x, 50);
    clip_mc.lineTo(0, 50);
    clip_mc.lineTo(0, 0);
    clip_mc.endFill();
}
```

The final thing left is to add the increment values to the color component values, so that next time around the colors will be slightly different. This will be done at the end of the drawShape() function, so the values get updated each frame.

```
r1 += rinc;
g1 += ginc;
b1 += binc;
```

One small thing I noticed at this point was the line defining the shape seemed a bit too harsh, giving it a cartoon feel. I just changed the `lineStyle` line to reduce the alpha down to about 20 and that gave it a much subtler effect. Here's the final code up to now:

```
r1 = 160;
g1 = 128;
b1 = 32;
r2 = 0;
g2 = 255;
b2 = 96;
rinc = (r2-r1)/40;
ginc = (g2-g1)/40;
binc = (b2-b1)/40;
ampX = 20;
wavelengthX = .3;
ampX1 = 3;
wavelengthX1 = 1.5;
ampY = 3;
wavelengthY = .24;
clipDepth = 0;
_root.onEnterFrame = drawShape;
function drawShape() {
   clip_mc = createEmptyMovieClip("clip"+ clipDepth, 1000- clipDepth++);
   clipY = 400-clipDepth*10;
   if (clipY<0) {
     delete _root.onEnterFrame;
   }
   clip_mc._y = clipY;
   clip_mc.lineStyle(1, 0x000000, 20);
   shapeCol = r1 << 16 | g1 << 8 | b1;
   clip_mc.beginFill(shapeCol, 100);
   angleX = Math.sin(angleY += wavelengthY)*ampY;
   for (i=0; i<56; i++) {
     x = i*10;
     y = Math.sin(angleX += wavelengthX)*ampX
     +Math.sin(angleX1 += wavelengthX1)*ampX1;
     clip_mc.lineTo(x, y);
   }
   clip_mc.lineTo(x, 50);
   clip_mc.lineTo(0, 50);
   clip_mc.lineTo(0, 0);
   clip_mc.endFill();
   r1 += rinc;
   g1 += ginc;
   b1 += binc;
}
```

Lastly, just to easily explore the infinite possibilities, I assigned random numbers to all of the initialization values. I threw the whole first block of code in an `init()` function, and set that function as the `onMouseDown` handler. Now each time you click the mouse, you draw a new landscape. This kind of thing keeps me busy for hours (OK, I'm strange!). Here's what that looks like:

```
onMouseDown = init;
function init() {
    r1 = Math.random()*128;
    g1 = Math.random()*128;
    b1 = Math.random()*128;
    r2 = Math.random()*128+127;
    g2 = Math.random()*128+127;
    b2 = Math.random()*128+127;
    rinc = (r2-r1)/40;
    ginc = (g2-g1)/40;
    binc = (b2-b1)/40;
    ampX = Math.random()*20+5;
    wavelengthX = Math.random();
    ampX1 = Math.random()*10;
    wavelengthX1 = Math.random()*3;
    ampY = Math.random()*10;
    wavelengthY = Math.random();
    clipDepth = 0;
    _root.onEnterFrame = drawShape;
}
```

This is simply followed by the existing `drawShape` function.

Run this full screen, do a screen capture and save it as a picture file – it makes some cool wallpaper!

My final version can be downloaded from www.friendsofED.com as `project_01.fla`.

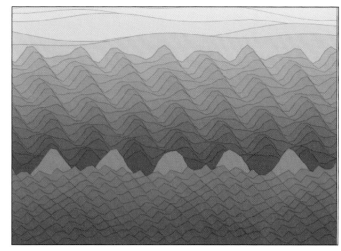

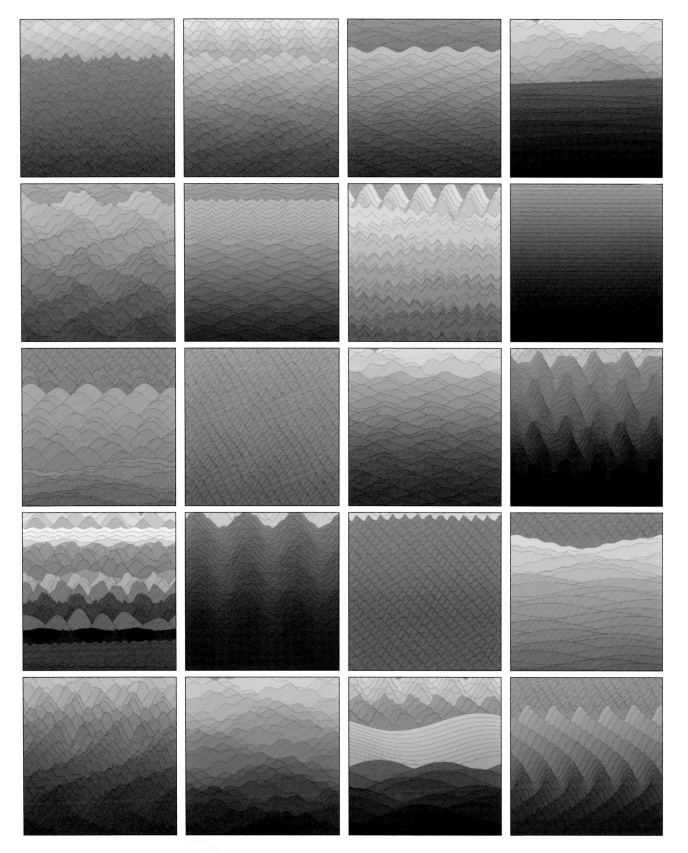

Curving

The next function I wanted to check in on is curveTo. As exciting as lineTo is, as you can see, it can take a lot of work to make a simple curve. Luckily our friends at Macromedia threw in this command for us to play with.

curveTo works a lot like lineTo. It starts wherever the pen happens to be located and draws a line to the coordinates you give it. However, you must specify an additional two parameters, which make up a control point which tell the curve how to curve.

As they say, a picture is worth a thousand words, and a SWF has got to be worth several times more than that. We'll specify two points, x1, y1 and x2, y2 and draw a curve between them. For the control point, we'll use the mouse pointer (_xmouse, _ymouse). In a new FLA, start with this code in the first frame:

```
x1 = 100;
y1 = 200;
x2 = 450;
y2 = 200;
onEnterFrame = function () {
   _root.clear();
   _root.lineStyle(1, 0, 100);
   _root.moveTo(x1, y1);
   _root.curveTo(_xmouse, _ymouse, x2, y2);
};
```

That was pretty simple. Now I know my first reaction when I first created this was, "Hey, the curve isn't *touching* the mouse! That's not too useful." So, I'm guessing you might be thinking the same thing. The control point is where the curve goes *toward*, but is not meant to hit there. Of course, it would be a lot more useful in many cases if you could dictate exactly where the curve landed. But how?

I wasn't the only one with that question. It started popping up around the web and the answer I got came from Robert Penner. If we call the point we want to hit as targetX, targetY, and the point we feed to curveTo is controlX, controlY, here's the formula:

```
controlX = targetX*2-(x1+x2)/2;
controlY = targetY*2-(y1+y2)/2;
```

Now, if I understood that in a lot more depth, I would no doubt explain how it works in a lot more detail. What I do know is that it does work, and it's pretty simple to remember. Now let's see it in action. We'll just apply that formula using the mouse position as a target. We'll compute the control point and feed that into curve to. Try this:

```
x1 = 100;
y1 = 200;
x2 = 450;
y2 = 200;
onEnterFrame = function () {
   controlX = _xmouse*2-(x1+x2)/2;
   controlY = _ymouse*2-(y1+y2)/2;
   _root.clear();
   _root.lineStyle(1, 0, 100);
   _root.moveTo(x1, y1);
   _root.curveTo(controlX, controlY, x2, y2);
};
```

Jello ball

Now that we have the basics down, let's move on to the next major project. This is a re-creation of one of the first files I did when I got a hold of Flash MX. I was excited about the possibilities of using curveTo to make dynamic, organic shapes. I feel like this project really captured what I wanted to do with it. Basically, we'll be using a series of curveTo's to create a circle. Then, by manipulating the points that make up the curves, with a little springiness thrown in, we'll have a big blob of jiggling jello on our screen. Don't worry though, it washes off easily.

First we will need a bunch of points and a way of storing them. There are a number of ways of doing this. I chose to use objects. An object is simply a piece of data stored in memory. But unlike a simple variable, an object can contain additional variables, called properties or members, and can even contain its own functions, usually called methods. To begin with, our objects will just have two properties, x and y. Later we'll add a few more, and the object will neatly package up all the data we need for each point.

There are two main ways of creating an object. One is to use the new keyword and say:

```
point = new Object();
```

You can then go along and create its properties:

```
point.x = 275;
point.y = 200;
```

...etc.

The alternate way is a bit of a shortcut that lets you create your object and its properties and even assign values to them all at once. You simply list your properties in curly braces. Use a colon after each property to specify its value, and separate each property/value pair with a comma:

```
point = {x: 275, y: 200};
```

We're going to make a set of 20 point objects and rather than assigning each to a variable, we'll store them in an array. This makes it very easy to handle them sequentially in a loop. In fact we'll use a loop to fill the array in the first place. Here's our code to begin with:

```
MAX = 20;
points_array = new Array();
for (i=0; i<max; i++) {
    points_array[i] = {x:275, y:200};
}
```

We just created a new array called points_array, and looped through it 20 times, filling each element with a new object. Each object has an x and y property, set to 275 and 200, center stage.

So far so good, but so what? We need the points arranged in a circle to begin with, not clumped together in the middle of the screen. We will space the points out evenly around the circle. So we'll need to slice our circle up like a pie. We need to know how big each slice is (what its angle is).

We already decided on 20 points, which makes 20 slices. A circle is 360 degrees, so 360/20 is 18 degrees each. Cool, but remember that Flash likes radians, not degrees. We could figure it in degrees and then convert, but that eats up a lot of overhead, and we may need all the CPU cycles we can spare once we start plugging in the formulas below. So if you can grit your teeth and deal with radians just a bit more, it'll pay off. It's good practice anyway!

OK, as we covered earlier, a circle is PI*2 radians, so one slice is Math.PI*2/20. Don't even worry what that number turns out to be. You don't need to know it or ever even see it. We'll just stick it in a variable and be done with it.

```
oneSlice = Math.PI*2/max;
```

There we go. Remember that max was already set to 20, so we'll use that. If we later decide we want more or less points, we just change the value of max, and everything will be recalculated and work just fine.

The last thing we need to decide before we plot our points is how big the circle will be. How's 200 pixels sound? OK. So its radius will be 100. We'll just define that at the start:

```
radius = 100;
```

Now we can jump back into the FOR loop and get some real values for each point's x and y. For this we use some basic trigonometry. You survived through it last time, so be brave. First off, we'll determine the actual angle of the current point. We know what oneSlice is, and the variable i, keeps track of the number of times through the loop, or how many slices there are. So the current angle will be i times oneSlice.

```
angle = oneSlice*i;
```

Now here's the trig part. These are the formulas for getting the x and y values of a point when you know its radius and angle:

```
xPosition = cos(angle) * radius
yPosition = sin(angle) * radius
```

Now that will give you the position in relation to the center of the circle. We'll have to add something that to align the center of the circle with the center of the screen. Here are those formulas fit into our current file so far:

```
MAX = 20;
oneSlice = Math.PI*2/max;
radius = 100;
points_array = new Array();
for (i=0; i<max; i++) {
    angle = oneSlice*i;
    xPos = Math.cos(angle)*radius+275;
    yPos = Math.sin(angle)*radius+200;
    points_array[i] = {x:xPos, y:yPos};
}
```

Now, you can go ahead and test that if you want, but you're not going to see much. Remember that an object is just a collection of data. It doesn't have any visual representation on the screen, unlike a movie clip, which usually contains graphic content. We need to take those x and y values and feed them to some drawing API command to see what we've created.

We'll start with the `lineTo` command we already know. We just do a `moveTo` to the first point, then loop through the array, drawing lines to each successive point, starting at point 1. When we finish the array, we draw one final line back to point 0 and close up the circle. Just type this in after all the last piece of code:

```
_root.lineStyle(1, 0, 100);
_root.moveTo(points_array[0].x, points_array[0].y);
for (i=1; i<max; i++) {
    _root.lineTo(points_array[i].x, points_array[i].y);
}
_root.lineTo(points_array[0].x, points_array[0].y);
```

Test that to see the circle come into being.

Now let's alter it to use `curveTo`. We'll start out the same, moving to point 0 and starting a for loop. But since `curveTo` takes four parameters, representing two points, we need to increment our counter by 2 each loop. We'll basically be using one point as the control point, and the next point as the end point of the curve.

We also need to change the test portion of the for statement to read `i<max-1`, so that in our final curve we have one point left over as a control point when we loop back to point 0. This code should be pretty self explanatory if you've followed everything so far:

```
MAX = 20;
oneSlice = Math.PI*2/max;
radius = 100;
points_array = new Array();
for (i=0; i<max; i++) {
    angle = oneSlice*i;
    xPos = Math.cos(angle)*radius+275;
    yPos = Math.sin(angle)*radius+200;
    points_array[i] = {x:xPos, y:yPos};
}
_root.lineStyle(1, 0, 100);
_root.moveTo(points_array[0].x, points_array[0].y);
for (i=1; i<max-1; i += 2) {
    _root.curveTo(points_array[i].x, points_array[i].y, points_array[i+1].x,
points_array[i+1].y);
}
_root.curveTo(points_array[i].x, points_array[i].y, points_array[0].x,
points_array[0].y);
```

This draws a somewhat smoother circle. Not perfect, but smooth enough for our purposes. We could use the trick from above – of placing the curve directly on the target point. That would create a near perfect circle. But again, that would also eat up a lot more processor time. So this somewhat lumpy circle will suffice!

Next up, we will throw in some springiness and really bring the circle to life.

For something to spring, we need a few more pieces of information:

A target – where is it moving *to*?   `xTarget, yTarget`
Velocity – how fast is it going, and in what direction?   `xVelocity, yVelocity`
Springiness – how much does it bounce?   `SPRING`
Damping – how soon will it come to rest?   `DAMP`

Each of our 20 points will be independently springing around. Therefore each will need its own target and its own individual velocity. Both of these factors will be broken down into x and y factors, giving us an `xTarget, yTarget, xVelocity, yVelocity`. In addition, each point will have its own springiness factor, so each will behave slightly differently. This will simply be defined as *spring*. These will become five additional properties that we will define when creating each object. So, going back to where we create the point objects, the line becomes:

```
points[i] = {x:275, y:200, xTarget:275, yTarget:200,
xVelocity:0, yVelocity:0, spring:Math.random()*.5+.5};
```

Here we reverted back to having x and y initialize center screen. We also used those values for the target, and set the velocities to zero. Spring was set to a random number between .5 and 1.0.

Now we jump up to the top of the file and throw in a damping factor. This will be a global factor, the same for all points. Here's the first part of the file (I temporarily removed the drawing part):

```
DAMP = .9;
MAX = 20;
oneSlice = Math.PI*2/max;
radius = 100;
points_array = new Array();
for (i=0; i<max; i++) {
    points_array[i] = {x:275, y:200, xTarget:275, yTarget:200,
    xVelocity:0, yVelocity:0, spring:Math.random()*.5+.5};
}
```

Now we have all the pieces in place, it's time to animate them. The way a spring works is that an object is attracted to a target point. The further away from the point it is, the stronger the attraction. Imagine snapping a rubber band. The further you pull it, the more power it snaps with. This force pulling it towards the target can be called acceleration. Acceleration essentially changes and object's velocity. The acceleration in a spring is proportional to the distance from the object to the target.

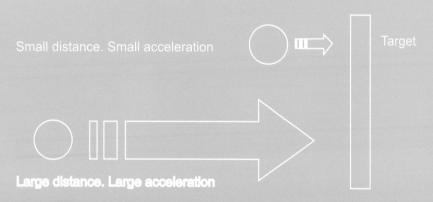

Small distance. Small acceleration

Target

Large distance. Large acceleration

So, the next thing we need to do is determine the point's target x and y. This will be the same code we used earlier to simply space the points in a circle, except we will use the mouse coordinates as a center point. Thus, the points will be *trying* to form a circle around the mouse cursor. We want this to be updated as the mouse moves, so we stick it in an onEnterFrame function:

```
_root.onEnterFrame = function () {
  for (i=0; i<max; i++) {
    angle = oneSlice*i;
    point = points_array[i];
    point.xTarget = Math.cos(angle)*radius+_xmouse;
    point.yTarget = Math.sin(angle)*radius+_ymouse;
  }
};
```

This should all look pretty similar. We just created a temporary variable, point, to use as we calculate the various properties. It's just easier to type "point" than "points_array[i]" over and over – and it is also executes faster in Flash!

Now that we've calculated the xTarget and yTarget for each point, we need to find the distance between the current value of each point and its target. Then we multiply this by the spring factor to come up with an acceleration for that point. This sounds harder than it looks. This code goes right in the for loop after we define the targets:

```
accelX = (point.xTarget-point.x)*point.spring;
accelY = (point.yTarget-point.y)*point.spring;
```

Distance (point x Target - point x)

point_x ● ○ xTarget

accelX will be a fraction of the distance from point to the target

We just subtract the current value from the target value and multiply times spring.

Now that we have the acceleration values, we simply add them to the point's current velocity. The next two lines are:

```
point.xVelocity += accelX;
point.yVelocity += accelY;
```

Here's what we have so far in our onEnterFrame function:

```
_root.onEnterFrame = function() {
  for (i=0; i<max; i++) {
    angle = oneSlice*i;
    point = points_array[i];
    point.xTarget = Math.cos(angle)*radius+_xmouse;
    point.yTarget = Math.sin(angle)*radius+_ymouse;
    accelX = (point.xTarget-point.x)*point.spring;
    accelY = (point.yTarget-point.y)*point.spring;
    point.xVelocity += accelX;
    point.yVelocity += accelY;
  }
};
```

This gives us the updated velocity with which the point will move. It is now time to throw in that damping factor. In the real world, nothing will bounce around forever. Even that ultra-mega-super-ball you bought as a kid eventually came to a rest – after freaking out the cat, knocking over your mom's vase and whacking Dad in the head. That's because as it moved and bounced, it was losing energy. If we don't take that into account, we won't have a jello ball, we'll have chaos.

To simulate the loss of energy, we just multiply each velocity factor by damp, which we've set at .9. Therefore, on each frame, the velocity becomes 90% of what it would have been, and eventually the points will slow down and come to a stop. Again, it's simpler when you see it:

```
point.xVelocity *= damp;
point.yVelocity *= damp;
```

Now we simply add the current velocity to the point's x and y values:

```
point.x += point.xVelocity;
point.y += point.yVelocity;
```

We're just about done. All we need to do now is close up that `for` loop and plug back in the drawing code we made before. Here's the final code:

```
DAMP = .9;
MAX = 20;
oneSlice = Math.PI*2/max;
radius = 100;
points_array = new Array();
for (i=0; i<max; i++) {
   points_array[i] = {x:275, y:200, xTarget:275, yTarget:200,
   ➥xVelocity:0, yVelocity:0, spring:Math.random()*.5+.5};
}
_root.onEnterFrame = function() {
   for (i=0; i<max; i++) {
     angle = oneSlice*i;
     point = points_array[i];
     point.xTarget = Math.cos(angle)*radius+_xmouse;
     point.yTarget = Math.sin(angle)*radius+_ymouse;
     accelX = (point.xTarget-point.x)*point.spring;
     accelY = (point.yTarget-point.y)*point.spring;
     point.xVelocity += accelX;
     point.yVelocity += accelY;
     point.xVelocity *= damp;
     point.yVelocity *= damp;
     point.x += point.xVelocity;
     point.y += point.yVelocity;
   }
   _root.clear();
   _root.lineStyle(1, 0, 100);
   _root.beginFill(0x00ff00, 100);
   _root.moveTo(points_array[0].x, points_array[0].y);
   for (i=1; i<max-1; i += 2) {
     _root.curveTo(points_array[i].x, points_array[i].y,
     ➥points_array[i+1].x, points_array[i+1].y);
   }
 _root.curveTo(points_array[i].x, points_array[i].y,
 ➥ points_array[0].x, points_array[0].y);
   _root.endFill();
};
```

Notice I also plugged in a `beginFill` and `endFill` statement there to give the ball some color. You now have a bouncing blob of green jello. Actually, when you first start it up, it may look more like a Picasso painting until it settles down a bit. Try messing around with some of the key variables — notably the `spring` definition and the `damp` variable, to control just how springy it is, and how quickly it quiets down. This file is `project_02.fla`, for download.

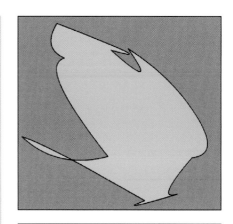

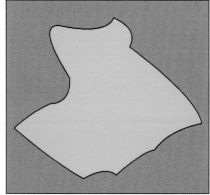

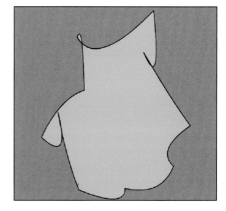

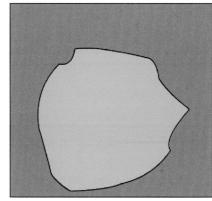

Gradients

The only thing we haven't hit upon in the drawing API yet is gradient fills. If everything else wasn't enough, this adds some real power to your ability to make stunning visual effects with Flash MX.

To create a gradient fill, we simply replace the command `beginFill` with `beginGradientFill`. OK, maybe my use of the word "simply" was a bit premature – in `beginFill` we merely had to specify a color and an alpha; with a gradient fill, we have to define we get to define the type of fill, the colors used, the alphas, the ratio of one color to the other(s), and the direction and size of the fill. Specifically, here is the syntax of the command:

```
beginGradientFill(fillType, colors, alphas,
ratios, matrix);
```

OK, let's take them one at a time...

- **fillType** – this is a string, which can be either radial or linear. A radial gradient will expand like a circle, with one color in the center and other colors radiating outward in rings. A linear fill goes from left to right, starting with one color and blending into any others as it goes.

- **colors** – this is an array, each element holding a color value. You can create an array using the new operator, and then fill it in:

```
col_array = new Array();
  col_array[0] = 0xff0000;
  col_array[1] = 0x0000ff;
```

    ...or you can use the shortcut method, similar to the object creation shortcut, just use square brackets, filling in each color value separated by commas:

```
col_array = [0xff0000, 0x0000ff];
```

You can define as many colors as you want for the array. If you just use two, it will blend from the first to the second. If you add more, you will get bands or rings of different colors.

- **alphas** – this is also an array. This array will contain values from 0 (fully transparent) to 100 (opaque). It is important to note that the colors, alphas and ratios arrays all must have exactly the same amount of element. You can't have two colors and three alphas. If you try, your gradient will fail silently, leaving you wondering what happened.

- **ratios** – another array. This accepts values from 0 to 255. These show where in the gradient each color starts. For a linear gradient, 0 is the far left and 255 is the far right of the gradient. If you have two colors and want them to blend evenly across the entire width, enter [0, 255]. If, for example, you entered [0, 128], the first color would blend completely into the second about half way across the gradient. Radials work the same way, but 0 is at the center and 255 at the outer edge.

- **matrix** – **not** an array this time, but an object. This object contains variables that control where the gradient starts, how big it is, and if it is rotated, how much so. Here is a typical object definition for a matrix:

```
matrix = {matrixType: "box", x: 0, y: 0,
➡ w: 100,h: 100, r: 0};
```

OK, lets go through those...

- matrixType is a string, "box". That's the only valid value for it.

- x and y are the coordinates where the gradient will begin.w and h are the width and height of the gradient.

- r is the rotation (in radians once again).

All right, enough explanations, let's put it to work and see it in action.

```
colors = [0xff0000, 0x0000ff];
alphas = [100, 100];
ratios = [0, 255];
matrix = {matrixType:"box", x:0, y:0, w:550,
➡ h:400, r:0};

_root.beginGradientFill("radial", colors,
➡ alphas, ratios, matrix);
```

```
_root.lineTo(550, 0);
_root.lineTo(550, 400);
_root.lineTo(0, 400);
_root.lineTo(0, 0);
_root.endFill();
```

We defined our colors, alphas, ratios and matrix, then plugged them into the `beginGradientFill()` statement, then just drew a simple box around the screen. Don't forget `endFill()`, which works the same whether your fill is plain or gradient.

This gives you a pretty gaudy red to blue circular gradient. Ugly, but effective at demonstrating what's going on. Now try changing the `fillType` parameter from "radial" to "linear". This shows you the linear gradient in action. Now, with "linear" still in place, change first three lines to:

```
colors = [0xff0000, 0x00ff00, 0x0000ff];
alphas = [100, 100, 100];
ratios = [0, 40, 255];
```

This shows you the effect of having three colors specified. Note that the green color is concentrated close to the left, because we put a value of 40 in `ratios` for the middle color. Try playing around with that to get the feel for it.

Now if it was just about setting up some numbers and creating a gradient that just sits there, that would be pretty boring. You may as well just use the gradient fill tool in the authoring environment – it's a lot more intuitive. When we use code to do things, we can change the numbers over time and start creating some really cool, dynamic effects, things you could never do with the authoring environment, and never in Flash 5 either!

Earlier we used `Math.sin` to create some waves. This is one of the most useful functions I have ever found. I use it for so many things – any time I want some value to cycle back and forth smoothly. If you combine a couple of `sin` statements with different parameters, you can get what looks like completely random, chaotic results. Even though it's just a couple of waves, each of which are very logical and easy to follow, the combination seems completely random. We'll be using that here.

What we will do is take a color value and break it down into its three separate components, red, green and blue. Each one of these can be a value from 0 to 255.

As we saw earlier, `Math.sin()` returns a value from -1 to +1. If we multiply that times 127, we get -127 to +127. If we add that to the value of 128, we get a result that loops back and forth from 1 to 255. Perfect! Now we can start.

Here is our code for one of those component colors:

```
redSpeed1 = .1;
_root.onEnterFrame = function () {
    redAngle1 += redSpeed1
    red1 = Math.sin(redAngle1)*127+128;
}
```

Here, we assign a value to `redSpeed1` of .1, and then in an `onEnterFrame` function, we add that value to `redAngle1`. We then feed that to `Math.sin`. As we take the `redAngle1` around in a circle, we'll get a result looping through 0, 1, 0, -1, 0, etc. Multiply the result by 127 and it will go up and down from -127 to +127. Add that to 128. This will result in `red1` cycling from 1 to 255 continuously.

Now we just do the same thing with green and blue, using slightly different speeds:

```
redSpeed1 = .1;
greenSpeed1 = .07;
blueSpeed1 = .04;
_root.onEnterFrame = function () {
    redAngle1 += redSpeed1;
    greenAngle1 += greenSpeed1;
    blueAngle1 += blueSpeed1;
    red1 = Math.sin(redAngle1)*127+128;
    green1 = Math.sin(greenAngle1)*127+128;
    blue1 = Math.sin(blueAngle1)*127+128;
}
```

We now have a valid value for red, green and blue. As we covered earlier in the chapter, we can combine these into a value Flash can understand for color:

```
col1 = red1 << 16 | green1 << 8 | blue1;
```

OK, we are half way there. We have defined one cycling color. The good news is, the second color is just as easy, just copy everything above and change the 1s to 2s! I also picked some other different values for the speed variables.

```
redSpeed1 = .1;
greenSpeed1 = .07;
blueSpeed1 = .04;
redSpeed2 = .09;
greenSpeed2 = .06;
blueSpeed2 = .03;
_root.onEnterFrame = function () {
    redAngle1 += redSpeed1;
    greenAngle1 += greenSpeed1;
    blueAngle1 += blueSpeed1;
    redAngle2 += redSpeed2;
    greenAngle2 += greenSpeed2;
    blueAngle2 += blueSpeed2;
    red1 = Math.sin(redAngle1)*127+128;
    green1 = Math.sin(greenAngle1)*127+128;
    blue1 = Math.sin(blueAngle1)*127+128;
    red2 = Math.sin(redAngle2)*127+128;
    green2 = Math.sin(greenAngle2)*127+128;
    blue2 = Math.sin(blueAngle2)*127+128;
    col1 = red1 << 16 | green1 << 8 | blue1;
    col2 = red2 << 16 | green2 << 8 | blue2;
}
```

Now we have two color values, col1 and col2, which are composed of red green and blue components, which are constantly changing. We just need to plug these into a colors array and feed that into our beginGradientFill command and we are just about done.

```
colors = [col1, col2];
alphas = [100, 100];
ratios = [0, 255];
matrix = {matrixType:"box", x:0, y:0, h:400, w:550, r:0};
_root.clear();
beginGradientFill("linear", colors, alphas, ratios, matrix);
_root.lineTo(550, 0);
_root.lineTo(550, 400);
_root.lineTo(0, 400);
_root.lineTo(0, 0);
_root.endFill();
```

Now we have some *dynamic* colors in our array, rather than the fixed ones we had before. Note that you can do this with any of the numeric parameters – alpha, ratios, x, y, h, w, r! I'll leave you to investigate all the possibilities. For my final file, I just chose to mess with the rotation factor. I set a rotSpeed variable and a rotAngle and used the sin of that times Math.PI. This left me with a value of −Math.PI to +Math.PI radians of rotation, which is equivalent to -180 to +180 degrees.

Here's the final code, `project_03.fla`. It kind of feels like flying through a rainbow!

```
redSpeed1 = .1;
greenSpeed1 = .07;
blueSpeed1 = .04;
redSpeed2 = .09;
greenSpeed2 = .06;
blueSpeed2 = .03;
rotSpeed = .01;
_root.onEnterFrame = function () {
    redAngle1 += redSpeed1;
    greenAngle1 += greenSpeed1;
    blueAngle1 += blueSpeed1;
    redAngle2 += redSpeed2;
    greenAngle2 += greenSpeed2;
    blueAngle2 += blueSpeed2;
    red1 = Math.sin(redAngle1)*127+128;
    green1 = Math.sin(greenAngle1)*127+128;
    blue1 = Math.sin(blueAngle1)*127+128;
    red2 = Math.sin(redAngle2)*127+128;
    green2 = Math.sin(greenAngle2)*127+128;
    blue2 = Math.sin(blueAngle2)*127+128;
    col1 = red1 << 16 | green1 << 8 | blue1;
    col2 = red2 << 16 | green2 << 8 | blue2;
    rot = Math.sin(rotAngle += rotSpeed)*Math.PI;
    colors = [col1, col2];
    alphas = [100, 100];
    ratios = [0, 255];
    matrix = {matrixType:"box", x:0, y:0, h:400, w:550, r:rot};
    clear();
    beginGradientFill("linear", colors, alphas, ratios, matrix);
    lineTo(550, 0);
    lineTo(550, 400);
    lineTo(0, 400);
    lineTo(0, 0);
    endFill();
};
```

Summary

Well, there, we've covered just about all the new drawing API functions. But as much of a cliché as it sounds, this isn't the end, it's just the beginning. The drawing functions are a way to visualize various mathematical formulas and physics concepts. You can take one example, a sine wave, and go crazy with it. You could literally go through every parameter of every drawing command and figure out how to apply a sine wave to it. We did it for the positions of lines, and the composite colors in a gradient fill. You could try it on the width of lines you are drawing, creating lines that get thin and thick. Or apply it to alpha, having lines or shapes that fade in and out. Or rotation, scale, position, alpha of movie clips that you are drawing into.

When you've completely exhausted `Math.sin`, grab another concept like springs. Don't just spring positions of things — spring their scale or color or rotation! (hmmm...I just gave myself an idea...) Then see how you can combine sine waves with springs.

There are probably about a dozen mathematical formulas and physics principles that I base all my work on. I just think up new ways of combining pieces of this with bits of that and imagine new ways to visualize things. Sometimes I even come up with something that amazes me!

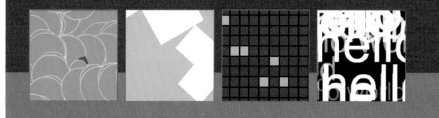

the power of the interval

jared tarbell

Essentially, the *Interval* has given us the ability to control time. Quantified time. The ability to control execution based on the passage of time is fundamental to Flash: objects spring to life from their slot on the timeline.

The timeline, however, while being linear and tidy, is not a precise progression of time. The developer specifies each movie's frame rate (measured as frames per second), but that point of reference morphs uncontrollably as it passes through the Flash player. Affected by variable processor demand and speeds, the frame rate can be seriously offset from the specification.

When we are controlling objects and their behavior in digital space, time becomes the only reference point we have to what's really going on. The sleek and efficient use of the Interval delivers us from anomalous imprecision of the frame rate to a more precise system of events and function.

The Interval is a pragmatic concept that enables the developer to define periods of time in which certain functions will be executed.

Why is the Interval so powerful?

The new Interval and its associated functions `setInterval`, `clearInterval`, and `updateAfterEvent` get me most excited about Flash MX. The Interval object provides a framework by which to execute functions at some predefined interval of time, measured in milliseconds. The object is created and destroyed by the two methods `setInterval` and `clearInterval`, respectively. The third method, `updateAfterEvent`, exists to enable the refreshing of the display when Interval events begin to occur faster than the frame rate.

The Interval is precise

The time span between Interval events is measured in milliseconds. Keep in mind that there are one thousand milliseconds in each second. The interval is not as susceptible to frame loss as other movie clip methods. This enables the programmer a high degree of trust when using the Interval. This trust promotes confidence. Confidence makes for better programs. Better programs will save the world from tedium.

The Interval allows faster than normal computation

Previously in Flash, any change made to objects on the stage required that they be rendered before another change could occur. While Flash is exceptionally well adapted for fast rendering (even with anti-aliasing!), this 'render after change' method hindered the programmer from performing complex multi-step interactive computations faster than the frame rate of the movie. The Interval is not bound to the frame rate of the movie. Although not entirely possible on all processors, setting the Interval for a time span of one-millisecond produces an equivalent computational frame rate of about 1000 frames per second.

The Interval can be created and destroyed at will

Not only can the interval be created and destroyed at will but the Interval can also be assigned to multiple objects. Also, multiple Intervals can be assigned to a single object. This has far reaching potential, as we will see in one of our example programs later in the chapter.

The Interval is fast
Side by side comparisons of the Interval and an equivalent frame looping movie clip show that the Interval is far less likely to experience latency. Although I don't entirely understand the object model used to implement the Interval, I can imagine that it's a bit closer to the metal, and has a much cleaner bit-wise representation during execution.

How do we use the Interval?

Many Flash developers are familiar with the two frame looping movie clip. Typically, the first frame contains some kind of logical computation to be performed, and the second frame contains a single `gotoAndPlay(1)`, sometimes with a terminating conditional. The first advantage to the interval is that it can be instantiated anywhere within the timeline, at any scope, without an object on stage. The interval is set much like an internal register. The interval is now the perfect alternative for anyone who is accustomed to creating small frame looping movie clips as logical controllers.

In Flash 5, the standard two frame loop basically went like this:

Frame 1:
```
Some actions to perform:..
```

Frame 2:
```
gotoAndPlay(1);
```

Often these objects would exist on the stage to be used as controllers. The same thing can be accomplished using `setInterval` with only one line of code and requiring no movie clips on stage or in the library.

Transcendence from the two frame loop has the advantage of allowing the explicit generation of computational structures. By replacing the for loop with an Interval,

```
for(i;i<limit;i++) {
    // build some stuff...
}
```

becomes...

```
function buildSomeStuff(i) {
if (i>=limit) clearInterval(forInterval);
// build some stuff...
}
forInterval = setInterval(stage,"buildSomeStuff",30,i++);
```

We can display the progress of our iterative loop *as it happens*. This is advantageous when the construction process is interesting, or when the final form has some special meaning derived from the process.

Let's look at an example of the `setInterval` function in its most basic form:

```
// ActionScript from helloworldtrace.fla, root, Frame 1, Layer logic
setInterval(function() { trace("hello world"); },1000);
```

From the developer's perspective, the output of the above would look something like this:

```
Output
                                                          Options
   hello world
   hello world
   hello world
   hello world
   hello world
   hello world
```

That's not very exciting, so let's do the same thing with a little bit of what Flash excels at, the dynamic creation of vectored text.

Most of the code for the project exists in the first frame of the root timeline:

```
// ActionScript from helloworld.fla, root, Layer logic, Frame 1
function helloWorld() {
    neo="mc"+String(depth++);
    this.attachMovie("mCHello",neo,depth);
    this[neo]._x=_xmouse;
    this[neo]._y=_ymouse;
}
setInterval(this, "helloWorld", 100);
stop();
```

While the function and the `setInterval` method that references it are both on the same frame and layer, this does not necessarily have to be the case. As long as the function and the `setInterval` that references it are in the same scope, the process will work.

A movie clip named mcHello exists in the library that is basically a "hello world" text object with a simple expanding shape tween spanning 80 frames. Once instantiated, the movie clip slowly fades forward and decreases in opacity, with a sharp and sudden death as a result of a single line of ActionScript in the very last frame:

```
// ActionScript from helloworld.fla, Movieclip mcHello, Layer logic,
Frame 1
this.removeMovieClip();
```

The final effect of this movie is a one second clock that beats out a smoothly animated 'hello

setInterval

The `setInterval` method encapsulates the core functionality of the new Interval and is the most commonly used of all three Interval methods. In short, the `setInterval` function defines a specific function to be called as some specified time interval, as applied to a specific object within the movie.

clearInterval

The `clearInterval` method is used to clear an Interval set by `setInterval`. If we plan on removing an Interval at some point in the future, we need to keep track of it. This is accomplished by grabbing the name of the Interval through the return object of the function. When calling `clearInterval`, we simply pass to it the name of the Interval we wish to be destroyed.

```
myInterval = setInterval( function () { trace("ping") },1000);
```

Later we rid ourselves with...

```
clearInterval(myInterval);
```

updateAfterEvent

An interesting feature of the `setInterval` function is the ability to create Intervals that are faster than the frame rate of the movie clip. This has some peculiar consequences because the Flash player only draws the screen after the calculation of each frame. When computations begin to occur multiple times within the same frame, some computations are not rendered to the screen.

The `updateAfterEvent` function exists to force the Flash Player to redraw the screen, regardless of frame rate. The method is processor intensive, and essentially involves a temporary increase in frame rate to compensate for Intervals faster than the frame rate or in between frames.

A particularly useful thing to know about Flash MX is that it will halt frame execution to completely process all script within a particular frame. The positive aspect of this behavior is that we are assured all code will be executed. The negative effect of this behavior is that in cases where the code's execution time is great, animation frames can be lost, resulting in a lower frame rate. This is often referred to as frame loss. The Interval helps us avoid this pitfall by not requiring the Flash player to redraw the screen after every step. In cases where it is important to see each step of interface generation, the `updateAfterEvent` function will force the display to redraw regardless of the current position of the playhead.

Use the `updateAfterEvent` method if it's important that a computational update be immediately represented on the display.

Variations of use

Macromedia has allowed us a couple of different ways to assign Intervals to objects other than object indifferent assignment in the root timeline. We'll go through each of these methods by applying them to the specific instances where they are most useful. In each case the FLAs I've made are available for download from www.friendsofED.com, and as we're investigating the new features of MX here you may like to investigate these to further understand how the effects are created – looking at other people's work is a great way to learn. Before every piece of script in the chapter I've added a comment showing exactly where in the FLA it can be found.

Building a clock with parameterized intervals

I have often found myself obsessing over the construction of a time display with each new programming language I begin working in. Flash is no exception, nor am I the only one who does this. The clock is sometimes an unnecessarily heavy gravitation in a programmer's life. Quite simply, building clock faces is an interesting recreation.

Let's use the new found simplicity of setInterval to build ourselves a parameterized clock. By allowing our clock to work off a set of custom definable parameters, we unhinge ourselves from the standard system clock. This detachment from 'real time' will provide a nice space to get more creative.

The approach in previous versions would be to periodically read values from the Date object and interpret them in some graphical way. Values would be stored as commonly held units of time in the form of seconds, minutes, hours, and sometimes a specific day in the human continuum. The setInterval defines frequency of execution using milliseconds, still a common time unit, but small enough as to be practically indistinguishable to most humans. Remember that there are 1000 milliseconds in one second. I might take a guess and estimate that over 500,000 milliseconds have flown by since you began reading this chapter.

Our movie is exactly one frame, it is stack.fla - available for download at www.friendsofED.com. At the root level of our movie, frame 1 has this script:

```
// ActionScript stack.fla, root, Layer logic, Frame 1
// basic unit of time
scalar=30;
// clock stack intervals
picoInterval = setInterval(function () {
colorColA.gotoAndStop(colorColA._currentframe+1);},scalar);
nanoInterval = setInterval(function () {
colorColB.gotoAndStop(colorColB._currentframe+1);
colorColA.gotoAndStop(1); },scalar*50);
decoInterval = setInterval(function () {
colorColC.gotoAndStop(colorColC._currentframe+1);
colorColB.gotoAndStop(1); },scalar*500);
stop();
```

Note the use of a multiplier in the form of a variable called scalar. Setting up the relationships between clock units in this fashion allows us a quick and easy way to adjust the timing of all three intervals with a single variable.

Our clock will work on a basic premise. We have three movie clips at the _root level. Each of the movie clips contains a number of frames, each frame with a stack of colored bars one greater than the frame before. Playing one of these movie clips straight through would show what would appear to be colored bars, stacking up on top of each other.

Using Intervals, we will control the rate by which each of these three movie clips plays itself. Each passing of time will advance the playhead for the corresponding movie clip by exactly one. Movie clips that represent higher orders of time (units of time that contain other units of time) also reset the playheads of those units back to frame 1. The end result is a stacking clock that works independent of the system Date object and on arbitrarily defined units of time.

Each movie clip contains only one bit of logic on the first frame:

```
stop();
```

Really, that's all we need to do. We are free to use the rest of the _root's timeline for what-ever purposes we wish. The clock will run until the movie is closed because that is the nature and fundamental power of the Interval.

Running our clock produces a beautiful cascading representation of time slipping by. Watching the clock for only a few seconds shows us the patterns by which it is operating.

To produce astounding effects, we might make quick modifications to the graphic content stored on each frame of the three clock unit movie clips. Even simpler, we could replace the movie clips with something new altogether. Try placing a short animation you may have from another project into the Library. Drag three instances of the animation onto the main stage, and name them ColorColA, ColorColB, and ColorColC, respectively. The resulting clock will be an abstract collage of animation across multiple frames of time.

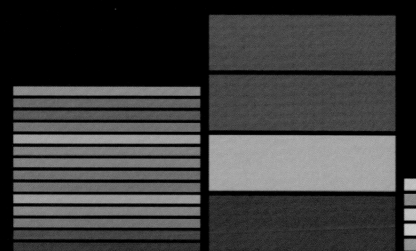

Generative computations using the Interval

If I could cast a magic spell, my first spell would be the creation of an eternal vine, thick with strength, green and soft. A vine big enough to climb, right up into the clouds to an unknown world of swirling water vapor, tiny bacterium, and thunderous electrical activity. I suppose I would probably want to dress up a bit, and pack some food. Or could I conjure up that as well?

It's a ridiculous question. Casting magic spells is simply not possible. Perhaps that's why we program. The majesty and wonder of programming is conjuring the ethereal out of nowhere, and forming it into your heart's desire. Even better, these apparitions of light, magic, and code are reactive! They live, and as they do, they make decisions, they respond to interaction, they learn, they accumulate, they combine, and they die. No need to get too attached to these guys, for perhaps the most wonderful thing about them is that their reality is defined as a repeatable statement, spread across wire and replicated on storage devices around the globe. Killing one of them off is not necessarily the end of their existence as a species. We'll just instantiate another one or maybe another few thousand.

A dilemma of generative design is showing the construction process of a computationally generated structure as it happens. Normally, the programmer has a few choices that are basically grouped in one of two ways: those processes that show the construction of the computations as they happen, and those processes that show the generated structure after all computations have been done. From the user's perspective, the former is often more exciting (unless the process takes too long). Of course it is also often more difficult to program. This is especially true in older versions of Flash, where both computation and display were frame-based processes. Flash MX is still primarily the same, however the Interval allows us to circumnavigate this restriction.

Let's get to work on our first incantation!

Time-based texturing

Here's a fun example that provides the user direct control over two unique generative Intervals through the press of a button. For demonstration purposes, I've written each function using two alternate methods of setInterval.

The movie is simple: two frames, two layers (called logic and button). On the layer called button, frame 1, we have a button that sends the playhead to frame 4. On layer button, frame 4, we have a button that sends the playhead to frame 1.

On the layer named logic, frame 1, we have the following code:

```
// ActionScript from texture.fla, root, Frame 1, Layer logic
clearInterval(intvTwo);
intvOne = setInterval(function() {
    neo="dot"+String(_root.depth++);
    _root.createEmptyMovieClip(neo, _root.depth);
    with (_root[neo]) {
        lineStyle(1,0x746963,30);
        curveTo(10,10+random(30),500,0);
```

```
    lineStyle(1,0x736975,30);
    curveTo(-10,10+random(30),-500,0);
    _x=random(500);
    _y=random(500);
    }
}
intvTwo = setInterval(this,"makeNeo",10);
stop();
```

The logic performed on both frames is equivalent. Frame 1 uses a style in which the function definition is embedded as a parameter to the `setInterval` method. It draws brown lines. Frame 4 uses a style in which a function is defined externally, and referenced by name as a parameter of the `setInterval`. It draws blue lines. Both styles work equally well. Both have their own advantages.

Notice that both styles clear the Interval of the other as a first step. Failing to do this would result in a 'doubling' generative effect each time the user pressed the button. It would also creep dangerously towards the heart of the CPU like a tiger in the brush.

The result of this movie is a system in which nicely colored curves slowly populate the display area, producing a polychromatic feathered texture. Since we're giving the user some degree of control (they decide which Interval is executed and for how long), the results of the system are unique and boundless.

Let's get to work on a level two incantation: the beanstalk!

Recursive beanstalk and the 'one time' Interval

The recursively-generated object is now a familiar form. It would be interesting to watch such a form take shape under the constraints of a series of time Intervals. We might grow a vine or stalk that would ebb and flow to an unseen season. That would be nice.

Let's attempt to do this, the FLA we're about to create is available for download as beanstalk.fla. First, for reasons we will discuss later, we will set an Interval on the root level that periodically calculates a sine curve based on a randomly increasing value. Then we stop. The code on frame 1 looks like this:

```
// ActionScript beanstalk.fla, root, Layer logic, Frame 1
// curly effect
sinusoidal = new Object();
sinusoidal.wobble = function() {
        _root.t+=random(41)/2;
        _root.sint=30*Math.sin(Math.PI / 180 * _root.t);
          }
setInterval(sinusoidal,"wobble",60);
stop();
```

This simply sets up an oscillating vector at the root level that can be referenced by instantiated movie clips to determine their rotation. The end effect of such a system is an irregular curling effect. We will need no additional code on the root level.

Let's now create the basic building block of our beanstalk, the 'node' movie clip. Two instances of this movie clip sit in the center of the stage in the root timeline. They are the basic building blocks of our magic vine.

Create a new movie clip, called 'node', and link it for ActionScript export with the same name. Draw a basic geometric shape on stage and center it to the origin of the movie clip. This shape, whatever it may be, will be the repeated shape that eventually builds our beanstalk.

Now create a new layer called logic and place the following ActionScript on the first frame:

```
// ActionScript beanstalk.fla, node Movieclip, Layer logic, Frame 1
// do not grow beyond 100 nested nodes
if (depth<100) {
    growInterval=setInterval(this,"grow",30);
    // at random, generate an offshoot
    if (!random(depth+5)) sproutNewGrowth();
}
stop();
```

Notice that we are essentially doing three things: checking the depth to see if we are not too deep to continue, setting up an Interval to call the function 'grow' every 30 milliseconds, and we're creating a quick random test to occasionally create new sprout growth.

We also need to write the two functions that are referenced by the above. For consistency, let's create a new layer called functions and put them there. They look like this:

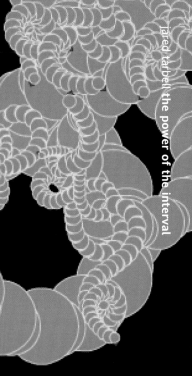

```
// ActionScript beanstalk.fla, node Movieclip, Layer functions, Frame 1

// function grow
// Adds a new node of recursive growth to the vine
function grow() {
    // attach a new Movieclip called 'nd'
    neo="nd";
    this.attachMovie("node",neo,0);
    this[neo]._y=-100;
    // reference the sinusoidal on the root level to twist gracefully
    this[neo]._rotation=_root.sint;
    // slight reduction in size
    this[neo]._xscale=99;
    this[neo]._yscale=99;
    this[neo].depth=this.depth+1;
    // no need to grow more than once
    // clear the growing interval
    clearInterval(this.growInterval);
}


// function sproutNewGrowth
// Creates a small branch of growth (sprouts)
function sproutNewGrowth() {
    // attach a new Movieclip, uniquely named 'limb1', 'limb2', 'limb3'...
    neo="limb"+String(_root.depth++);
    _root.attachMovie("node",neo,_root.depth);

    // determine the root level position to put the growth
    var point = new object();
    point.x = 0;
    point.y = 0;
    localToGlobal(point);
    _root[neo]._x=point.x;
    _root[neo]._y=point.y;

    // half growth to the left, half grow to the right
    if (random(2)) {
      _root[neo]._rotation=_root.sint+90;
    } else {
      _root[neo]._rotation=_root.sint-90;
    }

    // make the new sprout very small
    _root[neo]._xscale=5;
    _root[neo]._yscale=5;
```

```
// offshoots can be shortened by presetting their depth
_root[neo].depth=depth;
}
```

Both of these functions are standard recursive processes that attach the same movie clip within itself, over and over again, each time with some small twist (determined by the vector at the root level) and a slight reduction in size. Notice however, the `clearInterval` function at the very end of the `grow` function. This `clearInterval` function clears the very Interval that called the function in the first place. Why would we want to do this? Well, quite simply, we only want the function to be called once. In this case, we are leveraging the Interval as a delay.

What would happen if we didn't clear the Interval? Due to the recursive nature of this function, we would end up establishing Intervals exponentially, quickly consuming all available resources on the host machine, most probably bringing the operating system to its knees.

Using this simple structure as a basis of experimentation, we can climb great distances into far away clouds. Before I could help myself, I was already changing the color of the 'node' movie clip and even added a second frame to it that contained a flower. Since flowers are not as common as the node structures upon which they grow, I only allow the 'node' movie clip to stop on this frame every 42 or so instantiations (approximately 2% of all nodes will also have a flower). To accomplish this, we need only one additional line of code in the first frame of the 'node' movie clip:

```
// ActionScript beanstalk2.fla, node Movieclip, Layer functions, Frame 1
if (random(42)) stop();
```

Of course we would also need to place a `stop()` on frame 2 so that we don't loop back to the beginning. This particular version of the beanstalk is available for download as `beanstalk2.fla`.

It's always nice to be able to create an object in Flash and then forget about it. Objects that allow this usually have some degree of logical intelligence, or in sharp contrast, are quite boring, just sitting around on the stage often exactly where you left them. For this next example, I would like to demonstrate how we might create a small universe of the former type of object using the `setInterval` as the mechanism of intelligence.

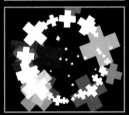

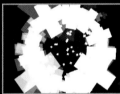

Flyers

Create a new movie clip. Call it 'ringSource' and place exactly one copy onto the stage. Export the movie clip for ActionScript using the same name for its link identifier. Inside the movie clip, rename the single layer 'logic' and apply the following ActionScript to frame 1:

```
// ActionScript from flyers.fla, ringSource Movieclip, Frame 1, Layer logic
function produceFlyer() {
    neo="fly"+String(depth++);
    this.attachMovie("flyer",neo,depth);
    rot=random(360);
    this[neo]._rotation=rot;
    this[neo].vy=6*Math.sin(Math.PI/180*rot);
    this[neo].vx=6*Math.cos(Math.PI/180*rot);
}
rotInterval = setInterval(function () { _rotation-=1 },30);
proInterval = setInterval(this,"produceFlyer",100);
stop();
```

By this code segment, we can see that there are two functions to assign to the ringSource. One function simply rotates it by one degree every 30 milliseconds and the other is used to produce something called a flyer that we will soon discuss.

The flyer is a movie clip that we will need to create; it's a small graphic object that follows the 'create and abandon' methodology we discussed earlier. It contains two functions, die and move. These functions do basically what they describe. The functions are executed as part of an Interval, however, only one function is executed at a time. This is because we want the 'flyer' to move about and live for a while before we send him off into a confused death spiral, where ultimately, we force him to remove himself.

```
// ActionScript from flyers.fla, flyer Movieclip, Frame 1, Layer logic
function die() {
    this._y+=vy;
    this._x+=vx;
    this._xscale+=vs;
    this._yscale+=vs;
    vx+=(random(7)-3)/10;
    vy+=(random(7)-3)/10;
    vs+=(random(7)-3)/5;
    this._alpha-=1;
    age++;
    if (age>300) {
      clearInterval(dieInterval);
      this.removeMovieClip();
    }
}
function move() {
    this._y+=vy;
    this._x+=vx;
    this._xscale+=vs;
    this._yscale+=vs;
```

```
    vs+=(random(7)-3)/5;
    vx*=.97;
    vy*=.97;
    age++;
    if (age>200) {
      clearInterval(moveInterval);
      dieInterval = setInterval(this,"die",20);
    }
  }
  moveInterval = setInterval(this,"move",20);
  stop();
```

Notice how behavioral control of the movie clip is self-governing. Initially, the 'flyer' sets up a single Interval to be executed at the relatively short time space of 20 milliseconds. Within the function called by the Interval (namely move), an age variable is increment each time through. Once the 'flyer' reaches a certain age (201), the original Interval is cleared and a new one is set up, this time referencing the die function.

This same functionality could be accomplished using clip events, in particular, enterFrame. However, clip events apply only to movie clips already placed on stage, and thus do not persist when a movie clip is attached from the Library.

The die function does a number of things similar to the move function. Position is adjusted, velocities are modified, and age is incremented. The fundamental difference is that the die function introduces a heaping portion of chaos through randomization. There is also a more severe age conditional: when the age reaches a certain limit (300), the final Interval is cleared and the movie clip removes itself from existence. This is what is meant by create and abandon, as no computational work outside the movie clip is required once it has been instantiated.

A variation on this theme introduces an alternative graphic shape and new functionality.

Instead of each instantiated movie clip existing as a lonely nomad, oblivious to the entities around him, we'll allow each flyer movie clip to have precisely one friend. The friend will simply be the flyer previously created. Later, we'll write a function that shows these friendly relationships, but first, we must tell each newly created flyer exactly who his friend is. I'll use the variable friend, because that seems appropriate. Friend will store the name of the other flyer movie clip. The following code exists in the function produceFlyer() of the ringSource movie clip:

```
// ActionScript from flyers.fla, ringSource Movieclip, Frame 1, Layer logic
this[neo].friend="flyguy"+String(depth-2);
```

There are now many things a flyer can accomplish knowing the name of another flyer. For this example, we'll simply have each flyer draw a line to his friend. This is not just a normal line however. Our flyers are moving all over the place, so drawing a line must be a dynamic process. Again, an Interval will accomplish this task with ease:

```
// ActionScript from flyers.fla, flyer Movieclip, Frame 1, Layer logic
function lineToFriend() {
    this.clear();
    this.lineStyle(0,0xffffff,20);
    this.lineTo(_parent[this.friend]._x-this._x,_parent[this.friend]._y-this._y);
}
lineInterval =setInterval(this,"lineToFriend",30);
```

The result is an intricate relational system of friendly flyers.

Precision is an important part of simulation. In an object oriented environment, we must be mindful of concurrency. To demonstrate how we might use the Interval as the driver behind a successful simulation, let's build a network of interconnected switches, which if created successfully, will have some very unusual properties.

The premise for our network of movie clips is fairly straightforward. Each movie clip is a switch that can be either 'on' or 'off'. Switches are randomly connected to other switches. The state of the switch is determined by the state of the switches to which it is connected through some simple set of rules. For our example, let's use the following two rules (changing these rules would be a fruitful path of creative exploration):

Switching rules
Each switch is connected to at least two other switches.
A switch moves into the 'on' state if exactly one of the connected switches is also 'on'.

As a first step, let's create the binary switch.

Create a new movie clip and name it 'node'. Rename the first layer 'logic', and add another layer called 'graphic'. This way we can easily separate code from the graphic shapes, something we may be changing frequently until we get the look we desire.

Basically, the switch will be a three-frame movie clip. The first frame contains the logic we will use to set up the node's Interval and the other two frames are used to maintain node state:

```
// ActionScript from network.fla, node, Layer logic, Frame 1
connectList = new Array();
var nextState;
if (random(2)) gotoAndPlay("off");
```

Frames two and three in the Logic layer are labeled "on" and "off", respectively. By default, the switch will initially be set to some random state (see the script in frame 1). A unique graphic shape illustrates the node's state and sits on the stage of each frame. The appearance of the switch is entirely up to you. For this example, I've used a solid white square for the "on" state and a gray square outline for the "off" state. The idea here is that the "on" state is somehow lit up.

Each node has three functions. They are called by network control logic found in the root timeline, the details of which will be discussed later. The functions must be accessible to each state of the node, so rather than redefine each function on those frames in the Logic layer, let's create a new layer called Functions that spans all frames of the movie clip and contains the following ActionScript:

```
// ActionScript from network.fla, node, Frame 1, Layer functions
function connectTo(esta) {
    lineStyle(0,0xffffff,20);
    moveTo(0,0);
    lineTo(_root[esta]._x-this._x,_root[esta]._y-this._y);
    connectList.push(esta);
}
function calcNext() {
    var charge=0;
    for (n=0;n<connectList.length;n++) {
        if (_root[connectList[n]].state=="on") charge++;
```

```
    if (charge%2) nextState="on";
    else nextState="off";
}
function setNext() {
    this.gotoAndPlay(nextState);
}
```

As a final step, export the switch movie clip for ActionScript using the link identifier 'node'. We now have a fully configured binary switch, ready to be assembled into a network.

Our movie then, really consists of three stages: build the network, randomly connect the switches and as a final step, watch the simulation unfold.

We have a couple of thousand choices on how we might arrange nodes within our network. Fortunately, the physical laws of microelectronic circuitry do not bind us. To keep things simple, I have decided to arrange our network in a simple grid of equal length and width. The algorithm to build such a network is as follows:

```
// ActionScript from network.fla, root, Layer logic, Frame 1
network = new Array();
// make network
for (x=0; x<4; x++) {
    for (y=0; y<4; y++) {
        neo = "node"+String(depth++);
        this.attachMovie("node", neo, depth);
        this[neo]._x = 120+x*40;
        this[neo]._y = 120+y*40;
        // register the name of the switch by placing it in an array
        network.push(neo);
    }
}
```

Notice we used two simple `for` loops. We could have done the same thing with an Interval, but for this specific purpose (arranging items in a grid) the loop is absolutely perfect. Besides, soon enough we'll have plenty of Intervals running.

Next, we need to connect our nodes to each other in a sufficiently random fashion. For this, we will use another for loop in the next frame. It is not critical that we avoid overloading connections (connecting to the same switch twice), nor is it one of our rules. However, as a logical precaution we will avoid connecting switches to themselves. As such, the following will work just fine:

```
// ActionScript from network.fla, root, Layer logic, Frame 2
for (m=0;m<2;m++) {
    for (n=0;n<network.length;n++) {
        neo=network[n];
        esta=n;
        while (esta==n) {
            esta=random(network.length);
        }
        this[neo].connectTo(network[esta]);
```

```
      var n;
      // compute next state for all switches
      for (n=0; n<network.length; n++) {
        _root[network[n]].calcNext();
      }
      // change state of all switches
      for (n=0; n<network.length; n++) {
        _root[network[n]].setNext();
      }
  }
  cycleInterval = setInterval(cycle, "interval", 100);
  stop();
```

Although not exactly simple, that's it! We've now defined a system often referred to as a randomly connected binary network.

Generate a few random networks and observe the switching behavior of the nodes as a collective. Do you see isolated areas of pattern? Do you see randomness? Do you see waves of repeated switching sequences traveling the network? Stare long enough, and you will observe all of these phenomena.

The most interesting aspect of building any system is discovering properties of that system that one wouldn't normally expect. Such is the case with the randomly connected binary network. In addition to producing surprising behavior, the binary network is a useful tool for emulating computational neurosciences, including memory and analytical thinking.

Building networks with sufficiently large numbers of switches promotes environments of adaptation and thought process. The question then becomes one of magnitude. What is the threshold of complexity required for an adaptive, thinking system? Certainly it is well above the 49 or so switching elements we are using in our Flash example. Still, there are some interesting effects that can be observed through watching these small-scale binary networks.

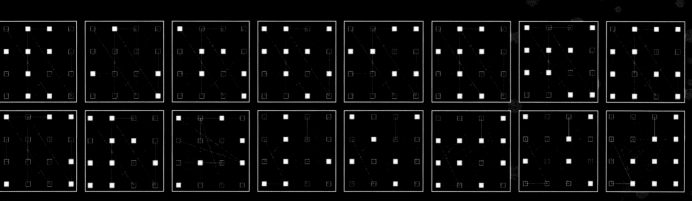

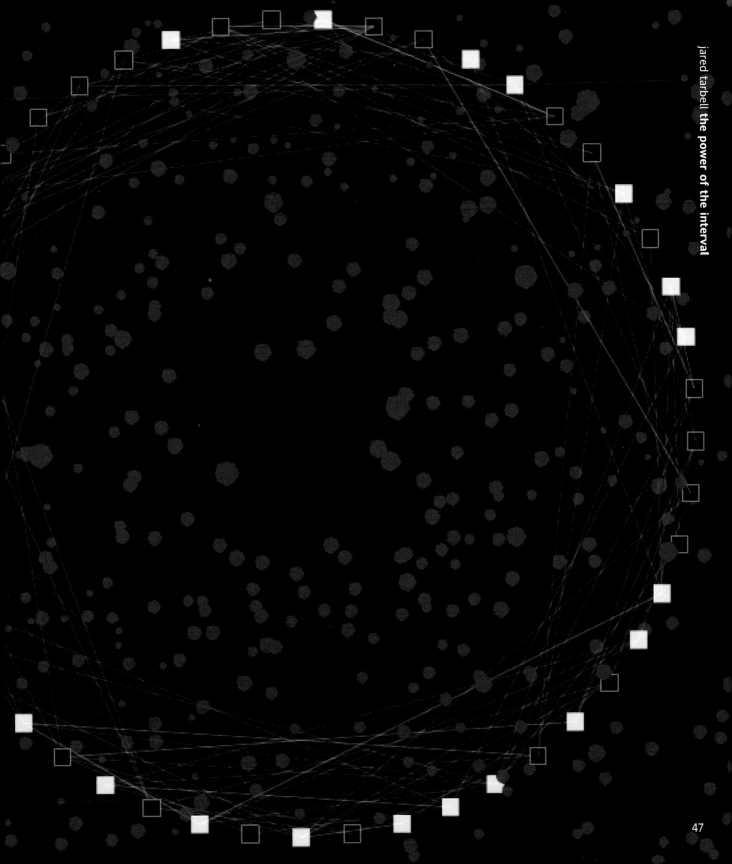

Particles exhibiting variable blur

Let's look at an example that uses the Interval to govern the extent by which user control is monitored. This is a useful method for conserving CPU usage when precision user control is not necessarily required or when user control has profound effects on computational requirements. A high animation frame rate can be maintained while the user's input is only periodically collected at a substantially slower rate.

In this example, small spherical objects wander mindlessly in three-dimensional space. Using the position of the mouse, interaction with the objects adjusts the hysteria and speed by which they wander. This is done through clever use of the Interval and is a good example of what could not be done in Flash 5 using the frame-loop. In previous versions of Flash, we would have run into a brick wall trying to force these objects to run faster than the frame rate.

First, create a layer named logic and assign the following ActionScript to it:

```
// ActionScript from blurbits.fla, _root, Frame 1, Layer logic

// set up mousewatch
mouseWatch = new Object();
mouseWatch.interval = function() {
  // watch the mouse and do stuff
  bitChange=Math.ceil(60*Math.abs(_xmouse/600));
  bitSpeed=Math.ceil(30*Math.abs(_ymouse/350));
  for (n=0;n<_root.bitList.length;n++) {
    _root[_root.bitList[n]].updateInterval(_root.bitSpeed);
  }
}

// set the user input interval around 10 fps
mouseInterval = setInterval( mouseWatch, "interval", 100);
```

The above has accomplished a few important things for us. First, we've created an object called `mouseWatch` and defined a single function for it, called `interval`. Using the current position of the mouse, this function sets two important root level variables called `bitChange` and `bitSpeed`. They are measurements in milliseconds that all moving objects on stage reference to determine behavior.

`BitChange` controls how often the moving objects on stage will arbitrarily choose a new destination. `BitSpeed` determines how fast the objects move.

There's a bit of mathematics used to adjust the value ranges of both `bitChange` and `bitSpeed` to acceptable levels.

`BitChange` is computed starting from the inside out. First, we unitize the horizontal position of the mouse into a range of [0...1]. This is assuming that the width of the stage is exactly 600 pixels. What we can't assume is that the mouse will stay within the stage. It may move to the left of zero, and this would give us a negative value. We do not want negative values! To avoid this we take the absolute value. Multiplying this by a constant of 60 should then return a number between 0 and 60 (maybe higher). As a final step, we take the ceiling value, which rounds the number up to the nearest whole number. In our case, this value represents the nearest millisecond.

`BitSpeed` is computed similarly, the only differences lying in the constants and the cardinality of the mouse.

Basically, the closer the mouse is to the top left corner, the faster and more wild the bits on the screen are going to fly around. As a final step, the function iterates through the list of existing bits and adjusts their Intervals to reflect the new values of the bit variables.

The root timeline also contains two additional lines of code:

```
// ActionScript from blurbits.fla, _root, Frame 1, Layer logic

// registry of all bits
bitList = new Array();

// some bits on the screen incantation (x origin, y origin, number of bits)
genRandomBits(300,175,10);
```

The first sets up an array for bits to register themselves when they are created. The second generates a few random bits to get things started.

Create another layer named functions. Here we will keep the `genRandomBits` function, used to create some iBits.

```
// ActionScript from blurbits.fla, _root, Frame // 1, Layer functions
function genRandomBits(x,y,num) {
    // create a number of bits at a position: x,y
    for (n=0;n<num;n++) {
      neo="bit"+String(depth++);
      this.attachMovie("ibit",neo,10+depth);
      this[neo]._x=x;
      this[neo]._y=y;
      // register the name of this new iBit
      this.bitList.push(neo);
    }
}
```

Now let's create the movie clip that we will be instantiating. Draw a circle on the root stage and convert it into a movie clip. Call the new movie clip 'iBit' and link it with the same name so that it can be exported for ActionScript. Now edit the movie clip by double-clicking it.

On the first frame, create a layer called logic and apply the following ActionScript to it:

```
// ActionScript from blurbits.fla, iBit
// Movieclip, Frame 1, Layer logic
// set initial destination
dx=random(600);
dy=random(350);
dz=random(100);
// set up interval
intervalMove = setInterval( this, "wander", 30);

stop();
```

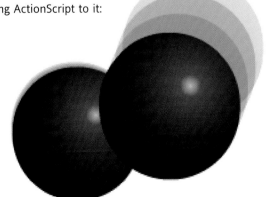

Now apply the following ActionScript to the functions layer:

```
// ActionScript from blurbits.fla, iBit Movieclip, Frame 1, Layer functions
function pickDestination() {
    // pick some nearby place to go
    dx+=random(201)-100;
    dy+=random(201)-100;
    dz+=random(50)-25;
    // make sure this hasn't picked some place offstage
    if (dx<0) dx=0;
    else if (dx>600) dx=600;
    if (dy<0) dy=0;
    else if (dy>350) dy=350;
    if (dz<0) dz=0;
    else if (dz>80) dz=80;
}
function updateInterval(newSpeed) {
    // set up intervals - test
    clearInterval(intervalMove);
    intervalMove = setInterval( this, "wander", newSpeed);
}
function wander() {
    // randomly pick new destination
    if (!random(_parent.bitChange)) pickDestination();
    // move to destination
    vx+=(_x-dx)/30;
    vy+=(_y-dy)/30;
    vz+=(z-dz)/30;
    _x-=vx;
    _y-=vy;
    z-=vz;
    _xscale=_yscale=100-z;
    this.blur0._x=vx*.9;
    this.blur0._y=vy*.9;
    this.blur1._x=vx*.6;
    this.blur1._y=vy*.6;
    this.blur2._x=vx*.3;
    this.blur2._y=vy*.3;
    vx*=.8;
    vy*=.8;
    vz*=.8;
}
```

All three functions are critical to the correct behavior of the movie clip, although their specific implementations can be modified to create any number of unusual effects. The wander function is used to move the object to its destination in an elegant fashion using an elastic vector and some friction. This is also where the blur circles are offset according to velocity. The pickDestination function does exactly what it sounds like it does. These two functions are fairly standard ways to move an object about the screen. It is the updateInterval function that is of particular interest to us within the context of this chapter, as that is where the movie clip's movement Interval is adjusted. If you recall, a mouse-watching function in the root timeline makes iterative calls to the updateInterval function for each iBit. The function clears the old Interval, then sets a new one with the parameter passed in as an argument. Notice how we've assigned a name to this setInterval. This is critical if we are to later remove it.

To reinforce the illusion of fast movement, several layers of additional circles have been placed on lower layers. By offsetting their position relative to the velocity of the object, a blurring effect is created that is quite believable.

The only additional element of the movie is an optional large button that sits in the background. Each time the button is pressed, additional iBits are created through the genRandomBits function.

Remove the first the iBit we created on the main stage, and we're ready to set this movie in action.

So what does this 'iBit' behavior look like, exactly? Well, it's basically small spherical object that seems to fly around the screen in three dimensions. The regularity and speed with which is does this is controlled by the position of the mouse, in real time. What's most amazing is when the speed of the bit moves beyond what one would normally consider to be the highest speed possible, given the frame rate. This is nice. Of course this is only possible using the Interval.

Experimental uses and the danger of recursion

Recursion is a particularly dangerous but potentially exciting use of the Interval. Recursion is simply a process where a function is allowed to call itself. Recursion can also be a collection of functions that through their inter-linking, form a kind of feedback loop. Because the `setInterval` calls a function as part of it's execution, creating a recursive structure would simply involve the embedding of another `setInterval` somewhere within the invoking function.

Why is this dangerous?

Recursion is a dangerous proposition because if left unchecked, the process quickly consumes all available resources on a machine and renders its host program emaciated, confused, and useless. This is particularly evident with the use of `setInterval`. `SetInterval` does not make a single call to some function, but rather, makes repeated calls to a function at potentially rapid rates, an infinite number of times, or until it is cleared. It's not hard to understand the severity of what would happen if we started calling Intervals within Intervals.

Let's abandon caution and get right into it!

Even with careful consideration, we have a considerably high chance of locking our machine during these experiments. For this reason, save often! Do not keep open, unsaved work in other applications. Do not expect to halt ActionScript execution by answering 'Yes' if we should hit an infinitely dense computation rate. We may not see that dialog.

Perhaps we should start safely and work our way towards tighter, more elegant algorithms. In this light, here is a recursively defined Interval definition that uses only trace statements to represent its progress:

```
setInterval(function() { trace("army of Intervals");
setInterval(function() { trace("shot fired") },900) }, 1000);
```

The output of the above is a series of messages sent to the Output window. It goes something like:

Let's build an example that does the same thing, but with movie clips.

Create a new movie. Rename the main layer to `logic`. Place the following code on the first frame:

```
function stackBrick(bcolor) {
        neo="brick"+String(depth++);
        this.createEmptyMovieClip(neo,depth);
        this[neo]._x=stackWidth;
        this[neo]._y=stackHeight;
        if (bcolor=="blue") {
            this[neo].lineStyle(0,0x94abda,100);
            this[neo].beginFill(0x94abda,100);
        } else {
            this[neo].lineStyle(0,0x454545,100);
            this[neo].beginFill(0x454545,100);
        }
        this[neo].lineTo(0,8);
        this[neo].lineTo(8,8);
        this[neo].lineTo(8,0);
        this[neo].lineTo(0,0);
        stackHeight+=10;
        if (stackHeight>500) {
            stackHeight=0;
            stackWidth+=10;
        }
}
    mainInterval = setInterval( function() {
            stackBrick("blue");
            setInterval(function() { stackBrick("brown") },90);
        },100);
    stop();
```

Basically, we're setting up the same recursive interval definition as in the previous example. Instead of calling the trace function, we're calling a function of our own, called `stackBrick`.

`StackBrick` is a fairly straightforward MX specific function that leverages the new drawing API. This example simply draws a square, and colors it a specific color based on the function parameter `bcolor`. To stack the bricks properly (not that we necessarily need to avoid unconventional methods), we track the stack's height and width using to incrementally determined variables, `stackHeight` and `stackWidth`, respectively.

That's it! But believe me, this is plenty enough to get us into some serious trouble. Save your work. Some machines may be able to render the background image on this page.

During the execution of this movie, small colored squares stack themselves both vertically and horizontally, filling the screen. The color of each square is determined by the Interval that called it. In this example, we have two Intervals, one associated with blue and the other with gray.

By instantiating a movie clip each time an Interval is called, we can observe the frequency and patterns of their periodicity. The pattern of this example is not as simple as it first appears. For each blue movie clip created, an additional brown movie clip is scheduled to be created. The effect is a cascading series of gray movie clips.

Adjusting the time of the Intervals can produce interesting variations of effect. The time difference between the two Intervals is the important part of the adjustment, not necessary the magnitudes of the time. Adjusting the magnitudes only speeds up or slows down the construction of the pattern.

For this example, I have discovered that I most like Intervals that are very close in their periods of execution. Self-similarity produces subtle variations of pattern. I am hesitant to encourage the experimentation of recursive Interval definition. If you do decide to explore, be sure to save your work often. Avoid malicious publishing, and start off with large time intervals.

scriptable masks

lifaros

I always start by drawing my experiments on a piece of paper, just like a storyboard. Then I try to define the functions that I need to achieve the correct behavior of the movie. Sometimes I need to solve some equations or a complex math problem and once they're solved, I begin the ActionScript process. I turn on my PC, open Flash, and start turning my sketches into ActionScript.

I've been experimenting with masks a lot recently. Dynamic masks can be used to develop a lot of interesting visual effects, and since Flash 4, advanced Flash developers have coded draggable masks to create magnifying glasses, jigsaw puzzles, liquid images, and many other things. This was a bit complex because masks were not scriptable, so they had to learn a lot of tricks to solve these tasks.

Macromedia have added a lot of new ActionScript features in Flash MX. For instance we don't need to draw or insert movie clips on the stage. Now we can create all the necessary objects with code, which is pretty amazing. Best of all, dynamic masking in MX is so easy, we don't need to use the old Flash 4/5 tricks.

There is a lot of code in this chapter, so to save your tired fingers you can download all the source files from www.friendsofed.com.

Who is that masked man?

Not the Lone Ranger - but it could be - you can mask anything with the new setMask feature. Within the ActionScript Dictionary, you will see that:

"... Usage
myMovieClip.setMask (maskMovieClip)

Parameters
myMovieClip The instance name of a movie clip to be masked.
maskMovieClip The instance name of a movie clip to be a mask.

I prefer to use this notation, because is self-explanatory.

```
masked.setMask (masker)
```

We define the movie clip that needs to be *masked* and the movie clip that will act as mask (*masker*). For instance we've got a movie clip (yellow square) that will be masked by a draggable movie clip (blue circle).

```
circle.startDrag(true);
square.setMask(circle);
```

before masking

after masking

The golden rules of dynamic masking

Rule 1: A masker movie clip can't be used to mask more than one object at the same time.

If we script like this:

```
masked1.setMask (masker)
masked2.setMask (masker)
masked3.setMask (masker)
```

...only masked3 will be masked!

For example we have a draggable red circle over a yellow square and a green triangle. This piece of code doesn't work properly because only the yellow square is masked, as you can see in the second picture here.

```
circle.startDrag(true);
triangle.setMask(circle);
square.setMask(circle);
```

The solution is to nest both movie clips (the yellow square and green triangle) within a "holder" movie clip, as seen in the third right-hand picture.

```
circle.startDrag(true);
holder.setMask(circle);
```

no mask

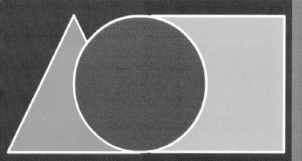

wrong mask

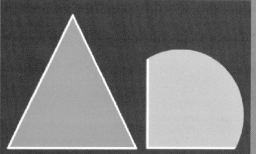

correct mask

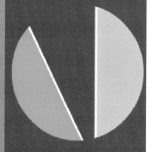

Rule 2: A movie clip can't be masked by more than one "masker" movie clip at the same time.

If our script looks like this:

```
masked.setMask (masker1)
masked.setMask (masker2)
masked.setMask (masker3)
```

...only masker3 will act as a mask.

We have a red circle and a green triangle over a yellow square. If we try to use both shapes as maskers, only the last one will act as mask, as seen in the center image.

```
square.setMask(circle);
square.setMask(triangle);
```

If you need to use multiple movie clips as masks over the same movie clip, you can create a "holder" movie clip and then embed all the maskers, seen here in the image on the right.

```
square.setMask(holder);
```

no mask   **wrong mask**   **correct mask**

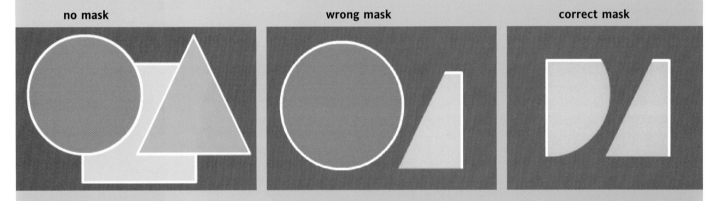

Rule 3: Drawing API lines or curves can't be used as masks.

Only filled drawing API shapes can be act as masks. Lines can't be changed to filled shapes so I have developed a method to draw filled lines and Bezier curves (This is explained in greater detail within my Drawing API chapter).

Rule 4; You can't mask an external image if it hasn't been loaded completely.

For instance this code doesn't work properly because the `setMask` function was called before the external image is on the stage.

```
holder.loadMovie("blue.jpg");
holder.setMask(mask);
mask.startDrag(true);
```

We need to include an image preloader; this way the `setMask` command will be called once the image has been loaded.

This piece of code will create a draggable square that will mask an external JPG image (named `blue.jpg` - you can use any you like, as long as it's in the same directory) after it's 100% loaded.

```
MovieClip.prototype.loader = function(file) {
    this.createEmptyMovieClip("image", 1);
    this.image.loadMovie(file);
    this.onEnterFrame = function() {
      if (this.image.getBytesLoaded() ==
➡this.image.getBytesTotal() && this.image.getBytesTotal()>0) {
        this.image.setMask(mask);
        mask.startDrag(true);
        this.onEnterFrame = null;
      }
    };
};
MovieClip.prototype.drawBox = function(x, y, xsize, ysize,
strokewidth, strokecolor, strokealpha, fillcolor, fillalpha) {
    this.clear();
    this.beginFill(fillcolor, fillalpha);
    this.lineStyle(strokewidth, strokecolor, strokealpha);
    this.moveTo(x-xsize/2, y-ysize/2);
    this.lineTo(x+xsize/2, y-ysize/2);
    this.lineTo(x+xsize/2, y+ysize/2);
    this.lineTo(x-xsize/2, y+ysize/2);
    this.endFill();
};
this.createEmptyMovieClip("holder", 1);
this.createEmptyMovieClip("mask", 2);
this.mask.drawBox(0, 0, 100, 100, 0, 0xffffff, 100, 0x0000ff, 100);
holder.loader("blue.jpg");
stop();
```

masking an external image without preloader

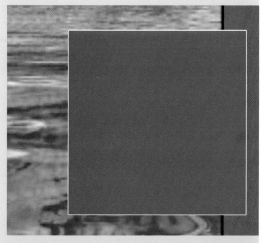

masking an external image with preloader

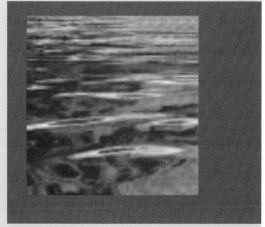

Well, we've now got the foundations of dynamic masking covered, let's take a look at masks in action.

59

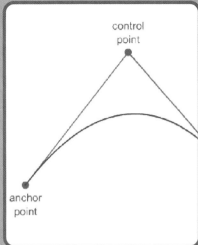

Learning curves

The purpose of these experiments is to prove that we can combine the new dynamic mask features with the drawing API methods. I'm also going to use the new event handlers and some object-oriented programming (OOP) concepts.

To this end, we're going to draw and animate some organic shapes, and then we are going to use these shapes as dynamic masks.

We'll use lines (`lineTo`) and curves (`curveTo`) to join some points. `LineTo` draws a straight line between two points, while `curveTo` draws a parabolic segment (quadratic Bezier spline) between two points (anchor points). The shape of the curve is controlled by a third external point named the control point.

Bezier splines are an interesting property: the slope of the Bezier curve at the anchor point and the slope of the straight line between the anchor point and the control point are the same.

These type of curves were developed by a French mathematician named Pierre Bézier, and will be the basis of our experiments.

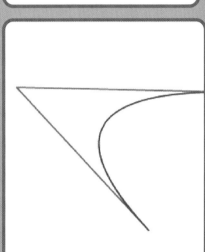

Throwing shapes

First of all we need to learn a method or trick to soften a shape. For instance we've an irregular polygon with seven vertices and seven sides, and we want to draw a continuous curve that passes through the polygon. How?

First we calculate the midpoint of each side.

Then draw a number of Bezier curves, using each vertex as the control point and use the midpoints of the adjacent sides as the anchors.

As you can see, if we want a closed shape with *n* vertices, we must draw *n* Bezier curves.

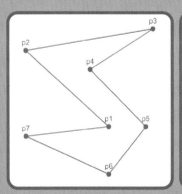

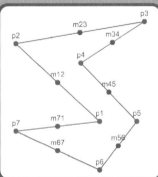

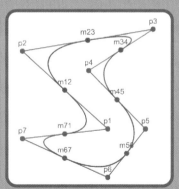

We can use the same idea to soften an open shape, but this time we must draw *n-2* Bezier curves. For instance, we've got an open shape with nine vertices and eight sides – the procedure is the same, except that the extreme vertices (p1 and p9) are used as anchor points instead of the midponts of the extreme sides (m12 and m89) that are not used.

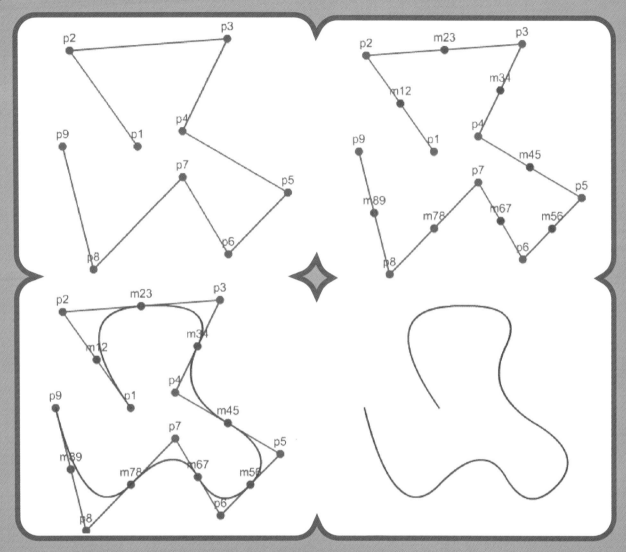

It's really easy!

You can appreciate that there are neither corners nor discontinuities, so the curve is smooth, soft, organic...

Try drawing complex shapes in order to assimilate this method. If you are an advanced math developer, try coding a 3D version of this Bezier spline. The method is the same, although you will need to use x, y, z triplets to define each point.

Bezier waves

I want to simulate waving horizontal surfaces, but I also want movement, motion, something like the waves of the sea. The solution could be defining some points, that will move softly up and down, and then drawing straight lines or Bezier curves between them.

The vertical position of each point will be modulated at a random amplitude and frequency, so every time we've got a different result.

Code and file structure

I usually include all the functions and methods within the first frame, while the second frame is used to define variables, creating objects and to set up the onEnterFrame loop. I keep the functions and methods definitons stored on the first frame, and performm all of the calls on the second frame. I use this file structure just for order and because it is easy to read and debug (if you'd like, you can put all the code within the first frame).

I'm going to create, at first, a starting point with the first piece of code, and then in the proceeding versions of the experiments I'm going to show variations, just adding or removing some lines of code or changing some variables on the second frame.

Remember that I have included all the source files, so open the mx_bezier_waves_01.fla file and follow me.

The first step is to develop an OOP wave class using a constructor function. Within the constructor we define all the properties of our wave, the number of points, radius (amplitude), x, y position, etc. Each "wave object" has a "bodyholder" movie clip, that holds all of the graphical elements.

mx_bezier_waves_01

This is the ActionScript in the first frame:

```
function wave(points, radius, offset, wavewidth, xpos, ypos, strokewidth,
strokecolor, strokealpha, fillcolor, fillalpha) {
    this.body = createEmptyMovieClip("bodyholder"+k, 1000+k++);
    this.x = [];      // this array holds the horizontal position of each point
    this.y = [];      // this array holds the vertical position of each point
    this.mx = [];     //this array holds the horizontal position of each midpoint
    this.my = [];     //this array holds the vertical position of each midpoint
    this.frec = [];   //this array holds the modulation frequency of each point
    this.wavewidth = wavewidth;
    this.xpos = xpos;
    this.ypos = ypos;
    this.radius = radius;
    this.offset = offset;
    this.points = points;
    this.strokewidth = strokewidth;
    this.strokecolor = strokecolor;
    this.strokealpha = strokealpha;
    this.fillcolor = fillcolor;
    this.fillalpha = fillalpha;
    for (var i = 0; i<points; i++) {
        this.frec[i] = 1.2*(Math.random()+.5);
    }
}
```

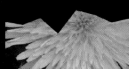
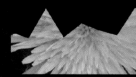
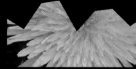

...then we define the following methods:

This one modifies the vertical value of each point, generating a sinusoidal movement. So every time we call this method, the new coordinates of the points (x,y) and midpoints (mx,my) are calculated:

```
this.wave.prototype.modulate = function(t) {
    for (var i = 0; i<this.points; i++) {
        this.x[i] = this.xpos+(this.wavewidth/(this.points-1))*i;
        this.y[i] = this.ypos+this.radius+this.offset*Math.sin(this.frec[i]*t*dtr);
        this.mx[i] = (this.x[i]+this.x[i-1])/2;
        this.my[i] = (this.y[i]+this.y[i-1])/2;
    }
};
```

This method draws straight lines between each adjacent point or vertex of our shape. As you can see we are using some drawing API methods to draw lines and fill surfaces.

```
this.wave.prototype.drawLines = function() {
    this.body.beginFill(this.fillcolor, this.fillalpha);
    this.body.lineStyle(this.strokewidth, this.strokecolor, this.strokealpha);
    this.body.moveTo(this.xpos, this.ypos);
    this.body.lineTo(this.x[0], this.y[0]);
    for (var i = 1; i<this.points; i++) {
        this.body.lineTo(this.x[i], this.y[i]);
    }
    this.body.lineTo(this.x[this.points-1], this.ypos);
    this.body.endFill();
};
```

This method, which is similar, draws Bezier curves between each vertex and its adjacent midpoints. We can see the smoothing method in action.

```
this.wave.prototype.drawCurves = function() {
    this.body.beginFill(this.fillcolor, this.fillalpha);
    this.body.lineStyle(this.strokewidth, this.strokecolor, this.strokealpha);
    this.body.moveTo(this.xpos, this.ypos);
    this.body.lineTo(this.x[0], this.y[0]);
    for (var i = 1; i<this.points-2; i++) {
        this.body.curveTo(this.x[i], this.y[i], this.mx[i+1], this.my[i+1]);
    }
    this.body.curveTo(this.x[this.points-2], this.y[this.points-2],
➡  this.x[this.points-1], this.y[this.points-1]);
    this.body.lineTo(this.x[this.points-1], this.ypos);
    this.body.endFill();
};
```

In my FLA this ActionScript lives on the second frame.. Finally we define some variables, create a movie clip to hold the image and generate our first "wave" object. The onEnterFrame event handler allows the wave movement.

Keep in mind that we're now dealing with a FLA file where the JPG image is an object in our library and is attached with the `attachMovie` command.

```
dtr = Math.PI/180;                    //degrees to radians conversion factor
speed = 5;//modulation speed
sx = Stage.width/2;                   // stage horizontal center
sy = Stage.height/2;                  // stage vertical center
wave[1] = new wave(10, -2*Stage.height/4, 30, Stage.width, 0,
➡ Stage.height, 2, 0xffffff, 100, 0x6633ff, 100);
createEmptyMovieClip("image", 1);
image.attachMovie("image01", "img", 1);
image._x=sx;
image._y=sy;
image.setMask(wave[1].body);
this.onEnterFrame = function() {
    wave[1].modulate(speed*fa++);
    wave[1].body.clear();
    wave[1].drawLines();
};
stop();
```

You can appreciate that `wave[1]` has 10 points, the fixed size is 2/4 of the stage height, the variable vertical offset is 30, the horizontal wave size is equal to the stage width and the bottom left corner of the wave is located at the bottom left corner of the stage.

This line of code is used to make the dynamic mask effect:

```
image.setMask(wave[1].body);
```

mx_bezier_waves_02

Now we want to draw curves instead of straight lines, so use `drawCurves` instead of the `drawLines` method and compare both results. In this FLA the `onEnterFrame` function becomes:

```
this.onEnterFrame = function() {
    wave[1].modulate(speed*fa++);
    wave[1].body.clear();
    wave[1].drawCurves();
};
```

...as you can see, the wave movement is better; very "liquid" and much more real, because there are no corners.

You can modify these parameters in order to obtain different shapes:

`points` = number of points or vertices of the wave
`radius` = fixed vertical value of the points
`offset`= variable vertical value of the points
`wavewidth` = horizontal wave size
`xpos`= horizontal position of the bottom left corner of the wave
`ypos`= vertical position of the bottom left corner of the wave
`strokewidth`, `strokecolor`, `strokealpha`, `fillcolor`, and `fillalpha` are self explanatory

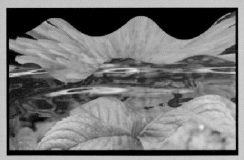

mx_bezier_waves_03

For this experiment, I'm drawing 3 waves, arranged in a vertical order, and each wave will be masking its own image. Remember that we are using the same body of the code, so we don't need to rewrite all again. Just modify the head.

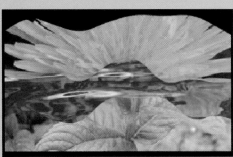

```
dtr = Math.PI/180;        //degrees to radians conversion factor
speed = 5;//modulation speed
sx = Stage.width/2;       // stage horizontal center
sy = Stage.height/2;      // stage vertical center
imageArray = ["image01", "image02", "image03"];
                          // array of linked images names
image = [];               // array of image holders
for (var i = 0; i<3; i++) {
    wave[i] = new wave(10, (i-3)*Stage.height/4, 20,
➡ Stage.width, 0, Stage.height, 2, 0xffffff, 100, 0x6633ff, 100);
    image[i] = createEmptyMovieClip("image"+i, i);
    image[i].attachMovie(imageArray[i], "img", 1);
    image[i]._x=sx,
    image[i]._y=sy;
    image[i].setMask(wave[i].body);
}
this.onEnterFrame = function() {
    for (var i = 0; i<3; i++) {
      wave[i].modulate(speed*fa++);
      wave[i].body.clear();
      wave[i].drawCurves();
    }
};
```

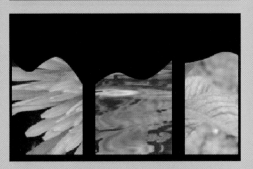

Each linked image needs a holder, so we generate these movie clips using `createEmptyMovieClip` method.

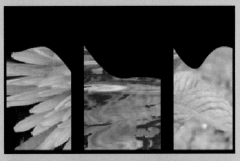

This time we've got 3 waves arranged in an horizontal order, side by side:

```
dtr = Math.PI/180;        //degrees to radians conversion factor
speed = 5;//modulation speed
sx = Stage.width/2;       // stage horizontal center
sy = Stage.height/2;      // stage vertical center
// array of linked images names
imageArray = ["image01", "image02", "image03"];
image = [];// array of image holders
```

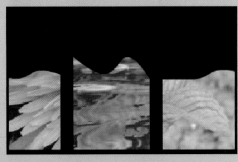

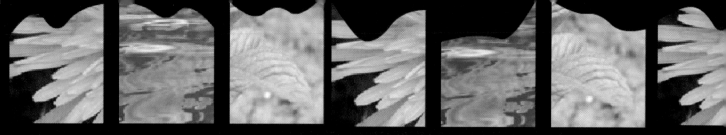

```
for (var i = 0; i<3; i++) {
    wave[i] = new wave(5, -.5*Stage.height, 20, Stage.width/3.5, i*Stage.width/3,
    ➡ Stage.height, 2, 0xffffff, 100, 0x6633ff, 100);
    image[i] = createEmptyMovieClip("image"+i, i);
    image[i].attachMovie(imageArray[i], "img", 1);
    image[i]._x=sx, image[i]._y=sy;
    image[i].setMask(wave[i].body);
}
this.onEnterFrame = function() {
    for (var i = 0; i<3; i++) {
        wave[i].modulate(speed*fa++);
        wave[i].body.clear();
        wave[i].drawCurves();
    }
};
```

mx_bezier_waves_05

This time I'm using 3 couples of waves, so we need to create 6 waves. Each wave is opposed to the other, so we get interesting double sided waves. I'm masking just one image, so I embed all the waves into a holder movie clip, named 'multiple'.

```
dtr = Math.PI/180,speed = 5;
sx = Stage.width/2, sy = Stage.height/2;
this.multiple = createEmptyMovieClip("mult", 50);
wave[0] = new wave(21, -.05*Stage.height, .047*Stage.height, Stage.width, 0,
➡ Stage.height/4, 2, 0xffffff, 100, 0x6633ff, 100);
wave[1] = new wave(21, .05*Stage.height, .047*Stage.height, Stage.width, 0,
➡ Stage.height/4, 2, 0xffffff, 100, 0x6633ff, 100);
wave[2] = new wave(21, -.05*Stage.height, .047*Stage.height, Stage.width,
➡ 0, 2*Stage.height/4, 2, 0xffffff, 100, 0x6633ff, 100);
wave[3] = new wave(21, .05*Stage.height, .047*Stage.height, Stage.width, 0,
➡ 2*Stage.height/4, 2, 0xffffff, 100, 0x6633ff, 100);
wave[4] = new wave(21, -.05*Stage.height, .047*Stage.height, Stage.width, 0, ➡
➡3*Stage.height/4, 2, 0xffffff, 100, 0x6633ff, 100);
wave[5] = new wave(21, .05*Stage.height, .047*Stage.height, Stage.width, 0, 3*Stage.height/4,
➡ 2, 0xffffff, 100, 0x6633ff, 100);
image = createEmptyMovieClip("image", i);
image.attachMovie("image01", "img", 1);
image._x=sx, image._y=sy;
image.setMask(multiple);
this.onEnterFrame = function() {
    for (var i = 0; i<6; i++) {
        wave[i].modulate(speed*fa++);
        wave[i].body.clear();
        wave[i].drawCurves();
    }
```

We also need to change just one line of code within the constructor function:

```
this.body = multiple.createEmptyMovieClip("bodyholder"+k, 1000+k++);
```

The result is a nice piece of abstract art!

You can easily modify a lot of parameters, such as the wave size, position, speed, amplitude, and so on, so there are millions of combinations. This is the magic of OOP programming!

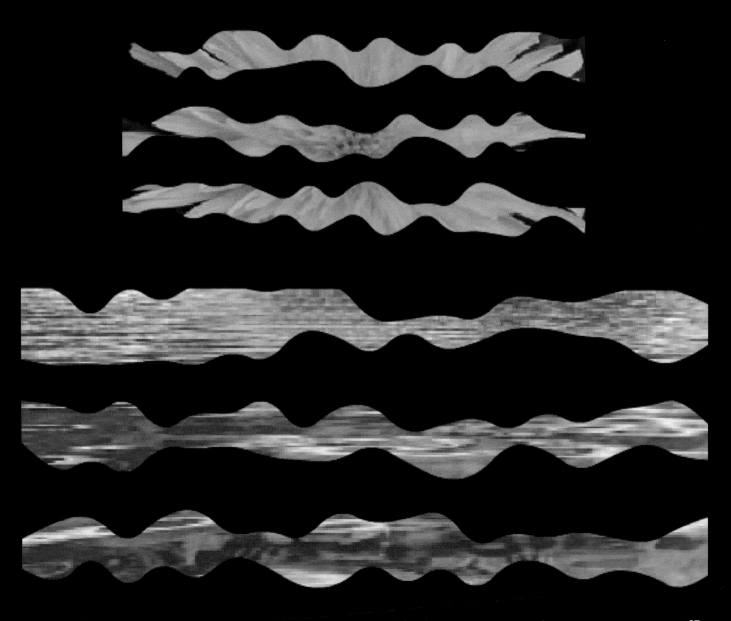

Bezier amoebas

These creatures are very nice. This time we use a radial pattern to plot the points, so the shape looks like a undulating amoeba or something like that.

Again, the radius of each point will be modulated at a random amplitude and frequency. The procedure is pretty similar to the former experiment. Once the functions and methods are in place, we can benerate a lot of variations just by changing the parameters in frame 2.

mx_bezier_amoeba_01

Firstly we need to create a constructor function in order to define all the object properties.

```
function amoeba(points, radius, offset, xpos, ypos, strokewidth, stroke
➡ color, strokealpha, fillcolor, fillalpha) {
    this.body = createEmptyMovieClip("bodyholder"+k, 1000+ k++);
    this.x = [];
    this.y = [];
    this.mx = [];
    this.my = [];
    this.xpos = xpos;
    this.ypos = ypos;
    this.radius = radius;
    this.offset = offset;
    this.frec = [];
    this.points = points;
    this.strokewidth = strokewidth;
    this.strokecolor = strokecolor;
    this.strokealpha = strokealpha;
    this.fillcolor = fillcolor;
    this.fillalpha = fillalpha;
    for (var i = 0; i<points; i++) {
        this.frec[i] = 2*(Math.random()+.5);
    }
}
```

...then we define a few other amoeba methods:

This one is to modify the radial value of each point, generating a sinusoidal movement. Here we must calculate the x and y position of each point, according to its angle.

```
this.amoeba.prototype.modulate = function(t) {
    for (var i = 0; i<this.points; i++) {
        var ran = this.radius+this.offset*Math.sin(this.frec[i]*t*dtr);
        this.x[i] = this.xpos+ran*Math.cos(i*2*Math.PI/this.points);
        this.y[i] = this.ypos+ran*Math.sin(i*2*Math.PI/this.points);
        this.mx[i] = (this.x[i]+this.x[i-1])/2;
        this.my[i] = (this.y[i]+this.y[i-1])/2;
    }
    this.mx[0] = (this.x[this.points-1]+this.x[0])/2;
    this.my[0] = (this.y[this.points-1]+this.y[0])/2;
};
```

The `drawCurves` method, will draw Bezier curves between each vertex and its adjacent midpoints, just applying the same smoothing method as we have before:

```
this.amoeba.prototype.drawCurves = function() {
    this.body.clear();
    this.body.beginFill(this.fillcolor, this.fillalpha);
    this.body.lineStyle(this.strokewidth,
    ➡this.strokecolor, this.strokealpha);
    this.body.moveTo(this.mx[0], this.my[0]);
    for (var i = 0; i<this.points-1; i++) {
      this.body.curveTo(this.x[i], this.y[i], this.mx[i+1], this.my[i+1]);
    }
    this.body.curveTo(this.x[this.points-1], this.y[this.points-1], this.mx[0],
      ➡ this.my[0]);
    this.body.endFill();
};
```

This method is to draw lines between each adjacent point or vertex:

```
this.amoeba.prototype.drawLines = function() {
    this.body.beginFill(this.fillcolor, this.fillalpha);
    this.body.lineStyle(this.strokewidth, this.strokecolor, this.strokeal-
pha);
    this.body.moveTo(this.x[0], this.y[0]);
    for (var i = 1; i<this.points-1; i++) {
      this.body.lineTo(this.x[i], this.y[i]);
    }
    this.body.lineTo(this.x[0], this.y[0]);
    this.body.endFill();
};
```

After defining the class constructor and its methods, we generate our first artificial amoeba. This amoeba has 21 points, and is located at the center of the movie stage. You can see that I'm using straight lines between adjacent points.

```
dtr=Math.PI/180, speed=5, sx=Stage.width/2, sy=Stage.height/2;
amoeba[1] = new amoeba(21, Stage.height/2.5, Stage.height/15,
➡ Stage.width/2, Stage.height/2, 2, 0xffffff, 100, 0x6633ff, 100);
createEmptyMovieClip("image", 1);
image.attachMovie("image01", "img", 1);
image._x=sx, image._y=sy;
image.setMask(amoeba[1].body);
this.onEnterFrame = function() {
    amoeba[1].modulate(speed*fa++);
    amoeba[1].body.clear();
    amoeba[1].drawLines();
};
stop();
```

We need just one line of code to set up the mask:

```
this.image01.setMask(amoeba[1].body);
```

The `onEnterFrame` event handler allows the amoeba movement. The key variables, which you can alter to mess with the effect, are:

`points` =number of points or vertices
`radius` = fixed radial value
`offset`= variable radial value
`xpos`= horizontal position of the amoeba center
`ypos`= vertical position of the amoeba center
`strokewidth, strokecolor, strokealpha, fillcolor,` and `fillalpha` are self explanatory

Now it's time to play by changing some values in order to generate different kinds of effects.

mx_bezier_amoeba_02

We have the same object configuration, but this time we use the `drawCurves` method in order to draw soft curves between adjacent points.

```
this.onEnterFrame = function() {
    amoeba[1].modulate(speed*fa++);
    amoeba[1].body.clear();
    amoeba[1].drawCurves();
};
```

mx_bezier_amoeba_03

Our amoeba is dynamic but lacking in interactivity, so I'm going to change the offset value according to the mouse distance. Add this piece of code within the body of the code (first frame). This new method returns the distance between the mouse and the amoeba's center.

```
this.amoeba.prototype.distance = function() {
    var dx = _xmouse-this.xpos,
    var dy = _ymouse-this.ypos;
    return Math.sqrt(dx*dx+dy*dy);
};
```

Within the `onEnterFrame` event handler, I have defined an exponential relation to set the modulation offset. The result is very interesting; the amoeba reacts to mouse proximity.

```
this.onEnterFrame = function() {
    amoeba[1].offset = 25*Math.exp(-(
    ➥ amoeba[1].distance())/50);
    amoeba[1].modulate(speed*fa++);
```

```
    amoeba[1].body.clear();
    amoeba[1].drawCurves();
};
```

mx_bezier_amoeba_04

This time I'm going to generate a bi-dimensional array of amoebas. Each one will react to mouse proximity. I need to mask just one image, so I've embedded all the amoebas' bodies into a holder movie clip, named "multiple".

```
dtr=Math.PI/180, speed=2, sx=Stage.width/
➥ 2, sy=Stage.height/2;
createEmptyMovieClip("image", 1);
image.attachMovie("image01", "img", 1);
image._x=sx, image._y=sy;
multiple = createEmptyMovieClip("mult", 50);
rows=4;
columns=6;
for (var i = 0; i<rows; i++) {
    amoeba[i] = [];
    for (var j = 0; j<columns; j++) {
        amoeba[i][j] = new amoeba(4, 25, 7,
        ➥ (j+1)*Stage.width/(columns+1),
        ➥ (i+1)*Stage.height/(rows+1), 2,
        ➥ 0xffffff, 100, 0x6633ff, 100);
    }
}
image.setMask(multiple);
this.onEnterFrame = function() {
    for (var i = 0; i<rows; i++) {
        for (var j = 0; j<columns; j++) {
            amoeba[i][j].offset = 25*Math.exp(-
            ➥ amoeba[i][j].distance()/50);
            amoeba[i][j].modulate(speed*fa++);
            amoeba[i][j].body.clear();
            amoeba[i][j].drawCurves();
        }
    }
};
stop();
```

We also need to change just one line of code within the 'constructor' function:

```
this.body = multiple.createEmptyMovieClip("body
➥ holder"+k, k++);
```

...you can also change the number of rows and columns in order to obtain other visual patterns. Use lower numbers if your processor is slow.

mx_bezier_amoeba_05

The amoeba will follow the mouse and the masked image will change dynamically when you press over the amoeba.

```
dtr=Math.PI/180, speed=2, sx=Stage.width/2,
sy=Stage.height/2, easing=.1;
image._x=sx, image._y=sy;
imageArray = ["image01", "image02", "image03"];
image = [];
for (var i = 0; i<3; i++) {
    image[i] = createEmptyMovieClip("image"+i, 3-i);
    image[i].attachMovie(imageArray[i], "img", 1);
    image[i]._x=sx, image[i]._y=sy;
}
amoeba[1] = new amoeba(15, 50, 15, Stage.width/2,
Stage.height/2, 2, 0xffffff, 100, 0x6633ff, 100);
image[0].setMask(amoeba[1].body);
this.onEnterFrame = function() {
    amoeba[1].move((1-easing)*amoeba[1].xpos+easing*_xmouse,
(1-easing)*amoeba[1].ypos+easing*_ymouse);
    amoeba[1].modulate(speed*fa++);
    amoeba[1].body.clear();
    amoeba[1].drawCurves();
};
amoeba[1].body.onPress = function() {
    d == 2 ? d=0 : d++;
    image[d].swapDepths(1000+dd++);
    image[d].setMask(amoeba[1].body);
};
stop();
```

We also include this new method:

```
this.amoeba.prototype.move = function(x, y) {
    this.xpos = x;
    this.ypos = y;
};
```

You can add or remove images as you want, just change the image array.

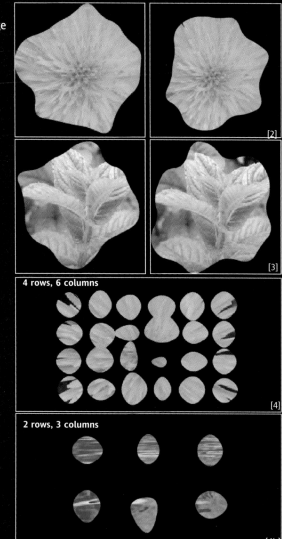

[2]

[3]

4 rows, 6 columns

[4]

2 rows, 3 columns

[4b]

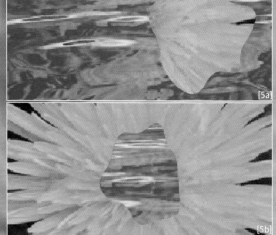

[5a]

[5b]

mx_bezier_amoeba_06

Finally we've got a new kind of shape, like a ring. This amoeba looks like a ring or "aura". We have added a new parameter: a circle radius that can be internal or external. I have modified the class constructor and methods so I need to write some new code.

We have added the x, y coordinates of the internal circle points (ix, iy) and its midpoints (imx,imy):

```
function amoeba(points, radius, offset, innerradius, xpos, ypos, strokewidth, strokecolor,
strokealpha, fillcolor, fillalpha) {
    this.body = createEmptyMovieClip("mybody"+k, 1000+k++);
    this.x=[], this.y=[], this.mx=[], this.my=[];
    this.ix=[], this.iy=[], this.imx=[], this.imy=[];
    this.innerradius = innerradius;
    this.xpos=xpos, this.ypos=ypos;
    this.radius=radius, this.offset=offset, this.frec=[], this.points=points;
    this.strokewidth=strokewidth, this.strokecolor=strokecolor, this.strokealpha=strokealpha,
    ➥ this.fillcolor=fillcolor, this.fillalpha=fillalpha;
    for (var i = 0; i<points; i++) {
      this.frec[i] = 2*(Math.random()+.5);
    }
}
```

This time the modulate method calculates the location of the inner circle points and midpoints too.

```
this.amoeba.prototype.modulate = function(t) {
    for (var i = 0; i<this.points; i++) {
      var ran = this.radius+this.offset*Math.sin(this.frec[i]*t*dtr);
      this.x[i] = this.xpos+ran*Math.cos(i*2*Math.PI/this.points);
      this.y[i] = this.ypos+ran*Math.sin(i*2*Math.PI/this.points);
      this.mx[i] = (this.x[i]+this.x[i-1])/2;
      this.my[i] = (this.y[i]+this.y[i-1])/2;
      var r = this.innerradius;
      this.ix[i] = this.xpos+r*Math.cos(i*2*Math.PI/this.points);
      this.iy[i] = this.ypos+r*Math.sin(i*2*Math.PI/this.points);
      this.imx[i] = (this.ix[i]+this.ix[i-1])/2;
      this.imy[i] = (this.iy[i]+this.iy[i-1])/2;
    }
    this.mx[0] = (this.x[this.points-1]+this.x[0])/2;
    this.my[0] = (this.y[this.points-1]+this.y[0])/2;
    this.imx[0] = (this.ix[this.points-1]+this.ix[0])/2;
    this.imy[0] = (this.iy[this.points-1]+this.iy[0])/2;
};
```

I have also modified the drawCurves method. As you can see it is not easy drawing a filled ring to use as a mask.

```
this.amoeba.prototype.drawCurves = function() {
    this.body.clear();
    this.body.beginFill(this.fillcolor, this.fillalpha);
    this.body.lineStyle(this.strokewidth, this.strokecolor, this.stroke
    ➥ this.body.moveTo(this.imx[0], this.imy[0]);
```

```
    this.body.curveTo(this.ix[this.points-1], this.iy[this.points-1], this.imx[this.points-1],
    ➥ this.imy[this.points-1]);
    for (var i = this.points-2; i>=0; i—) {
        this.body.curveTo(this.ix[i], this.iy[i], this.imx[i], this.imy[i]);
    }
    this.body.lineTo(this.mx[0], this.my[0]);
    for (var i = 0; i<=this.points-2; i++) {
        this.body.curveTo(this.x[i], this.y[i], this.mx[i+1], this.my[i+1]);
    }
    this.body.curveTo(this.x[this.points-1], this.y[this.points-1], this.mx[0], this.my[0]);
    this.body.lineTo(this.imx[0], this.imy[0]);
    this.body.endFill();
};
```

....and finally we create a couple of Bezier auras for the ring. .The big one has an inner fixed radius while the little one has an outer fixed radius (fig.21).

```
dtr=Math.PI/180, speed=2, sx=Stage.width/2, sy=Stage.height/2, easing=.1;
image._x=sx, image._y=sy;
imageArray = ["image03", "image02", "image01"];
image = [];
amoeba[0] = new amoeba(30, .15*Stage.height, .09*Stage.height, .25*Stage.height, Stage.width/2,
➥ Stage.height/2, 2, 0xffffff, 100, 0x6633ff, 100);
amoeba[1] = new amoeba(30, .45*Stage.height, .09*Stage.height, .35*Stage.height, Stage.width/2,
➥ Stage.height/2, 2, 0xffffff, 100, 0x6633ff, 100);
for (var i = 0; i<3; i++) {
    image[i] = createEmptyMovieClip("image"+i, 3-i);
    image[i].attachMovie(imageArray[i], "img", 1);
    image[i]._x=sx, image[i]._y=sy;
}
image[0].setMask(amoeba[0].body);
image[1].setMask(amoeba[1].body);
this.onEnterFrame = function() {
    for (var i = 0; i<2; i++) {
        amoeba[i].modulate(speed*fa++);
        amoeba[i].body.clear();
        amoeba[i].drawCurves();
    }
};
stop();
```

That's all, so go be creative and discover your own new Bezier shapes.

I'm sure by now you've learned a lot about the new dynamic mask functions and its unlimited posibilities. These examples may not be the most useful, but are useful for illustrating a lot of the new Flash MX ActionScript functions.

Image explosion

The purpose of this application is to show that we can break an image into a lot of small pieces in order to make some nice transition effects. This will be achieved using the power of dynamic masks (no more motion tweening or static masks!)

First of all, there is an image on the stage that I want to destroy, smashing it into small shards, so each and every time the pattern will have a different look. When this happens, each piece will be broken into smaller pieces – by a random fractal process, dependent on a set number of fractal levels.

Again, don't use more than 3 levels if you have a slow processor.

This is an OOP project, so the first step is to define our 'piece' class constructor function:

mx_explosion_01

This is the body script - entered in the first frame. You can see that this function receives the x, y coordinates of each vertex of the triangle, the fractal level and some drawing API values as parameters.

```
function piece(x1, y1, x2, y2, x3, y3, level) {
    this.initTriangle(x1, y1, x2, y2, x3, y3, level);
    this.drawTriangle();
    this.body.level<maxlevel ? this.loopFractalTriangle()  : null;
}
```

Now to add some of the fundfamental methods. This method will be used to set some properties of the body of the piece. The body is a movie clip that holds all the graphic elements of the object...

Inside the body movie clip, we've got 2 movie clips: the movie clip named 'masked' will be masked by movie clip named 'masker' (that should be obvious). `masked` holds the JPG image that is embedded via `attachMovie`, while masker holds the shape that will be drawn using the drawing API. Keep in mind that this time we are using a triangular shape, so we've got just 3 vertices (x1,y1), (x2,y2) and (x3,y3). The center of each triangle will be the baricenter (or gravity center) (x4,y4). We also perform some movements in order to set the baricenter as the movie clip x,y origin of each triangle.

We then apply some random color transformation to every triangle shape.

```
this.piece.prototype.initTriangle = function(x1, y1, x2, y2, x3, y3, level) {
    this.body = createEmptyMovieClip("bodyholder"+k, 1000+k++);
    this.body.level = level;
    this.body.ref = this;
    this.body.x1=x1, this.body.x2=x2, this.body.x3=x3, this.body.x4=(x1+x2+x3)/3;
    this.body.y1=y1, this.body.y2=y2, this.body.y3=y3, this.body.y4=(y1+y2+y3)/3;
    this.body.masked = this.body.createEmptyMovieClip("masked", 1);
    this.body.masker = this.body.createEmptyMovieClip("masker", 2);
    this.body.masked.attachMovie("image01", "img", 1);
    this.body.masked._x = sx-this.body.x4;
    this.body.masked._y = sy-this.body.y4;
    this.body.masked.setMask(this.body.masker);
    this.mycolor = new Color(this.body);
    this.ran = 200*(Math.random()-.5);
    this.mycolor.setTransform({ra:100, rb:this.ran, ga:100, gb:this.ran,
    ➡ ba:100, bb:this.ran, aa:100, ab:0});
    this.body._x = this.body.x4;
    this.body._y = this.body.y4;
};
```

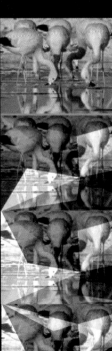

This method divides each triangle into three smaller triangles. We've got a conditional switch statement inside the `onEnterFrame` event handler in order to add color effects and some time delay between every triangle creation.

```
this.piece.prototype.loopFractalTriangle = function() {
  var counter = 0;
  this.body.onEnterFrame = function() {
    switch (counter) {
    case 1 :
      this.ref.mycolor.setTransform({ra:150, rb:this.ref.ran, ga:150, gb:this.ref.ran, ba:150,
bb:this.ref.ran, aa:100, ab:0});
      break;
    case 2 :
      this.ref.mycolor.setTransform({ra:100, rb:this.ref.ran, ga:100, gb:this.ref.ran, ba:100,
bb:this.ref.ran, aa:100, ab:0});
      break;
    case 3 :
      t[kk++] = new piece(this.x1, this.y1, this.x4, this.y4, this.x2, this.y2, this.level+1);
      break;
    case 5 :
      t[kk++] = new piece(this.x2, this.y2, this.x4, this.y4, this.x3, this.y3, this.level+1);
      break;
    case 7 :
      t[kk++] = new piece(this.x3, this.y3, this.x4, this.y4, this.x1, this.y1, this.level+1);
      break;
    case 9 :
      delete this.ref;
      this.removeMovieClip();
      break;
    }
    counter++;
  };
};
```

This method, `drawTriangle`, is just used to draw the triangle inside our masker movie clip, using some drawing API functions...

```
this.piece.prototype.drawTriangle = function() {
  this.body.masker.beginFill(0x000000, 100);
  this.body.masker.lineStyle(0, 0xffffff, 100);
  this.body.masker.moveTo(this.body.x1-this.body.x4, this.body.y1-this.body.y4);
  this.body.masker.lineTo(this.body.x2-this.body.x4, this.body.y2-this.body.y4);
  this.body.masker.lineTo(this.body.x3-this.body.x4, this.body.y3-this.body.y4);
  this.body.masker.lineTo(this.body.x1-this.body.x4, this.body.y1-this.body.y4);
  this.body.masker.endFill();
};
```

`newBox`: this method is used to draw a box on the stage that can be used as button.

```
MovieClip.prototype.newBox = function(xpos, ypos, mywidth, myheight, mytext, textsize,
➡ textcolor, textfont, textalign, strokewidth, strokecolor, strokealpha, fillcolor, fillalpha) {
  this.beginFill(fillcolor, fillalpha);
  this.lineStyle(strokewidth, strokecolor, strokealpha);
  this.moveTo(xpos-mywidth/2, ypos+myheight/2);
  this.lineTo(xpos-mywidth/2, ypos-myheight/2);
  this.lineTo(xpos+mywidth/2, ypos-myheight/2);
```

```
    this.lineTo(xpos+mywidth/2, ypos+myheight/2);
    this.endFill();
    this.createTextField("textum", 1, xpos-mywidth/2, ypos-myheight/2, mywidth, myheight);
    this.textum.text = mytext;
    this.myformat = new TextFormat();
    this.myformat.color = textcolor;
    this.myformat.font = textfont;
    this.myformat.align = textalign;
    this.myformat.size = textsize;
    this.textum.setTextFormat(this.myformat);
};
```

Finally, on the second frame, we define some variables and create the objects. The full image will be located at the center of the stage (sx,sy). We create a box that will be used as a button via an `onPress` event handler. Once pressed, the image will be divided into four triangles, where the corners and the center of the image are the vertex of the triangles. Well, the center (x0,y0) is not exactly the image center, because we are adding a random vector (r, angle) to the center coordinates (sx,sy).

```
maxlevel = 3;                              // number of fractal levels
dtr = Math.PI/180;                         // grades to radians conversion factor
sx = Stage.width/2;                        // stage horizontal center
sy = Stage.height/2;                       // stage vertical center
r = 20+30*Math.random();
angle = 360*Math.random();
rx = r*Math.cos(angle*dtr);
ry = r*Math.sin(angle*dtr);
x0=sx+rx, y0=sy+ry;                        // random center coordinates
this.createEmptyMovieClip("img", 1);
img.attachMovie("image01", "image", 1);
iw=img._width/2, ih=img._height/2;         // image center coordinates
img._x=sx, img._y=sy;
t = [];                                    // objects array
createEmptyMovieClip("but01", 2);
but01.newBox(sx, sy+ih+30, 90, 20, "break", 14, 0xffffff, "arial", "center", 1, 0xffffff, 100,
0x999999, 100);
this.but01.onPress = function() {
    but01._visible=0;
    img._visible=0;
    t[kk++] = new piece(sx-iw, sy+ih, x0, y0, sx-iw, sy-ih, 1);
    t[kk++] = new piece(sx-iw, sy-ih, x0, y0, sx+iw, sy-ih, 1);
    t[kk++] = new piece(sx+iw, sy-ih, x0, y0, sx+iw, sy+ih, 1);
    t[kk++] = new piece(sx+iw, sy+ih, x0, y0, sx-iw, sy+ih, 1);
};
stop();
```

mx_explosion_02

We are going to modify the body and the head of the code, so follow the instructions carefully. The next step is to add interaction, so we introduce this line of code at the bottom of the `piece` function:

```
    this.pieceButton();
```

Now add these new variables within the `initTriangle` method :

```
this.body.v = 40;                                         // initial speed
this.body.gravity = 13;                                   // gravity aceleration
this.body.angle = -90+90*(Math.random()-.5);;             // random initial angle
this.body.vx = this.body.v*Math.cos(this.body.angle*dtr); // horizontal speed component
this.body.vy = this.body.v*Math.sin(this.body.angle*dtr); // vertical speed component
this.body.vr = 80*(Math.random()-.5);                     // random rotational speed
```

... and the following methods:

Once the piece is pressed, the `loopJump` method will be triggered:

```
this.piece.prototype.pieceButton = function() {
    this.body.masker.onPress = function() {
      this._parent.ref.loopJump();
    };
};
```

The piece will jump according to parameters angle, v (speed) and gravity. You can see that each piece will describe a parabolic path.

```
this.piece.prototype.loopJump = function() {
    this.body.swapDepths(1000+k++);
    this.body.onEnterFrame = function() {
      this._x += this.vx;
      this._y += this.vy;
      this.vy += this.gravity;
      this._rotation += this.vr;
        if (this._y>=300) {
        this.onEnterFrame = null;
        delete this.ref;
        this.removeMovieClip();
      }
    };
};
```

Once you press the *break* button the image will be broken into many small triangles, and then every time you press a piece, it will jump, disappearing from the stage!

You can modify the code in order to generate different effects. For instance each piece can be moved disappearing to the right side of the stage instead jumping.

mx_explosion_03

We are ready to make our first image explosion – that means that all the pieces will jump at the same moment when we press a "explode" button. To dynamically draw our "explode" button we use the `drawBox` movie clip method

```
createEmptyMovieClip("but", 3);
but.newBox(sx, 350, 90, 20, "explode", 14, 0xffffff, "arial",
➡ "center", 1, 0xffffff, 100, 0x999999, 100);
but._visible = 0;
```

...then we add an event handler, so the box behaves as button. This `onPress` event handler creates a new array. The `st` array holds the objects that have survived the fractal process (remember that every time a triangle is broken, it disappears too).

```
st = [];
this.but02.onPress = function() {
  for (thing in t) {
    t[thing].body._name != null ? st.push(t[thing]) : null;
  }
  for (i=0; i<st.length; i++) {
    st[i].loopJump();
  }
  but02._visible=0;
};
```

Finally, change this line of code within the constructor function. This way the explode button will be visible once the fractal process has finished.

```
this.body.level<maxlevel ? this.loopFractalTriangle() : but02._visible=1;
```

...and removes the `pieceButton` method and this line of code:

```
this.pieceButton();
```

Press the break button to generate the fractal and then press the "explode" button to destroy the image. It's fun.

Remember that this process is very CPU intensive so my advice is don't use more than 3 fractal levels or your system may crash!

mx_explosion_04

Now we want to make it so that once the "explode" button is pressed, all the pieces start jumping one-by-one. Once the `st` array has been filled, it can be sorted using the following functions. :

```
function order(a, b) {
    return a.body._y<b.body._y ? -1 : a.body._y>b.body._y ? 1 : 0;
}

function disorder() {
    return Math.round(Math.random());
}
```

At this stage, we press the button and the jump process begins:

```
st = [];
this.but02.onPress = function() {
  but02._visible = 0;
  for (thing in t) {
    t[thing].body._name != undefined ? st.push(t[thing]) : null;
  }
  st.sort(order);
  index=0, frame=0;
  this.onEnterFrame = function() {
    frame==0 ? st[index].loopJump() : null;
```

```
      frame++;
      if (frame>=3) {
         index++;
         frame = 0;
      }
      index>=st.length ? this.onEnterFrame=null : null;
   };
};
```

We have included an `onEnterFrame` event handler to add some delay between every jump.

mx_explosion_05

We are ready to code our slide show. The first step is to generate an array of images for our slide show (keep in mind that you must set up the library linkage of every image).

```
maxlevel = 2;
dtr = Math.PI/180;
sx=Stage.width/2, sy=Stage.height/2;
images = 2;
image = 0;
imageArray = ["image01", "image02", "image03"]; //the array of images
this.createEmptyMovieClip("img", 1);
img.attachMovie(imageArray[image], "image", 1);
iw=img._width/2, ih=img._height/2;
img._x=sx, img._y=sy;
createEmptyMovieClip("but01", 2);              // "break" button
but01.newBox(sx, sy+ih+30, 90, 20, "broke", 14, 0xffffff,
➡ "arial", "center", 1, 0xffffff, 100, 0x999999, 100);
createEmptyMovieClip("but02", 3);              // "explode" button
but02.newBox(sx, sy+ih+30, 90, 20, "explode", 14,
➡ 0xffffff, "arial", "center", 1, 0xffffff, 100, 0x999999, 100);
but02._visible = 0;
function reset() {
   but01._visible = 0;
   img._visible = 0;
   angle = 360*Math.random();
   r = 20+30*Math.random();
   angle = 360*Math.random();
   rx = r*Math.cos(angle*dtr);
   ry = r*Math.sin(angle*dtr);
   x0=sx+rx, y0=sy+ry;
   t = [];
   st = [];
   t[kk++] = new piece(sx-iw, sy+ih, x0, y0, sx-iw, sy-ih, 1);
   t[kk++] = new piece(sx-iw, sy-ih, x0, y0, sx+iw, sy-ih, 1);
   t[kk++] = new piece(sx+iw, sy-ih, x0, y0, sx+iw, sy+ih, 1);
   t[kk++] = new piece(sx+iw, sy+ih, x0, y0, sx-iw, sy+ih, 1);
}
this.but01.onPress = function() {
   reset();
};

this.but02.onPress = function() {
   img._visible = 1;
```

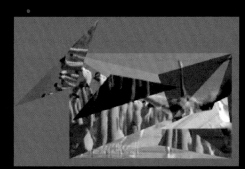

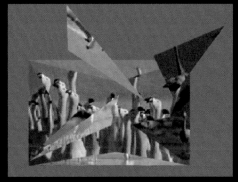

79

```
    index=0, frame=0;
    this.onEnterFrame = function() {
      frame == 0 ? st[index].loopJump() : null;
      frame++;
      if (frame>=2) {
        index++;
        frame = 0;
      }
      if (index == st.length) {
        this.onEnterFrame = null;
        but01._visible = 1;
      }
    };
  };
```

We have added a `reset` function that will be called every time we break a new image.

Every time the "explode" button is pressed, we attach a new image, and when the last piece of the broken image has jumped, the "break" button appears, so the process begins again.

Finally, change this line of code within the `init` method:

```
this.body.masked.attachMovie(imageArray[image], "img", 1);
```

mx_explosion_06sq

As a last experiment, I want to show you the automatic version of our slide show. I have also included another kind of shape. This time we are going to use rectangles instead triangles. The explosion process can be visualized in the following sequence of images.

This is the new `piece` constructor function

```
function piece(x1, y1, x2, y2, x3, y3, x4, y4, level) {
  this.initRectangle(x1, y1, x2, y2, x3, y3, x4, y4, level);
  this.drawRectangle();
  if (this.body.level<maxlevel) {
    this.loopFractalRectangle();
  } else {
    if (flag == 0) {
      flag = 1;
      pause(jump, jumpdelay);
    }
  }
}
```

I have also modified the methods because the rectangle shape has got 4 vertices. The new `baricenter` is the point (x5,y5).

```
this.piece.prototype.initRectangle = function(x1, y1, x2, y2, x3, y3, x4, y4, level) {
  this.body = createEmptyMovieClip("bodyholder"+k, 1000+k++);
  this.body.level = level;
  this.body.ref = this;
  this.body.x1=x1, this.body.x2=x2, this.body.x3=x3, this.body.x4=x4,
➡ this.body.x5=x1+(3+4*Math.random())/10*(x4-x1);
  this.body.y1=y1, this.body.y2=y2, this.body.y3=y3, this.body.y4=y4,
➡ this.body.y5=y2+(3+4*Math.random())/10*(y4-y2);
  this.body.masked = this.body.createEmptyMovieClip("masked", 1);
  this.body.masker = this.body.createEmptyMovieClip("masker", 2);
  this.body.masked.attachMovie(imageArray[image], "img", 1);
  this.body.masked._x = sx-this.body.x5;
  this.body.masked._y = sy-this.body.y5;
  this.body.masked.setMask(this.body.masker);
  this.mycolor = new Color(this.body);
  this.ran = -100+200*Math.random();
  this.mycolor.setTransform({ra:100, rb:this.ran, ga:100, gb:this.ran, ba:100, bb:this.ran, aa:100, ab:0});
  this.body._x = this.body.x5;
  this.body._y = this.body.y5;
  this.body.v = 40;
  this.body.gravity = 13;
  this.body.angle = -90+90*(Math.random()-.5);
  this.body.vx = this.body.v*Math.cos(this.body.angle*dtr);
  this.body.vy = this.body.v*Math.sin(this.body.angle*dtr);
  this.body.vr = 80*(Math.random()-.5);
};
```

```
this.piece.prototype.loopJump = function() {
  this.body.swapDepths(1000+k++);
  this.body.onEnterFrame = function() {
    this._x += this.vx;
    this._y += this.vy;
    this.vy += this.gravity;
    this._rotation += this.vr;
    if (this._y>=550) {
      this.onEnterFrame = null;
      delete this.ref;
      this.removeMovieClip();
    }
  };
};
```

We must generate 4 new rectangles each time:

```
this.piece.prototype.loopFractalRectangle = function() {
  var counter = 0;
  this.body.onEnterFrame = function() {
    switch (counter) {
    case 1 :
      this.ref.mycolor.setTransform({ra:150, rb:this.ref.ran, ga:150,
➡     gb:this.ref.ran, ba:150, bb:this.ref.ran, aa:100, ab:0});
      break;
    case 2 :
```

```
    this.ref.mycolor.setTransform({ra:100, rb:this.ref.ran, ga:100, gb:this.ref.ran, ba:100,
    ➥ bb:this.ref.ran, aa:100, ab:0});
      break;
    case 3 :
      t[kk++] = new piece(this.x1, this.y1, this.x1, this.y5, this.x5, this.y5, this.x5, this.y1, this.level+1);
      break;
    case 5 :
      t[kk++] = new piece(this.x1, this.y5, this.x2, this.y2, this.x5, this.y2, this.x5, this.y5, this.level+1);
      break;
    case 7 :
      t[kk++] = new piece(this.x5, this.y5, this.x5, this.y2, this.x3, this.y3, this.x3, this.y5, this.level+1);
      break;
    case 9 :
      t[kk++] = new piece(this.x5, this.y4, this.x5, this.y5, this.x3, this.y5, this.x4, this.y4, this.level+1);
      break;
    case 10 :
      delete this.ref;
      this.removeMovieClip();
      break;
    }
    counter++;
  };
};

this.piece.prototype.drawRectangle = function() {
  this.body.masker.beginFill(0x000000, 100);
  this.body.masker.lineStyle(0, 0xffffff, 100);
  this.body.masker.moveTo(this.body.x1-this.body.x5, this.body.y1-this.body.y5);
  this.body.masker.lineTo(this.body.x2-this.body.x5, this.body.y2-this.body.y5);
  this.body.masker.lineTo(this.body.x3-this.body.x5, this.body.y3-this.body.y5);
  this.body.masker.lineTo(this.body.x4-this.body.x5, this.body.y4-this.body.y5);
  this.body.masker.lineTo(this.body.x1-this.body.x5, this.body.y1-this.body.y5);
  this.body.masker.endFill();
};

function order(a, b) {
  return a.body._y<b.body._y ? -1 : a.body._y>b.body._y ? 1 : 0;
}
```

We include a pause function, that will be called every time we need a time delay. This function receives the name of the delayed function and the delay (number of frames) as parameters.

```
function pause(myfunction, mydelay) {
  var frame = 0, pausedfunction = myfunction;
  this.onEnterFrame = function(myfunction) {
    if (frame++ == mydelay) {
      this.onEnterFrame = null;
      pausedfunction();
    }
  }
```

We don't need buttons, so remove the "break" and "explode" buttons; we have 2 functions (`reset` and `jump`) that perform the animation.

```
maxlevel =3;
dtr = Math.PI/180;
sx=Stage.width/2, sy=Stage.height/2;
images = 2;
image = 0;
imageArray = ["image01", "image02", "image03"];
this.createEmptyMovieClip("img", 1);
img.attachMovie(imageArray[image], "image", 1);
iw=img._width/2, ih=img._height/2;
img._x=sx, img._y=sy;
jumpdelay = 30;
breakdelay = 50;
function reset() {
    flag = 0;
    t = [];
    st = [];
    var x1 = sx-iw, y1 = sy+ih;
    var x2 = sx-iw, y2 = sy-ih;
    var x3 = sx+iw, y3 = sy-ih;
    var x4 = sx+iw, y4 = sy+ih;
    t[kk++] = new piece(x1, y1, x2, y2, x3, y3, x4, y4, 1);
}
function jump() {
    image<images ? image++ : image=0;
    img.attachMovie(imageArray[image], "image", 1);
    for (thing in t) {
      t[thing] body._name != undefined ? st.push(t[thing]) : null;
    }
    st.sort(order);
    var index = 0, frame = 0;
    _root.onEnterFrame = function() {
      frame == 0 ? st[index].loopJump() : null;
      frame++;
      if (frame>=3) {
        index++;
        frame = 0;
      }
      if (index == st.length) {
        this.onEnterFrame = null;
        pause(reset, breakdelay);
      }
    };
}
pause(reset, 50);
stop();
```

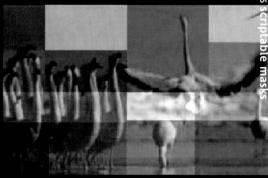
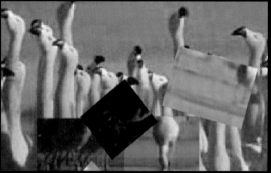

Done!, We have finished our advanced image slide show and the explosion effect using the new dynamic masking and drawing API functions. You can improve this application using external images (remember that you will need an image preloader in order to check if the image has been loaded).

I hope you've enjoyed our experiments with masks and masking. Mess with the code, the variables, and change the JPGs.. Remember, you can't break anything, and even if your SWFs crash and burn they might give you just the inspiration you've been looking for.

experimental interfaces
paul prudence

The movie clip object is at the core of Flash. ActionScript control of the movie clip has always been at the center of any great Flash work with its numerous methods and properties. Now in Flash MX it has been given a fabulous new set of methods, properties, and most importantly, event handlers to give us much greater control, more precision and greater versatility in the scripting environment. Exciting new features in MX include the ability to create new movie clips on the fly at runtime. The new drawing API allows us to dynamically populate such movie clips with lines, curves, fills and gradients on the fly as the movie is playing. A particularly brilliant new addition to the ActionScript lexicon is the ability to ascribe events to movie clips much in the same way you would give buttons event handlers. What's more, the old methodology of attaching code to movie clips and buttons has given way to a much more structured and centralized method akin to real OOP languages. It's now possible for all of your code to reside in one place. Other exciting advances include the ability to dynamically load external media such as JPGs and MP3s, I could go on but I would like to give each of these more time and look at them in more detail as I work through a set of creative experimental interfaces with variations utilizing many of these new features and more.

Advances in the MX scripting environment lend themselves amazingly well to interface design where quite often we have a situation where lots of buttons have similar traits and properties but remain unique in some functionality. For a non-programmer artist/designer like myself this is a breath of fresh air since I can concentrate on aesthetics without getting too lost in a pile of hermetic `hitTest` array loop checks! Put simply it's just a lot easier to accomplish certain tasks in MX – in Flash 5 the limitations of the scripting model meant often resorting to programming workarounds. Throughout this chapter I'll be offering explanations of how my code might have fared in Flash 5 and how in many cases the tasks in hand would have been impossible.

Experimental interface and the working process

The interface experiments I'm going to work through have been arrived at from an exploration of the use of multiple units arranged in non-ordinary interface configurations, geometric forms outside of the standard rectilinear formation (namely rows of buttons. I wanted an interface that had some discrete and unique beauty of its own apart from, and outside of, the site's content. As long as usability remained a key attribute and there was some sequential method for interaction I wanted an interface that you might want to play with for a little while, not something entirely functional to the point that it was only there to be clicked to get to something else. Running the risk of offending the usability police, I wanted something that on first encounter the user couldn't be quite 100% sure of.

The vast majority of my time in Flash is spent in explorative mode, making things, breaking things, adding new variables to the system, adding a new trig function here or there – quite often with no purpose in mind – it's a lot like playing with Meccano. Every now and then something happens, an interesting effect is produced and the start of a small adventure is embarked upon. I used to do a lot of painting and the same process occurs there, a form of alchemy when things start to flow and you say a-ha!

The files in this chapter are, I believe, at that point, at the end of the experimentation process and the start of the refinement process. It's interesting to note that quite often near the end of a refinement process I'll take a finished piece and start to break it again – adding antagonistic code to make something new. So this whole process of experimentation and refinement is cyclic and intermingled – experimentation is always at the heart of it somewhere, it's the food of the process.

As we shall see, Flash MX lends itself remarkably well to experimentation due to its improved internal code structure, it's now just a lot easier to hybridize our code, but more on that as we go on.

I'm going to work through two interfaces, each with a number of developed variations resulting from changes to the core code. I'll be looking at the core code in detail, with the variations I'll take a close look at the specific modifications. Finally I'll be offering possible routes to continue with in our experiments, so here we go.

Experiment 1 – An experimental drawing API interface created at runtime

Have a look at the code below all contained in frame one of the movie `API_circles01.fla`. You can download this, and all the other files for this chapter from www.friendsofED.com. Open it up, test it in your browser - then we'll delve into how it's created.

`API_circles01.fla`

```
// the links
// ———-
var link = ["circle09", "circle08", "circle07", "circle06", "circle05", "circle04", "circle03",
➡"circle02", "circle01", "circle09", "circle08", "circle07", "circle06", "circle05", "circle04",
➡"circle03", "circle02", "circle01", "circle09", "circle08", "circle07", "circle06", "circle05",
➡"circle04", "circle03", "circle02", "circle01", "circle09", "circle08", "circle07", "circle06",
➡"circle05", "circle04", "circle03", "circle02", "circle01", "circle09", "circle08", "circle07",
➡"circle06", "circle05", "circle04", "circle03", "circle02", "circle01", "circle09", "circle08",
➡"circle07", "circle06", "circle05", "circle04", "circle03", "circle02", "circle01"];


//draw circle proto
//———————-
MovieClip.prototype.drawCircle = function(xpos, ypos, radius, lWidth, lColor,
➡fColor,fAlpha) {
    x = xpos;
    y = ypos;
    r = radius;
    u = r*0.4086;
    v = r*0.7071;
    this.lineStyle(lwidth,lColor,100);
    this.beginFill(fColor, fAlpha);
    this.moveTo(x-r, y);
    this.curveTo(x-r, y-u, x-v, y-v);
    this.curveTo(x-u, y-r, x, y-r);
    this.curveTo(x+u, y-r, x+v, y-v);
    this.curveTo(x+r, y-u, x+r, y);
    this.curveTo(x+r, y+u, x+v, y+v);
    this.curveTo(x+u, y+r, x, y+r);
    this.curveTo(x-u, y+r, x-v, y+v);
    this.curveTo(x-r, y+u, x-r, y);
    this.endFill();
};
```

```
// create circles and add events
// ─────────────────────
for (i = 0; i < link.length; i++) {
    _root.createEmptyMovieClip("mc'+i, i);
    with ( _root["mc'+i] ) {
        drawCircle(0,0,20,1,0xFFffff,0xFD0E02*i/1,25);
        drawCircle(0,0,5,1,0xFFffff,0xFD0E02*i/1,25);
        _x = Math.sin (i)*(50-Math.sqrt(i)*15)+Math.sin(i)+250;
        _y = Math.cos (i)*(50-Math.sqrt(i)*55)+Math.cos(i)+250;
    }

    // the rollOver
    // ─────
    _root["mc"+i].onRollOver = function(){
        _root.createEmptyMovieClip("rol", 1000);
        rol.drawCircle(this._x,this._y,30,1,0xAFA374,0xffffff,40);
        this._yscale = this._xscale = 110;
        _root.createEmptyMovieClip("line", 1005);
        with ( _root.line ) {
            lineStyle( 1, 0xAFA374, 50 );
            moveTo( this._x, this._y  );
            lineTo(386,191);
        }
        _root.select = " " + _root.link[Number((this._name).substring(2)]
    }

    // the rollOut
    // ─────
    _root["mc"+i].onRollOut = function(){
        rol.clear();
        this._yscale = this._xscale = 100
    }

    // the release - load relative jpg
    // ─────────────────
    _root["mc"+i].onRelease = function(){
        _root.createEmptyMovieClip("line2", 1006);
        with ( _root.line2 ) {
            lineStyle( 1, 0xAFA374, 75 );
            moveTo( this._x, this._y  );
            lineTo(386,191);
        }
        toload = select + ".jpg";
        _root.createEmptyMovieClip("jpg_parent",-1);
        with ( _root.jpg_parent ) {
            _x = 384;
            _y = 106;
            loadMovie(toload, 0);
        }
    }
}
```

circle06

```
// the label
// ————-
_root.createEmptyMovieClip("label", 1002);
_root.label.createTextField("insidelabel",1003,100,-20,50,18);
_root.label.insidelabel.background = true;
_root.label.onEnterFrame = function () {
    yslide = (_root._ymouse - this._y) * .2;
    this._y += yslide;
    _root.label.insidelabel.text = _root.select;
}
```

circle02

Look at the ActionScript in Flash MX. Notice that there is nothing in the library, no symbols at all! Everything needed to generate the interface is contained within the single first frame of the movie – cool huh? When the movie is fired up this code does everything from drawing the circular buttons to attaching the event handlers (rollovers and press functions) to opening the desired files when the buttons are pressed. This is something that could never have been done in Flash 5 as the circular buttons would have to have been drawn manually and then added to the library from where they could have been referenced by a script often using the `attachMovie` method.

The movie clip object in Flash MX now has an exciting array of drawing methods that allow us to instruct Flash to draw lines, curves and fills and by extension any complex shape you care to imagine. This is all very well but what if we want to control these new shapes? Well we can, thanks to a new ability in MX to create empty movieclips as holders for anything we care to put inside them. Since an interface relies on user interaction to work there is one other great addition to the movie clip object in MX we can utilize and that is the ability to add an event chain to them and make them behave just like buttons. This may not seem so great at first glance since we already have buttons, and they too have had a wonderful overhaul in MX, but as we shall see, the implications are tremendous in more ways than one.

Enough talk, let's dip into the code a block at a time.

Picture this

First off I'm defining an array list of all JPGs that I want to load via my interface. This array could contain any number of items, the final number of buttons on the screen will be dependent on the amount of items in array, I've re-used the same JPGs a number of times, but it would be possible to have, say, 60 entirely different circles...

```
var link = ["circle60", "circle59", ... , "circle02", "circle01"]
```

The JPGs themselves need to be in the same directory as the published SWF – if you don't add the absolute URL or folder location of the images.

Draw!

Next I'm going to use the new MX API drawing methods to make a movie clip prototype called 'drawCircle'. This prototype function takes a number of arguments that allow us to use `drawCircle` as a movie clip method to make circles with specific properties such as radius, position and fill color. The drawing API is one of the most exciting new features in MX and in many cases will allow us to replace what would have been many lines of code in Flash 5 to just few in MX. The basic commands allow us to define line styles, i.e. line color, line thickness and line opacity (_alpha). We can draw lines and curves from point to point, and with the shapes made we can apply solid or gradient fills. We also have the option to pick up the pen and move it to another position on the screen without making a mark.

The circle code I've used is a little more complicated than we might expect. Surely we can make a circle using four curves at 90 degrees to one another? Well we can but MX has a habit of making non-perfect circles with this method, in fact they appear somewhat square, and a square circle is too non-conformist, even for me! MX fails on the accuracy front regarding curves of that angular size, however with a little bit of math and eight 45 degree angled curves we can achieve a perfect circle with ease!

```
//draw circle proto
//————-
MovieClip.prototype.drawCircle =
➡function(xpos, ypos, radius, lWidth,
➡lColor, fColor, fAlpha) {
    x = xpos;
    y = ypos;
    r = radius;
    u = r*0.4086;
    v =  r*0.7071;
    this.lineStyle(lwidth,lColor,100);
    this.beginFill(fColor, fAlpha);
    this.moveTo(x-r, y);
    this.curveTo(x-r, y-u, x-v, y-v);
    this.curveTo(x-u, y-r, x, y-r);
    this.curveTo(x+u, y-r, x+v, y-v);
    this.curveTo(x+r, y-u, x+r, y);
    this.curveTo(x+r, y+u, x+v, y+v);
    this.curveTo(x+u, y+r, x, y+r);
    this.curveTo(x-u, y+r, x-v, y+v);
    this.curveTo(x-r, y+u, x-r, y);
    this.endFill();
}
```

The possibilities for use of the drawing API in MX are virtually limitless. We can expect to see the hardcore few experimenting at the fringes of math and creativity producing some stunning work. More so, a great deal of files, like this one, will be published without a single movie clip or symbol in the library! A lot of 3D work in previous versions of Flash was hampered by processor unfriendly routines that worked hard just drawing these objects to be manipulated in 3D space. The ability to draw lines to points will really push such work to a new level and allow developers to concentrate solely on the 3D engines.

Next we are going to set a `for` loop to loop as many times as there are items in the array we have just defined. Length is a property of an array returning the number of items in the array, so in this case the loop will loop 60 times. The next line utilizes a new feature in MX, the ability to create an empty movie clip. Anyone familiar with Flash 5's `attachMovie` will be instantly at home as it has a very similar syntax requiring an instance name and a depth. The next line of code specifies a set of properties/methods for the `"mc"+i` instance within the curly braces using the `with` statement. This prevents you from having to repeatedly write the object's name or the path to the object. The first two lines within the `with` statement call upon the previously defined `drawCircle` function to make two circles in that particular instance of the newly created movie clip. The arguments passed to the `drawCircle` function that define these two circles are as follows in this order: x-position, y-position, radius, line width, line color, fill color and fill alpha. We can see for example that both circles are positioned top left within the new movie clip and the second circle is a quarter of the size of the first. We can further see that the colors of these circles will be different as they are dependent upon the value of i. Because the alpha is set to 25% for both, the result is a collection of hues pleasing to my eyes. The final two lines of code in this block set the x and y positions of each respective movie clip based on some math functions. I experiment quite a bit with plotting movieclips according to these kinds of functions, quite often I find unique shapes and geometric formations lying hidden and revealed by code tweaks and experimentation. I will come back to alter these lines quite a bit in later mutations of this file.

```
// Create circles and add events
// —————————
for (i = 0; i < link.length; i++) {
    _root.createEmptyMovieClip("mc"+i, i);
    with ( _root["mc"+i] ) {
        drawCircle(0, 0, 20, 1, 0xFFffff,
        ➥0xFD0E02*i/1, 25)
        drawCircle(0, 0, 5, 1, 0xFFffff,
        ➥0xFD0E02*i/1, 25)
        _x = Math.sin(i)*(50-Math.sqrt(i)
        ➥*15) + Math.sin(i)+250;
        _y = Math.cos (i)*(50-Math.sqrt(i)
        ➥*55) + Math.cos(i)+250;
    }
```

Play

The next step is to give our circles some interactivity and this is where one of the best new features in MX comes into play – and that is the ability to add button functionality to the humble movie clip object by virtue of a new set of event handlers. Not only can we add the kind of functionality previously only reserved for buttons but we don't even have to attach them to our movieclips as we did with our buttons. We can define event callback functions and attach them remotely to the movieclips via a centralized piece of code in this case in the first frame of our movie.

Let's digress from the circles code for a moment and take an example of how things have changed. In Flash 5 the syntax for adding *events* to buttons would have been something like this:

```
on ( release ) {
    perform the task
}
```

In MX we can do this – placing the code in the main timeline:

```
theMC.onRelease = function () {
    perform the task
}
```

This syntactical structure is much more in keeping with real OOP languages, in fact it is a subset of OOP rather like JavaScript. It has distinct advantages over the old Flash 5 way of doing things.

OK, now returning to our circles example, let's look at our code for the rollover state of one of our clip instances. We are still in the for loop and this allows us to attach an event to every single instance i.e. "mc"+i. The first line in our event function creates a new movie clip called rol with a depth of 1000. I've chosen a depth of 1000 so we can be sure it exists high enough in the stack never to be interfered with by other movie clip instances. The next line instructs Flash to draw a circle at the position of the mouse cursor, as this is directly over one of our "mc"+i clip instances it positions the circle exactly over the movie clip we are rolling over and in our movie actually gives a nice snap-to rollover effect. Following this we have set the scaling of our particular mc to 110% adding to the rollover effect. For schematic clarity in this interface I wanted to show a line connecting our rolled over mc to our loading area where our JPGs appear so again we create an empty movie clip and populate it with a line. An 0xAFA374 colored line 1 pixel wide with 50% alpha connects the registration point of our movie clip, which, by default conveniently for us, is the center of our specific mc, to position 386,191 on the stage – and this links to a circle containing the loaded content. Finally in this block of code, the _root variable select is set to a value in the link array dependent on the movie clip's instance name. This is a great way of individually identifying a particular movie clip amongst many that have been generated on the fly. What we have done is to convert the third character and onwards in the instance name string of the particular movie clip into a number which is useful for referring to that array. We have also added a character space at the start of this string for design purposes.

```
// the rollOver
// ———
_root["mc"+i].onRollOver = function(){
    _root.createEmptyMovieClip("rol",1000);
    rol.drawCircle(this._x, this._y, 30, 1,
    ➥0xAFA374, 0xffffff, 40);
    this._yscale = this._xscale = 110;
    _root.createEmptyMovieClip("line",1005);
    with ( _root.line ) {
        lineStyle( 1, 0xAFA374, 50 );
        moveTo( this._x, this._y );
        lineTo(386,191);
    }
    _root.select = " " + _root.link[Number
    ➥((this._name).substring(2))];
}
```

Now we will look at the rollout event. Using the clear method, which is also new to MX, we remove all the drawing commands associated the rol movie clip. This is essence makes the large white rollover circle disappear. We also want the individual mc to return to its original scale so we set the x and y scale back to 100%.

```
// the rollOut
// ———-
_root["mc"+i].onRollOut = function(){
    rol.clear();
    this._yscale = this._xscale = 100;
}
```

Next up are the events ascribed to clicking on one of our circles, the onRelease event. When the movie clip is released we have again created an empty movie clip called line2 at a free depth. Just like we did with the rollover function we draw a line from the center of the movie clip to 384,106 on the stage, this time with greater weight. We can see from the fact that these line clips are drawn freshly each time the onRelease is triggered that they will erase the previous versions of the drawn line. You can see in the final SWF that the combinations of movieclips line1 and line2 give a schematic representation of the circles to be clicked and the circles currently clicked.

The next three lines of code are the ones that load the JPG into the SWF. Previously in Flash the only external media we could load into SWFs were other SWFs. MX has now given us the wonderful ability to load both external JPGs and MP3s on the fly. This is great addition to MX because it means no more having to load all JPGs contained within a SWF before the file gets going. We can now load each JPG when a user requires it cutting down on preloading time dramatically, this will be of particular benefit to Flash photography portfolios for example. Going back to the code, first up we set the variable toload to add together the string variable select and the string ".jpg". Next we create an empty movie clip holder called 'jpg_parent' at a depth of -1 and position it in the correct spot on the stage ready for the final bit of code which is loadMovie(toload, 0). Remember toload will be equal to circle(x).jpg where x is a number between 1 and 60. That's all the code for movie clip interaction.

```
// the release + load relative jpg
// —————————-
_root["mc"+i].onRelease = function(){
    _root.createEmptyMovieClip("line2", 1006);
    with ( _root.line2 ) {
        lineStyle( 1, 0xAFA374, 75 );
        moveTo( this._x, this._y );
        lineto(386,191);
    }
    toload = select + ".jpg";
    _root.createEmptyMovieClip("jpg_parent",-1);
    with ( _root.jpg_parent ) {
        _x = 384;
        _y = 106;
        loadMovie(toload, 0);
    }
}
```

The last block of code is used to generate a label showing us the name of the item we are rolling over. Again we are going to generate this on the fly using the new MX `createTextField` method which creates a text field object inside of another newly created empty movie clip called 'label'. You can now see how indispensable the MX `createEmptyMovieclip` method is since we have used it a lot throughout this script and couldn't have got by without it.

Going back to the `createTextField` method we can see that it takes a number of arguments and in order they are: `instanceName`, `depth`, `x`, `y`, `width`, and `height`. Once created, the text field has a number of default properties that can be set that are both stylistic and of a functional nature, for example you can set the text to appear in password star form or add a border to the field. Here I've turned on the background, I can then go on to specify a color if I want but the default white is fine for now. Any text field created in this manner also gets its own default `TextFormat` object which defines the text formatting of the text field, for example font type, size, alignment etc. We'll look at this later in the second experiment. To give the label a bit of life I've added a sliding inertia `onEnterFrame` function so that the label glides towards the mouse pointer on the y axis. Last of all we need to populate the text field with the current movie clip name while rolling over it so we must set text to the value of `_root.select`, this is reset every frame so that text is kept up to date with whatever movie clip we are currently rolling over.

```
// the label
// ———-
_root.createEmptyMovieClip("label", 1002);
_root.label.createTextField("insidelabel",1003,100,-20,50,18);
_root.label.insidelabel.background = true;
_root.label.onEnterFrame = function () {
    yslide = (_root._ymouse - this._y) * .2;
    this._y += yslide;
    _root.label.insidelabel.text = _root.select;
}
```

That's it! A complete Flash MX interface generated at runtime weighing in at 1.33 Kilobytes and occupying one frame on the timeline! Not bad. The code is all in one place which means that on going back to this file everything will be easy to find, update and change. If I want to grab a portion of code and take it to another file I don't have to worry about importing the movie clip the code is attached to because it not attached to anything, this makes for great modular coding. I quite like this interface, its simplicity and tonal variation work – however Flash is all about motion, so let's develop this core code a bit further with a few tweaks and additions and give it some movement. Quite often the smallest of changes yield the greatest result, let's also make a few changes to the positioning of the movieclips.

API DNA

Some changes to the core code and we have an animated nucleic structured menu. The circle buttons are arranged in a spiraling chain and can be revolved in either direction with the mouse pointer, quite a large jump from the initial interface! Let's have a summary of the changes.

Open up `API_nucleic.fla` and look at the script. In the first part of our loop we can see that the two lines defining the size and color of our circles have been modified. The x and y positions of our newly made circles inside each movie clip are now dependent on some trigonometric functions of i, and this is what gives the final form a DNA look. The radii and colors have been changed as well as the x and y plotting positions.

```
drawCircle(Math.sin(i)*10,Math.cos(i)*20,17,1,0xFFffff,0xFD0E02*i/1,15);
drawCircle(Math.sin(i)*10,Math.cos(i)*20,10,1,0xFFffff,0xFD0E02*i/8.5,45);
_x = 275;
_y = 35+(i*16);
```

Regarding the rollout, rollover and release events – I've mainly taken code out. The lines pointing to the JPG load area have gone and the larger white rollover circle has gone. Only the relative scaling of the movie clip's remain. We have added a new event function to the movie clip's and this is:

```
// the enterFrame
// ———————
_root["movieclip"+i].onEnterFrame = function(){
    this._rotation-=8*(2-(_root._xmouse/150));
}
```

circle01

This piece of code is responsible for creating the twisting motion of the movieclips and is dependent on the relative position of the mouse.

As far as the label goes we've now added a few lines to make the text field slide in the x-axis as well as the y. However when we inadvertently rollover the text field it takes precedence over the circle buttons, and in effect, if the mouse pointer is over both it renders the button out of action. It's OK though, MX has an answer for this in the form of the selectable property of a text field. So we add the following line to our code:

```
_root.label.insidelabel.selectable = false;
```

Your history

I thought it would be interesting to add a history path to this next interface a bit like the one at the excellent uncontrol.com, this gives us a way of seeing the path we've traced as we click on successive items, the final result comes across as linear Hansel (as in Gretel) versus a shifting Venn diagram! Take a look at `API_historyPath.fla` — if you want the full effect you will have to publish and test in your browser. In Flash 5 it was possible to dynamically draw lines from and to specified points but it took a little bit of trickery. In essence you'd use a hairline line contained inside a movie clip and scale it from point to point. With MX using `lineTo` we can perform this task with ease. To draw a line from the last to the next clicked item is a relatively simple task. Included inside the `onRelease` events we've just added and modified a few lines of code. This file takes the last variation as a starting point and adds a few new lines of code. The `onRelease` block now looks like this:

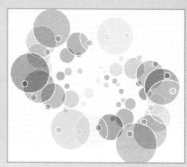

```
// the release - load relative jpg
// ———————————
_root["mc"+i].onRelease = function(){
    _root.createEmptyMovieClip("line2", 1005+count);
    with ( _root.line2 ) {
        lineStyle( 1, 0x684522, 10+count);
        moveTo( this._x, this._y );
        lineTo(lastx,lasty );
    }
    lastx = this._x ;
    lasty = this._y;
    count++;
    toload = select + ".jpg";
    _root.createEmptyMovieClip("jpg_parent",2000);
    with ( _root.jpg_parent ) {
        _x = 384;
        _y = 106;
        loadMovie(toload, 0);
    }
}
```

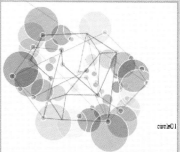

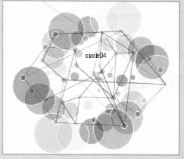

This time when a movie clip is clicked we are creating an empty movie clip at successive levels, this prevents the previous line from being erased when the new one is created. The linestyle's alpha value is set to increment by one each time an movie clip is clicked, this just gives an effect of history since the earlier path lines will be lighter and somewhat further off in distance. The line is drawn to the item we are currently clicking on from the previous item we have just clicked on. The most recently clicked items x and y positions are then set as variables `lastx` and `lasty` ready for the next line to be drawn. The variable `count` is incremented by 1 each time we draw a line, thereby increasing the depth of each newly created movie clip and also making path lines successively darker with each click.

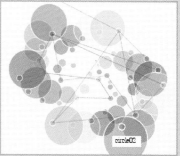

Apart from some color plotting position changes I have also rotated the initial positions of each generated movie clip by a factor of `i*60`.

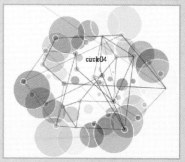

Gnomon the range

A gnomon is a self-repeating shape such as those found in spiral seashells and defined by Fibonacci sequences of numbers. The beautiful forms of the logarithmic (or equi-angular) spirals observed in nature occur when a region of active growth produces inactive material (such as the material of shells and horns) over time. All though our next variation isn't strictly a gnomon it does bare more than a passing resemblance to these kinds of forms, hence the name. Take a look a `API_gnomon30.swf`, then open up the corresponding `API_gnomon30.fla`.

Again, taking the last variation as a starting point we've changed the initial properties of the drawn circles, and the plotting positions of the movieclips that contain them. To indicate which item has been clicked this time, I've added a few lines of code that draws a colored line from the movie clip clicked, to the left hand side of the stage, this is contained in the `onRelease` event function.

```
with ( _root.line2 ) {
    lineStyle( 1, 0xFD0E02/count, 30 );
    moveTo( this._x, this._y  );
    lineTo(50, this._y-50 )
    lineTo(0, this._y-50);
}
```

If you experiment with the `drawCircle` arguments to change the properties of the circles and particularly the three lines of code directly after the `drawCircle` method you can get quite an amazing range of results.

```
drawCircle(i,0,i/1.5,1,0xffffff,0xFD0E02*i/1,50);
drawCircle(0,i/100,5,1,0xffffff,0xFD0E02*i/1.1,34);
_x = 325;
_y = i*10;
_rotation = i*30
```

The two lines containing the `drawCircle` movie clip prototype method allow us to define the size, coloring and positioning of the plotted circle buttons. We can, for example, dictate the size and color of the circles depending on the sequence of each created button and this makes for some very interesting effects. We can further effect the final positions of the circles with the next two lines, the last line deals with a rotational factor of each circle thereby further adding complexity to the plotting positions.

The following sub-variations have had these lines changed in some way or another:
`API_gnomon12.swf`, `API_gnomon30.swf`, `API_gnomon60.swf`, `API_gnomon120.swf`, `API_gnomon_tan.swf`.

All though the changes were often minimal, the result as seen in these files is quite varied.

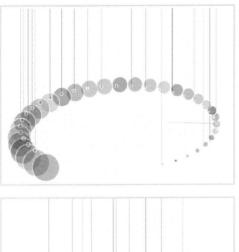

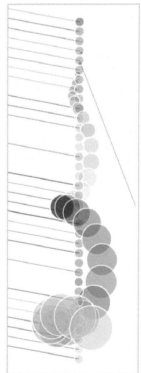

Sway

In the file `API_Undulating.fla` I've made a change to the circle button configurations and re-installed the history path function. The items move with a pleasing undulating effect the nearer the mouse pointer is to the bottom of the stage. This version is almost identical to `API_historyPath.fla` but with a few lines of code modified. The same four lines creating the circles and their respective positions have been changed.

```
drawCircle(0,i/5,2+i/2,1,0xFFffff,0x663300*i/1,25);
drawCircle(0,i/5,5,1,0xFFffff,0xFD0E02*i/1,44);
_x = Math.sin(i*60)*40+300;
_y = i*10;
_rotation = i*30;
```

The important line here is `_x = Math.sin(i*60)*40+300;` as it is what gives the circle buttons the final configuration – two curves intertwining.

The other important change is located in the `onEnterFrame` function, which governs the movement of the circle buttons.

```
_root["mc"+i].onEnterFrame = function(){
    this._rotation+=_root._ymouse/50;
    yslide=(_root._ymouse - this._y) *.1/number((this._name).substring(2));
}
```

The important line here is `this._rotation+=_root._ymouse/50` and this simply rotates each circle button by an amount dependent on _y position of the pointer, essentially giving the final file its undulating appearance.

In the second version (`API_Undulating02.fla` and its respective SWF) the sine function line is altered to become a log based calculation – and as math heads will know, this will change the positioning of our circles.

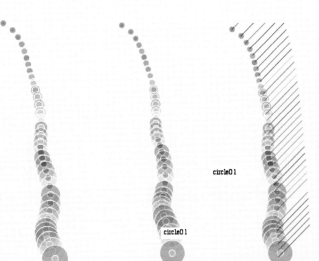

circle01

circle01

Experiment 2 – An experimental interface using movie clip buttons

This next experiment is closely related to the last in many respects, building up an interface using discrete units as building blocks. However this time instead of having static button objects I want to create a more animated rollover and click effect so I'm going to call to my aid the trusty timeline and do some frame-to-frame tween animation work. As I've mentioned the overhaul of the movie clip in Flash MX is excellent, but as well as movieclips being given new methods and properties the button has now been transformed into a real object with its own methods and properties and you can see that if you create a button and place it on the stage – in the property inspector it has a field to enter an instance name. Once on the stage you can now control with ActionScript its x and y positions, toggle its visibility and all the usual stuff and obviously it still retains all of its event methods, those you used to have to attach to the button in Flash 5. As we have already seen however, the common movie clip now also has these event methods and since you can use it as a button and reference its own timeline, it's actually a lot more powerful at behaving as a button than a button itself!

A button has four frames corresponding to different button states plus one for the hit area. Although we can add animations to these individual frames it can become very messy and often cumbersome, using movieclips as buttons solves this and also give you the possibility of making much more intricate and sophisticated rollover and release effects. Time to run through the file and explain what I mean. First though I must point out that the file uses some nested movieclips and this will help us to understand how the code works. If you have a look at the `unit` movie clip you will see that contained inside of it is another movie clip called `inner` and inside of `inner` is another called `inner2`.

Here's all of the code which resides in frames 1, 2 and 3:

Frame 1

```
_quality = "LOW";

// pick a rotation constant
// —————————
var degrees = [15,30,60,45,90,180,120,10,20];
var rota = degrees[Math.floor(Math.random()*8)];

var link = ["ta-ahet", "ta-khent", "ta-neter", "tchert", "tatau", "tebut",
➥"tem-ra", "tem-kheprer", "tem-thoth", "shepet", "set", "sehkmet",
➥"sheshu-heru", "maat", "annu", "sekhet-bast", "sekhet-nu", "sepes",
➥"nephthys", "net-ra", "amon", "ombos", "heru-em-het", "het-a-khet",
➥"anpu", "apzu", "asar-em-mena", "asar-em-seker", "amtet", "aper-ta"];

//button.Action.function
//—————————
bAction = function () {
    this.onEnterFrame = function () {
        this.inner._rotation+=2*(2-(_root._xmouse/150));
        this.inner.inner2._rotation-=2*(2-(_root._xmouse/150));
```

```
        if (this.inner.inner2._y < 300 ) {
            this.inner.inner2._y+=13; this.inner._rotation-=2;
        }
    }

    this.onRollOver = function(){
        _root.select = _root.link[number((this._name).substring(4))];
        _root.label._visible = true;
        this.inner.inner2.gotoAndPlay(2);
    }

    this.onRollOut = function (){
        _root.label._visible = false;
        this.inner.inner2.gotoAndPlay(11);
    }

    this.onRelease = function(){
        this.enabled = false ;
        this.inner.inner2.gotoAndPlay(21);
        toload = select + ".jpg";
        _root.createEmptyMovieClip("jpg_parent",2000);
        with ( _root.jpg_parent ) {
            _x = 584;
            _y = 106;
            loadMovie(toload, 0);
        }
    }

}

// the label
// ————-
_root.createEmptyMovieClip("label", 1002);
with ( _root.label ) {
    createTextField("insidelabel",1003,20,-20,50,18);
    insidelabel.text = "the label";
    insidelabel.background = true;
    insidelabel.selectable = false;
    insidelabel.autoSize = true;
}
_root.label.onEnterFrame = function () {
    yslide = (_root._ymouse - this._y) * .2;
    this._y += yslide;
    xslide = (_root._xmouse - this._x) * .2;
    this._x += xslide;
    _root.label.insidelabel.text = _root.select;
}
```

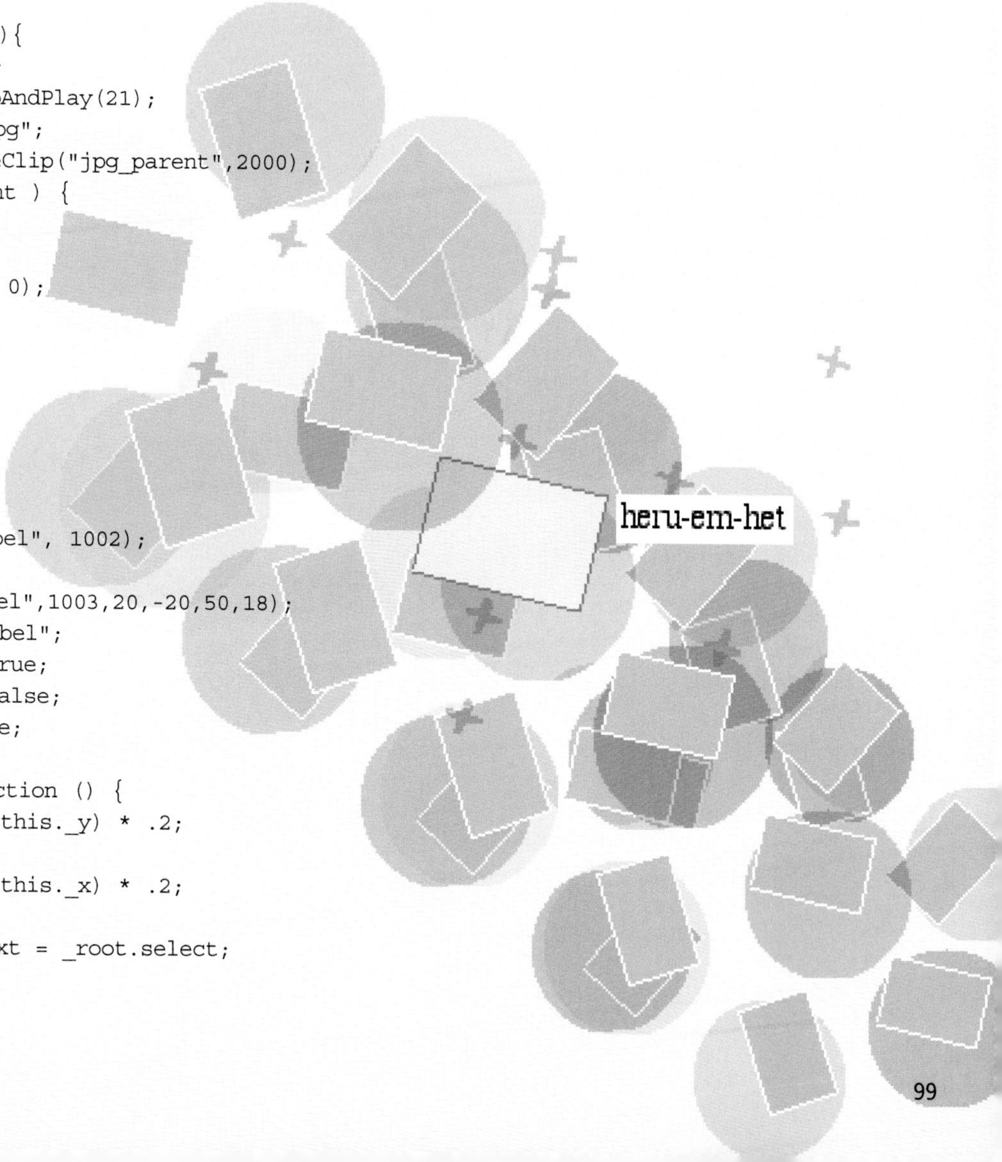

heru-em-het

Frame 2

```
// generate button pos. | color code | attach events
// ————————————-
i++;
attachMovie ("unit", "unit" + i, i);
with ( _root["unit" + i] ) {
    _y = Math.log (i)*(50-Math.sqrt(i)*20)+Math.sin(i)+330;
    _x = Math.log (i)*(50-Math.sqrt(i)*20)+Math.cos(i)+350;
    _rotation = i*rota;
    _yscale = _root["unit" + i]._xscale = 17+(i/4);
    inner.inner2.lineStyle( 60, 0xAFA374*i/9, 20 );
    inner.inner2.moveTo(this._x,this._y);
    inner.inner2.lineto(this._x-1,this._y);
}

bAction.apply(_root["unit" + i]);
if ( i > link.length-2 ) {
    var select="touch.a.sqr"; _root.stop();
}
```

Frame 3

```
gotoAndPlay (2);
```

Now let's run through the codein chunks.

Ra Ra Ra

First up we are going to set the movie quality to low. I've done this for two reasons. The primary reason is that sometimes I think the graphics in Flash look better aliased, and secondly it allows processor unfriendly movies to run real smooth. Next, I define a variable called rota with one of 9 possible values. These nine values have been derived entirely from experimentation and have been found to have useful properties regarding rotation and placement of movieclips. Quite often when you are experimenting you find that certain key variables do unique things to the system, it's good to write them down and use them in a random manner using an array and picking one at random to be used like this. Next up, we have an array defined similarly to the one in the first experiment, so not too much to explain here other than the fact that the names are of Egyptian gods and goddesses, some of them lesser known.

```
_quality = "LOW";

// pick a rotation constant
// ———————
var degrees = [ 15,30,60,45,90,180,120,10,20];
var rota = degrees[Math.floor(Math.random()*8)];

var link = ["ta-ahet", "ta-khent", "ta-neter", "tchert"];
```

The main event

Have a look at the second block of code starting with the comment `//button.Action.function`. You can see we have defined a number of event functions and they themselves have been encapsulated inside a function called `bAction`. Later we'll attach this whole block of events to our button movieclips. The `onEnterFrame` function takes care of the onscreen animation – notice the use of this is now required whereas in Flash 5 you could omit it as the code would have been attached as an `onClipEvent` function to the actual movieclip – so therefore Flash assumed you were talking to that movieclip's timeline if you left this out. While we're on the subject this illustrates another reason why we should favor movie clip buttons over standard buttons, standard buttons have no timeline to refer to and therefore we cannot refer to them using this.

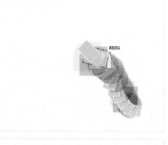

The effect achieved in this file would require quite a bit of trickery if we were to use standard button objects. More to the point, the fact that movieclips can now have event methods solves another problem. we find ourselves up against in previous versions of Flash,. if we were to dynamically generate many buttons on the fly and have events. In Flash 5 if you wanted to give movieclips event functions like rollovers you had to use `hitTest` to test whether the mouse pointer had moved within the boundary of the movieclip. Code would have been attached to each of your movieclip buttons. So whenever the mouse pointer moved over the clip { `do something` } would have been triggered,. But when you add an `else` statement you start having arguments between each movie clip. For example, if you had attached the script below to all the *movieclips* and you rolled over one of the clips it would try to set x to 1 while all the other clips would be setting it to 0, so you have a conflict.

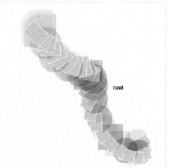

```
onClipEvent (enterFrame) {
    if ( this.hitTest(_root._xmouse, _root._ymouse, true) ) {
        x=1;
    } else {
        x=0;
    }
}
```

Of course, you can get around it by looping through an array of all the clips and checking their states individually, but it's processor unfriendly and messy. MX relieves us of exactly this problem by giving us proper event methods for our movieclips. If you look down at the rollover and rollout states, we set the visibility as on and off for the label clip – much easier!. In Flash 5, we would have to have checked all the movie clip states to perform this task, in MX we only have to look at the one we are interested in.

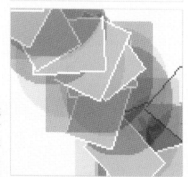

Inner space

Remember the nested movieclips, `unit` contains `inner` and `inner` contains `inner2`. The first two lines of the `onEnterFrame` function rotates these clips by a certain amount relative to the y co-ordinates of the mouse pointer, what the math actually does is rotate the clips clockwise or anticlockwise depending on how displaced the mouse pointer is from the center, check it out and see.

The next line conditional sets a further rotation and y axis movement dependent on the value of its own inner2's `_y` value. The onRollOver function determines the value of the variable select in much the same way as previous examples. As we have already mentioned the label is set to `_visible`. The next line instructs inner2 to play frame 2 of its own timeline. Let's have a look at inner2's timeline.

What I've done basically is to make rollover, rollout and release states that have shape tweens between each state. That way we have an animation for each state – much better than the four frames we get given to play with in a standard button. It allows us the luxury of making very nice animated buttons very easily and without hassle – all we need do is reference the start frame for each state with a gotoAndPlay in each event function as shown below. When we rollover the button the playhead moves to frame 2 and this starts the rollover animation, in this case the movie clip increases in size, changes to white and a plus appears on it. On rollout the button returns to its untouched state. Finally if it is clicked, the playhead moves to frame 21 of inner2's timeline at which point the plus explodes using a shape tween.

One thing to notice in the onRelease function is that fact that button has been set to disabled. This is another new property of movieclips in MX and it comes in handy. Disabling the button at this point is crucial for this movie to work in the way I intend it to. I have an animation tween in the timeline of inner2 and I want it to play right through with the cursor still over the movie clip – without the onRollOver function stepping in and moving the playhead back to a different point in inner2's timeline. If you look at the last frame of inner2's timeline you will see the following code:

```
this._parent._parent.enabled = true ;
```

So after the onRelease part of the animation has been played, the movie clip is brought back to life with button functionality thereby avoiding any timeline conflicts, all thanks to this simple new MX syntax. The rest of the code in this block has already been looked at in the first experiment; it deals with the loading of an external JPG.

```
//button.Action.function
//————————
bAction = function () {

    this.onEnterFrame = function () {
        this.inner._rotation+=2*(2-(_root._xmouse/150));
        this.inner.inner2._rotation-=2*(2-(_root._xmouse/150));
        if (this.inner.inner2._y < 300 ) {
            this.inner.inner2._y+=13; this.inner._rotation-=2
        }
    }

    this.onRollOver = function(){
        _root.select = _root.link[Number((this._name).substring(4))]
        _root.label._visible = true;
        this.inner.inner2.gotoAndPlay(2);
    }

    this.onRollOut = function (){
        _root.label._visible = false;
        this.inner.inner2.gotoAndPlay(11);
    }
```

```
this.onRelease = function(){
    this.enabled = false ;
    this.inner.inner2.gotoAndPlay(21);
    toload = select + ".jpg";
    _root.createEmptyMovieClip("jpg_parent",2000);
    with ( _root.jpg_parent ) {
        _x = 584;
        _y = 106;
        loadMovie(toload, 0);
    }
}

}
```

The last block of code in frame 1 generates a label like the one in the first experiment. This time we set some of the text field's properties. The `autoSize` property is set to `true` so that the text field automatically resizes according to the length of the string inside it – nice and handy. There is a whole arsenal of text field properties at your disposal. Married up with the `textFormat` object we can expect to see a dizzying array of funky typographical motion experiments in time!

```
// the label
// ——-
_root.createEmptyMovieClip("label", 1002);
with ( _root.label ) {
    createTextField("insidelabel",1003,20,-20,50,18);
    insidelabel.text = "the label";
    insidelabel.background = true;
    insidelabel.selectable = false;
    insidelabel.autoSize = true;
}
_root.label.onEnterFrame = function () {
    yslide = (_root._ymouse - this._y) * .2;
    this._y += yslide;
    xslide = (_root._xmouse - this._x) * .2;
    this._x += xslide;
    _root.label.insidelabel.text = _root.select;
}
```

Frame 2

The block of code in the second frame generates the interface button movieclips. This time I've used a frame loop to build up the interface sequentially. Once the loop has 'read' all the items in the array the value of `touch.a.sqr` is assigned to the variable `select` and the frame loop stops. This time we are plotting button movieclip positions according to log and sin/cos functions of `i` and as you can see in the final file it gives quite an interesting effect. If you try reloading the file you will see that it builds up a different configuration each time based on those rotational constants we randomly picked earlier – we are rotating each successively generated button movieclip by a factor of `i*rota`. The scaling of each is also determined by a factor of `i`.

103

Again, I'm going to use the drawing API to color-code each individual movieclip by drawing a very short line but with a large thickness thus making a large circle. I've set the linestyle color to be dependent on the sequence of the movieclips thereby giving some basic form of color coding. If, for example, you replace the line _rotation = i*rota with _rotation = i*180 the code will generate two distinct columns of button movieclips, one column containing red and blue coded buttons and the other green and beige. Its great that you can multiply hexadecimal color values in this way to subtly shift the hues of duplicated clips. You could try changing the divisor of i in the line inner.inner2.lineStyle(60,0xAFA374*i/9,20); to produce different color-coding effects. Lastly, while we are still in the frame loop we'll attach the event functions included in the bAction function to each generated button movieclip using apply.

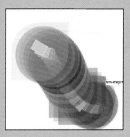

```
// generate button pos. | color code | attach events
// ——————————————————-
i++;
attachMovie ("unit", "unit" + i, i);
with ( _root["unit" + i] ) {
    _y = Math.log (i)*(50-Math.sqrt(i)*20)+Math.sin(i)+330;
    _x = Math.log (i)*(50-Math.sqrt(i)*20)+Math.cos(i)+350;
    _rotation = i*rota;
    _yscale = _root["unit" + i]._xscale = 17+(i/4);
    inner.inner2.lineStyle( 60, 0xAFA374*i/9, 20 );
    inner.inner2.moveTo(this._x,this._y);
    inner.inner2.lineTo(this._x-1,this._y);
}

bAction.apply(_root["unit" + i]);
if ( i > link.length-2 ) {
    var select="touch.a.sqr" ;
    _root.stop();
}
```

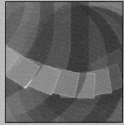

Some of the variations of this file I've produced blur the line between art and interface. In the ubiquitous tug of war between aesthetics and usability, sometimes aesthetics wins out and form dissolves function. To return the desired functionality to a few of these variations we would probably need do some more work in the scripting environment.

Shape changing

Try out the files rota_face_02a.fla to rota_face_02g.fla (or their published SWFs). In variation 2a, I've merely increased the size of the color code circles; the interface is larger and more pronounced. In 2b, I've stretched the color-code circles into tabular shapes and fixed the rotational factor of the generated movieclips to to i*15. In 2c, I've shifted the colors of the tabs and fixed the rotational factor to i*120. I really like the scale of 2d with its large rotating color fields, here I've just upped the scaling and played with the colors again. The rotational movement gets quite complex in variation 2e as the clips spin into and out of particularly defined geometric configurations which I find pleasing to the eye. To achieve this I've modified the respective rotations of the movieclips inner and inner2 inside the onEnterFrame event function in the first frame. Again I've also changed the colors. In variations 2f and 2g I've played with the scaling attributes and the final result I find quite interesting even if the interfaces begins to lose functionality.

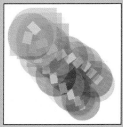

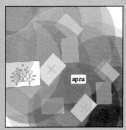

Wheels of fortune

As well as color and scaling changes the plotting positions of the movieclips have changed in variation 3a; these changes that been made in frame 2 are shown below. We now have a wheel of information.

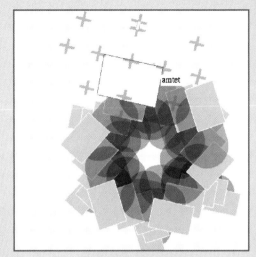

```
with ( _root["unit" + i] ) {
    _y = Math.sin (i)* (50- Math.sqrt(i)*20)
    ➥ + Math.sin(i)+250;
    _x = Math.cos (i)*(50-Math.sqrt(i)*20) +
    ➥ Math.cos(i)+380;
    _rotation = i*60;
    _yscale = _xscale = 25+(i/4);
    inner.inner2.lineStyle(40,
    ➥ 0x6600FF*i/0.85, 30 );
    inner.inner2.moveTo(_parent._x,
    ➥_parent._y);
    inner.inner2.lineto(_parent._x-i,
    ➥_parent._y);
}
```

In 3b, the final configuration of the interface wheel is rendered static by removing any rotation on `inner` or `inner2`. Resembling a flower form, I thought it would be nice if the 'petals' fell off of the interface as they were clicked. This simultaneously lets us know what petal we've clicked on and aids the navigational sequence. I've done this by adding a few new lines to the `onRelease` event function in frame 1 and these are:

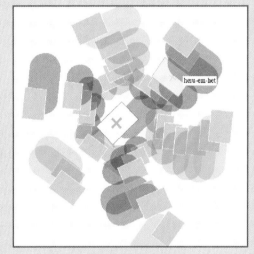

```
this.onEnterFrame = function () {
    if ( this._y < 600+random(20) ) {
        this._rotation-=10;
        this._y+=10;
    }
}
```

Variation 3c uses the same theme. Often, because of the animation, items become hidden behind other items in the interface. This type of interface would perhaps only be of use if there was a sequential hierarchy in which the information was to be read, such as pages in a book for example.

In the real world

Finally, I've given an example of this interface opening some Flash artwork I've produced. The work deals with ideas regarding structure and particle. As I've said before the line between interface and art in these files is often fine and I like it this way. Indeed the Flash files here have all been made from code based on these interface experiments. The `index.swf` loads up the interface, `rota_face_03a.swf` into `_level9` of the player. Clicking on a movieclip button then loads a specific SWF into `_level2` of the player – this means that the interface always appears above the content.

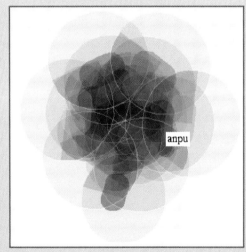

het-a-khet

Onwards

These interface experiments were produced during a few days of rain in summer 2002, I think each could benefit with some extra development, however they serve their purpose as starting prototypes for something more. In a world full of structured grid interfaces with rows and columns of buttons, I though it would be fun and interesting to look at alternative formations for presenting links.

Perhaps the next move would be to develop a way of navigating through different levels in each of these interfaces using a graphical representation of the drill down method. Smaller modules of grouped buttons could be used in a recursive fashion. So, perhaps when you click on one button a new atoll of buttons would appear, each atoll presenting successive layers or levels of information. Another obvious path to move down would be to link in an external data source, so the patterns of buttons would build up according to dynamic external data. Still further what about an interface that evolves aesthetically as it is being used? Better still, an interface whereby online users get to configure the interface themselves and leave a new formation of buttons for the next user who comes to the site.

Using the new MX way of adding events to movieclips in the timeline has allowed us to write organized and centralized code. The drawing API has given us the opportunity to make shapes on the screen as the Flash player runs eliminating the need for a library full of movieclips. A new set of objects such as the `textfield` object make tasks in Flash 5 that were pretty impossible very easy to accomplish in MX. The ability to import external media means we only have to wait for what we want to see or hear and not preload entire contents of Flash sites. More to the point, amends to sites can be carried out without even touching an FLA if we are only changing some JPGs for example. Because of these advances, and also because of enhancements to MX's internal compiling methods, file sizes for both FLAs and SWFs are considerably smaller than before. Indeed working on these files has afforded me the luxury of returning to floppy disks for backups!

From an artist-coder point of view, Flash is the most interesting tool on the planet, and this multi-dimensional design/development application just got a lot better with MX. With a lot of art made with computers, people quite often get obsessed with the idea that the technology is the message. As a creative tool, and by looking at some of the great work people are making with Flash, it seems so obvious that it's the personal showing through again and again to reveal truly great individual work. Not the case that it's the program that's talking. Flash MX has so many new elements to explore that by the time I will be just getting to grips with it, the new version of Flash will be out!

reacting to sound

ty lettau

The sight of sound

The first time that I really became interested in sound was during a trip to an antique store. While perusing the aisles, I noticed a small box. I was drawn to it because of the small graphic on the side. I picked it up and opened it. In the box was a roll of paper. Still curious, I began to unroll it and what I saw changed the way I think about things. I saw a pattern of holes cut into the paper. It was sort of like Braille, only much more complex, and clearly more linear. It was just a pattern of holes in paper, and I was amazed. I was amazed because the object was a reel for a player piano, and what I was looking at was a representation of a song. These holes were sound. I was actually looking at sound. I had seen wave patterns of sound before, but this was different. I think what made this interesting was that when I first saw it I had no idea what it was.

So began the journey into sound.

It also just so happens that a great friend of mine, Craig Kroeger (www.miniml.com) creates audio under the name Kemlus. I use his audio for almost everything I do. This project uses 6 of Craig's tracks. So thank you to Craig for allowing the use of those.

Anyway, what we are going to do here is to create several "engines" that generate patterns based on sound. The piano reel was actually a pattern that created sound. We are going to reverse this and use sound to create patterns and interactive toys.

FlashAmp

You may choose to skip this step as it requires you to download a piece of software. If you do not wish to purchase it, skip ahead to the next section.

For this all to work, we need a way to take our audio and translate it into numerical values which will represent the data in the audio. I use FlashAmp which can be downloaded at www.marmalademedia.com.au/flashamp/download.htm. It costs $30.00, but in my opinion it is well worth it. You can download a demo version, but it will only let you record a small portion of audio which isn't enough to use. If you want to get into this, the $30.00 is a small price for what it can do for you. If you don't think that it is something you will use often, I suggest skipping this step and simply using my prerecorded files. You can do this entire chapter with the files provided, but if you want to customize it for your own use or if

you want to use this idea on a project, you will need to buy FlashAmp.

There are other utilities to use. If you are using another utility to record data, this process will be slightly different and you will need to figure it out on your own. I am not familiar with all of the software for doing this, but most software comes with documentation. If you can find a free application that does this, or if you already have one, it should tell you how to use it.

Source audio files (01.aiff, 02.aiff, 03.aiff, 04.aiff, 05.aiff, 06.aiff)...

To start, we will need several sound files (here we use six). I typically use AIFF format audio and compress in Flash, but we can use anything. We *will* need an AIFF format for FlashAmp data recording later, so it's easier to start with AIFF files; I've named mine "01.aiff" – "06.aiff". If you wish to try your own audio, find six audio files and name them the same way.

Being that these audio files are very large, I have only included one of the AIFF files and one of the FLA files for the audio. To do this first step in full, you will need to find or create five more audio files.

Open FlashAmp and follow the steps using the settings below.

Select an Audio File: "01.aiff"
Amplitude List: Yes (Checkmark)
Cue Point Name List: No (X)
Frames Per Second: "15"
Value Scale: "100"
Smoothing: Yes (Checkmark)
Save FlashAmp File: Name it "01.as"

Other settings will produce other results. For example, setting the FPS to 90 will give a smoother data scale with much more data, but it will choke Flash. Feel free to experiment with the values, but for now, keep them as shown above.

Data files (01.as, 02.as, 03.as, 04.as, 05.as, 06.as)...

FlashAmp will write a text file. If we open it, we see this:

```
amplitude = (100,86,63,58,55,53,49,49,48,
........49,32,0)&ampDone=1
```

We now have a list of values, separated by commas (convenient, seeing as this is how arrays are structured in Flash) that range from 0 to 100. These numbers represent the volume of the audio from start to finish.

We need to make a few changes to the text file in order to use this file how we want to. First, change the variable name from "amplitude" to "amp". We do this so that later in Flash it will be easier to refer to. Next, add the code to make it into an array. We write "new Array" in front of the parentheses to declare that what follows is an array. Lastly, we remove &ampDone=1.

```
amp = new Array
(100,86,63,58,55,53,49,49,48,........49,32,0)
```

Save the file. Now we have a usable array that Flash can understand. Remember in FlashAmp when it asked for the filename to save as? We added the suffix .AS to it. This stands for ActionScript and will signal Flash (along with the method we use to bring the data in) that this is to be read into the ActionScript of the movie.

Repeat this process for all six audio clips, so we end with 6 text files named `01.as − 06.as`.

Flash audio files(01.fla, 02.fla, 03.fla, 04.fla, 05.fla, 06.fla)...

We have our sound file, and from it we have recorded our data file. So now we need to get into Flash. Open Flash and make a new file. It doesn't matter what size the stage is. The only thing that matters about the movie is the Frames Per Second. Set it to 15 because that is what FPS our data file was recorded at. Save the file as "01.fla".

If at any time, we load in any movie with a FPS lower than 15, everything will slow. To remedy this, we just need to be sure that all files with a frame rate are set to 15.

Now we need to import the "01.aiff" file. From the library, bring up the audio info and apply the following settings:

Compression: MP3
Bit Rate: 16 kbps
Quality: Best

Again, this is what I use. Try different settings to see what they do.

Next, we need to create two layers in this movie. Call one 'Audio' and the other 'Actions'. In frame 1 on the Audio layer, add the sound. Set the sound properties in Flash as follows:

Sync: Stream
Loop: 0 times

Now, extend the frames in this layer out by adding blank frames until you see the end of the sound. A streaming sound will only play while there are frames there for it to play on. In order to stream the sound, we need to extend the frames. If we don't, the sound will stop. Basically, streaming sound means that Flash isn't downloading all of the sound before it plays. It starts playing and downloads as it goes. This makes the download quicker (a huge benefit) but this is not the reason we use this method. Flash handles streaming sound by playing through frames. Imagine that the frames and the sound extend in the same way so that if the playhead is on the 140th frame, the sound is also at the 140th "frame". The exact reason that we are using streaming sound and frame passage will become clear a little later, so for now, let's just move on.

Go back to frame 1 and select the Actions layer. On frame 1, add this code:

```
#include("04.as")
```

We don't need any other code here anyway, but for further reference, do not ever put another action on a frame with an `#include` command. It needs to be alone.

This code is the other part of Flash understanding that the data file is actually ActionScript. The `#include` command tells Flash that the text it is importing is valid ActionScript. If there is a problem in the code syntax of the 01.as file, the Flash file will reflect the error. If we encounter a problem later on, it is best to first check the data file. It can be easy to make syntactical errors in it. It is also important to note that the `#include` command operates on export, not in real time. As long as the data file is there for Flash to call to it doesn't need to be there anymore. For example, if you upload to a web server, you do not need to upload the `01.as` file, as it is already a part of the Flash file.

We can now export the movie by pressing Command/Control and Return. Since we named it `01.fla`, our exported file will be `01.swf`.

Now repeat this process to create six individual FLA files and export them all to individual SWF files. Be sure that you replace the audio clip being imported *and* the `#include` command.

Main files...

Everything that we have created thus far will become our audio library. No matter which file we are working on, we will draw from this library of six audio tracks. Note that if you are creating your own audio, you should now have 24 files (six AIFF files, six AS files, six SWF files and six FLA files). Also note that I only have 14 (one AIFF file, six AS files, six SWF files and one FLA file) because the FLA and the AIFF files get big and there isn't room for them all.

In this chapter, we are going to be creating 3 different experiments in sound. They will be named by letter (A,B,C). So let's get started on A.

We are starting off with different sound files in each project. The defaults are:

A = 04.swf
B = 03.swf
C = Random (and an interface to select tracks)

Project A (The Basic Engine)...

Now that we have the entire framework in place, we can finally create our main Flash movie. Make a new file and save it as `A_01.fla`.

FPS: "15"
Size: "400 x 400"

Create two layers and call them 'Objects' and 'Actions'. We will be writing *all* of the code for this movie on the Actions layer in frame 1 unless otherwise noted. To save time, if we are writing code and we haven't specified an alternate location for it, then we are writing it here. Let's start with some parameters:

```
_quality="low";
fscommand(allowscale="false");
loadMovieNum("audio/04.swf",10);
stop();
```

Most of this is quite self-explanatory. `_quality="low"` simply sets the movie quality to non-anti-aliased. `fscom-`

`mand(allowscale="false")` makes the movie unscalable. The next line is what we have been doing all of the other steps for. `loadMovieNum("audio/04.swf",10)` brings the `audio.swf` file into the main movie. Notice we are loading it on level 10.

We need to take a moment to understand the hierarchy at work here. The key to this whole process is the array called amp which houses all of our volume data. This array (called 'amp') exists in the data file called `04.as`. Since we used `#include` to add the data file when we exported `04.swf`, the amp array is now in the `04.swf` file. Finally, since we just loaded in `04.swf` into the main movie on level 10, our amp array is now on level 10 in relation to the main movie. So if we want to call to this array to retrieve or use the values in it, we will say `_level10.amp[?]`.

Finally, we end the frame passage of the main timeline by saying `stop()`. We do this for performance reasons. It takes Flash more energy to chug through frames than it does to run code, so all of our motion will occur with loops and `clipEvents`.

Now we need to add a fair amount of code to what we just wrote.

```
_quality="low";
fscommand(allowscale="false");
loadMovieNum("audio/04.swf",10);
stop();

this.onEnterFrame=function() {
    if (C<_level10.amp.length) {
        C++;
    } else {
        C=0;
    }
};
```

The first part of this code is to declare a loop function. `this.onEnterFrame=function()` is actually a lot simpler than it looks. `this` simply declares that the target is the `_root` level. So anything that happens in this loop will be relative to the `_root` level. `onEnterFrame` is just like the Flash 5 syntax of MC `clipEvents`. The only difference is that now Flash MX can remotely target a `clipEvent` without the code actually being on the objects. Lastly, we need to declare a blank `function()` to hold all of the code that we want to happen.

Remember that although everything in this movie is stopped, the 04.swf on level 10 is actually cycling real frames.

We also need to understand frame passage. The first set of code included a stop() to pause the _root timeline's playhead. But onEnterFrame doesn't mean literally that it needs to pass frames, it just means that 15 times per second (because our movie is at 15 FPS), this code is going to execute.

So, every time the movie cycles through a frame (specifically, on the entrance of that frame), the _root timeline will enlist a function and run all of the code inside of it.

Now, let's look at the next part; the if statement simply gives us a conditional situation. When something is true, do part A; otherwise, do part B. All we need now is to determine what that something is. We need to create a counter which will cycle through the entire amp array. This counter will eventually be used to extract the corresponding value from the amp array. Think of it like this: every frame that passes is a frame that the 04.swf file has passed through. So we need a way to keep a counter in the main movie that will coincide with the frame of audio that 04.swf is on. If we look at the if statement, we see that our condition set so that if some value named C is less than the length of the "amp" array, then the code runs. C will be our counter variable. If we look to where it says C++, we see where C counts. C++ means that each frame, C will increase by one (this is called "incremental"). So each "frame", C is a value one higher than it was the last frame. Also, as C counts, 04.swf on level 10 also plays real frames. So on the 220th frame cycle of the main movie, level 10 is at real frame 220 and C equals 220.

Our movie will do this until the number that C represents is greater than the amount of values in the amp array (represented by the property .length). _level10.amp.length means that we look to level 10, find amp and see how long it is. When C is greater than this, we do something else.

Since amp is an array, the length is the amount of values in it, not the amount of characters. If we write varMyName="SoundOfDesign" and then find varMyName.length, we will get a result of 13 because it counts characters if the target is a variable.

The something else that we need to do is to reset C to 0. When the C value is greater than the length of the amp array, we also know that audio.swf on level 10 will be out of frames. When streaming audio runs out of frames, it restarts. When the audio restarts, we need C to restart, thereby also restarting where we call into the amp array to the beginning.

OK, we have the overall code structure in place, but there are a few more steps to go. Before we write any more code, we will need to make an object that we can later set to *react* to the audio. But even before we do this, let's discuss how this is all happening. We are going to make a movie clip in a moment. We are then going to control the properties (such as _x, _y, etc.) of this MC. To control these properties, we aren't actually using the audio stream, but rather the data in the "amp" array. The "amp" array, and the values in it, are directly related to the volume of the audio on any given part of the audio stream. So we can make the movie clip look as though the audio is affecting it, when it is actually the array values that are affecting it.

Let's make a 4x4 square of any color. Do not put a stroke on it. Make it into a movie clip by pressing F8. Name it 'MC_Clip'. Next, select the movie clip and give it an instance name of 'Clip'. Place the clip on the stage using the info palette. Set it to X = 0, Y = 0. Before we move on, let's also set the MC's _alpha to 25%. This will help later. Now we have an object that is ready to be given instructions.

Add the following line to the code we have written already:

```
_quality="low";
   fscommand(allowscale="false");
   loadMovieNum("audio/04.swf",10);
   stop();

   this.onEnterFrame=function() {
      if (C<_level10.amp.length) {
         C++;
         Clip._y=_level10.amp[_level10.
      ➥ _currentframe];
      } else {
         C=0;
      }
   };
```

This will finally give us an object that reacts. It is very simple at this point. All it does is move up and down based on the data, though it appears as though the volume is actually moving it. Also note that we aren't even using the C counter yet. We need that framework in place, but the _y position is controlled by another value. Notice that we are setting the _y to look at level 10, find "amp" and extract a value. The value is not C (as we might expect), but rather, _currentframe. The reason we do this is to ensure that we are calling to the *exact* part of the array that the audio is on. The frame that audio.swf on level 10 is on represents the exact part of the audio that is playing. So, if we use that to get the array value, we ensure that the array value is the right one. If we use C and the audio lags a bit or some other discrepancy occurs, the two will not be in sync. Also note that to call into an array, we use square brackets. Whatever is inside these brackets is the part of the array that is drawn out. So if level 10 is on the 160th frame, then the 159th value in the array is being drawn. Arrays operate on zero scale. This means that the 1st member of the array is actually the 0th member. So calling to the 160th wil actually bring up the 159th.

After writing this, save and export. (The file should be very much like A_01.fla)

Again, again!

Now that we have the basic movement in place, we can go in many different directions. In order for this to serve our purposes, we need to spruce it up a bit more. To do this, we have options. The best course of action at this point (read: what will give up the best potential for experimentation later) is to create a small replication engine so that we can affect more than just one MC. Let's add two new lines of code, and let's also change the last one we added.

```
_quality="low";
fscommand(allowscale="false");
loadMovieNum("audio/04.swf",10);
stop();

this.onEnterFrame=function() {
    if (C<_level10.amp.length) {
        C++;
        // Replicate
        Clip.duplicateMovieClip("Clip"+C,C);
        _root["Clip"+C]._x=C;
        _root["Clip"+C]._y=_level10.amp[_level10._currentframe];
    } else {
        C=0;
    }
};
```

Again, we have added code which *looks* more confusing than it *is*. The first new line simply tells "Clip" to duplicate. Notice we are finally using C. We need to use C for two reasons. The first involves the first part of the parentheses. We say Clip.duplicateMovieClip() to duplicate the movie clip. This gives us a new movie clip every time we run this line. But we need to consider the parameters of the new duplicate. Inside the parentheses exist to parameters which can be expressed as (what we want to name the new clip, what depth the new clip goes onto). If we want to duplicate a movie clip, we can't name the duplicate the exact same thing as the original. So we need to change its name. If we only wanted one duplicate, we could just call it 'Clip2'. But, we want to continually make duplicates. This is why we created C. As C counts, duplicates are being made. Notice in the first part of the parentheses it says "Clip"+C. This means that we are using the string "Clip" as a literal term. But we are also adding (the + means append whatever is next to the end of the string "Clip") the C value. So the first duplicated movie clip is called 'Clip1' and the second is called 'Clip2' and so on. This serves the need for unique naming. Next we need to determine the new duplicate's depth. Depth is like a level of the movie but is within the main movie. So far, we have the main movie on level 0 and the audio.swf file on level 10. When we duplicate a movie clip, it creates layers of depth in level 0. To duplicate a movie clip, we *must* put it on a new level, and we *must not* use a level already taken. If we do, we will overwrite what was there. Also, if we duplicate 100 movie clips, the 80th is on depth 80, but is still below level 10 because depth is all within level 0. As for depth and levels, the higher the number the more in front it is. So by using C as the depth we get a unique depth every frame just as we got a unique name.

Now what we have is objects being replicated constantly, all ready to react to the audio. We can do this one of two ways. We can set the movie based on the audio just when it loads, or we can set it to always follow the audio data. Before, when we just had one clip, it was always looking to the data and updating. This time we are going to set each clip just when it loads.

To call to the clips as they are made, and to call to them only once, we again use C. We say _root["Clip"+C]._x to call to the duplicate that was just made. If we think about how C behaves; that is that it counts up, but on any given frame is the same value for the entirety of that one frame, we can more easily understand this. We just used C to name the dupli-cate. On the 40th frame, C is 40 so the duplicate is named 'Clip40' and is on a depth of 40. When the movie gets done doing this, the movie has other code to run before it recycles and changes C to the next increment. So when the movie hits _root["Clip"+C]._x, C is still 40. So this line of code really just reads _root.Clip40._x. This means for that frame Clip40 is being affected, just once. Then the next frame, C will have counted to 41 and there-fore Clip40 is no longer the same as _root["Clip"+C] because that now means Clip41. This is just a way to apply and run this code on each clip as it loads and then leave it alone.

We target our clip with _root["Clip"+C]._x and we set it to C. Since C is counting, each time a clip is made, it will be one pixel farther to the right than the one before it. So now we have what appears to be movie clips replicating across the screen.

We edit the _y property to target the same as the _x code did, and we leave the value the same and we are left with... _root["Clip"+C]._y=level10.amp[_level10._current-frame];

Save a new version as 'A_02.fla' and export, (or look at our file A_02.fla). We now see a lot more happening. We are now basically tracking the audio and creating a map of it.

Between the lines

At this point, we are starting to see something that has potential. For the next iteration, we will try to utilize some of the new features of Flash to add to our project. First, let's try a simple Line Method.

```
_quality="low";
fscommand(allowscale="false");
loadMovieNum("audio/04.swf",10);
stop();

this.onEnterFrame=function() {
    if (C<_level10.amp.length) {
        C++;
        // Replicate
        Clip.duplicateMovieClip("Clip"+C,C);
        _root["Clip"+C]._x=C;
        _root["Clip"+C]._y=_level10.amp[_level10._currentframe];
        // Draw Lines
        this.createEmptyMovieClip("Draw", C+100000);
        Draw.lineStyle(.25, 0xFF3399, 25);
        Draw.moveTo(_root["Clip"+C]._x, _root["Clip"+C]._y);
        Draw.lineTo(_root["Clip"+(C-1)]._x, _root["Clip"+(C-1)]._y);
    } else {
        C=0;
    }
};
```

Yet again, we have added code that isn't very complicated once we understand how it works. The Draw features are new to Flash MX. Thus, they require a bit more imagination than what we were used to in Flash 5. The main reason why this is different is because Flash is actually *creating* a shape on the fly.

First, we need to create a movie clip for this shape to be stored. We could just make a MC by hand, but for this purpose, creating one through code works well. We create a MC by writing `this.createEmptyMovieClip("Draw", C+100000)`. This works very much like how we duplicated an MC earlier. We choose a name and a depth, and that's it. Notice that we add 100000 to the depth. We do this because if we use C, we will overwrite the Clip movie clips. Adding 100000 insures that the line being drawn is well out of the range of possible Clip movie clip depths. Next, we need to supply information for Flash to use as the line style. `Draw.lineStyle(.25, 0xFF3399, 25)` declares that we are talking about the movie clip Draw and any parameters within the parentheses will apply to that movie clip. We have three parameters to fill in. They are stroke, color, and alpha. The next two lines control the positioning of the line to be drawn. These are little more than a start point and an end point and then Flash connects the dots. `Draw.moveTo(_root["Clip"+C]._x, _root["Clip"+C]._y)` declares the current Clip movie clip as the start point. There are two values because we need to declare both the _x and the _y. `Draw.lineTo(_root["Clip"+(C-1)]._x, _root["Clip"+(C-1)]._y)` is what actually makes the line and connects the dots.

Each time this code cycles, it enters the Draw movie clip and adds the next line segment. Save a new version as 'A_03.fla' and export. (or see our version of the file A_03.fla). We see this:

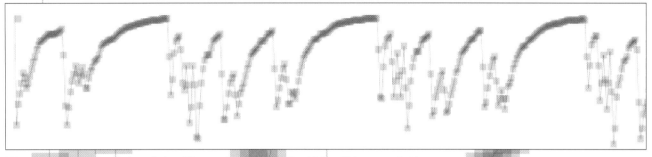

We can also set the alpha of the Clip movie clips to 0% which will leave only the lines of the Draw movie clip visible, like this:

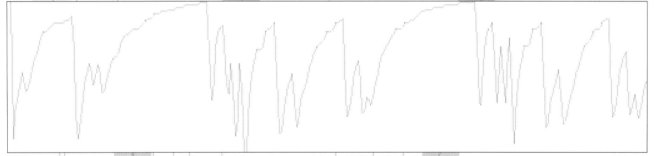

We can also start to randomize a bit so that the placement is determined by the audio, but it isn't as precise:

```
_quality="low";
fscommand(allowscale="false");
loadMovieNum("audio/04.swf",10);
stop();

this.onEnterFrame=function() {
    if (C<_level10.amp.length) {
        C++;
        // Replicate
        Clip.duplicateMovieClip("Clip"+C,C);
        _root["Clip"+C]._x=C+(Math.random(20)-10);
        _root["Clip"+C]._y=_level10.amp[_level10._currentframe] +(Math.random(20)-10);
        // Draw Lines
        this.createEmptyMovieClip("Draw", C+100000);
        Draw.lineStyle(.25, 0xFF3399, 25);
        Draw.moveTo(_root["Clip"+C]._x, _root["Clip"+C]._y);
        Draw.lineTo(_root["Clip"+(C-1)]._x, _root["Clip"+(C-1)]._y);
    } else {
        C=0;
    }
};
```

All we have to do is to declare a range for the random to choose from. The value returned will be between 0 and 19 (Math.random() is a zero based scale also) and then we minus 10. This gives us equal probability that the number will be positive versus negative. Adding this random range to the placement on both axes gives us a bit more of a chaotic map.

Next, a simple change in the stroke weight and alpha yields a different result.

```
_quality="low";
fscommand(allowscale="false");
loadMovieNum("audio/04.swf",10);
stop();

this.onEnterFrame=function() {
    if (C<_level10.amp.length) {
        C++;
        // Replicate
        Clip.duplicateMovieClip("Clip"+C,C);
        _root["Clip"+C]._x=C+(Math.random(20)-10);
        _root["Clip"+C]._y=_level10.amp[_level10._currentframe]
                                            +(Math.random(20)-10);
        // Draw Lines
        this.createEmptyMovieClip("Draw", C+100000);
        Draw.lineStyle(20, 0xFF3399, 10);
        Draw.moveTo(_root["Clip"+C]._x, _root["Clip"+C]._y);
        Draw.lineTo(_root["Clip"+(C-1)]._x, _root["Clip"+(C-1)]._y);
    } else {
        C=0;
    }
};
```

Feel free to experiment doing different things.

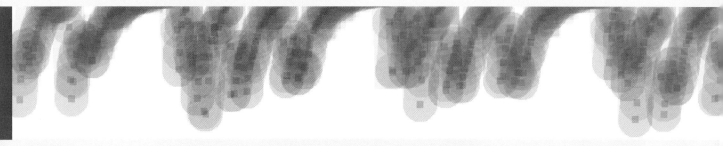

The equalizer

Before we move on to a completely different project, let's use this engine to build a quick equalizer. It isn't a true equalizer in that it is only using volume as its guide, but it is better than the arbitrarily tweened animations that we see often enough. Let's start by changing our code a bit.

```
_quality = "low";
fscommand(allowscale="false");
loadMovieNum("audio/02.swf", 10);
stop();
//
this.onEnterFrame = function() {
    if (C<6) {
        C++;
        // Replicate
        Clip.duplicateMovieClip("Clip"+C,C);
        Clip1._alpha = 25;
        _root["Clip"+C]._x=(C*5)+186;
        _root["Clip"+C]._y=200;
    } else {
        C = 0;
    };
};
```

We are loading in a new audio clip. Then we adjust the counter to only loop through six values instead of hundreds (stated before as the length of the array). Since we are now making only six duplicates, we reset C every 6th pass, thus the entire engine is very compact because of the x value. `_root["Clip"+C]._x=(C*5)+186` uses the C value times 5 (our clip is 4 pixels wide, so C x 5 moves each subsequent duplicate over one pixel past the last one). Then we add 186 to keep it all centered. We do this because our equalizer is 28 pixels wide and our movie is 400 pixels wide, so the center is 200. If we halve the equalizer, we get 14. 200 – 14 = 186. Last, we set the y axis to 200.

`Clip1._alpha = 25` just keeps the first clip in the line at 25% alpha. Now is a good time to change the physical alpha of Clip to 10% so that the other five will be lighter. We do this because the first one is reacting real-time and the other five are subsequently behind. This way, it is more obvious what the "master" level bar is.

Now all we do is write a few lines on the "Clip" MC:

```
onClipEvent (load) {
    C = _root.C;
}
onClipEvent (enterFrame) {
    _yscale = _level10.amp[_level10._currentframe-C]*10;
}
```

All the load `ClipEvent` does is to localize the `C` value to the MC. As `C` changes on the root, we want each duplicate to know what `C` was when it was "born". Then we set the `_yscale` property to the audio level times 10. As we target the frame to pull from the "amp" array, we minus `C`, because each duplicate understands its own `C` as something different from the others. `C` acts as an identifier for each MC. So by subtracting `C`, we ensure that each movie clip is getting a different value from the array. For example, the 5th duplicate is actually getting a value 5 less than what the amp array is actually on. If the `_currentframe` of `_level10` is 230, then the 5th duplicate is actually pulling the 225th value because it has subtracted its own `C` (5).

Lastly, we need to double-click into "Clip" and set the center point to Y = -4. This way, as we adjust the `_yscale`, the center point is on the bottom and will therefore scale upward. Finally, place Clip somewhere off the stage. It doesn't matter where, just anywhere outside the boundary of the stage. We can also write `_visible = 0` which is 'cleaner' but i'ts also more code. It's up to you. There are so many different ways to do the same thing in Flash, it's really just a matter of preference. I try to write code so that I need the fewest lines possible, but you may wish to do things differently. Again, try experimenting and moving things round to see what they do.

Save a new version as 'A_04.fla' and export. (or refer to the file `A_04.fla`).

Before we move on, let's try one more thing. Make a square 8 x 8 pixels in size. Make it a button and name it 'NavButton'. On this button, add the ActionScript:

```
on (release) {
    loadMovieNum("audio/0"+MyNumber+".swf", 10);
}
```

Now, select the button and make it into a movie clip. Name it 'NavMC'. Select the movie clip and give it an instance name of 'Nav'. Then, on the root create an Actions layer, and add this:

```
_quality = "low";
fscommand(allowscale-"false");
loadMovieNum("audio/02.swf", 10);
this.onLoad = function() {
    for (N=1; N<7; N++) {
        // Replicate
        Nav.duplicateMovieClip("Nav"+N, N+100);
        _root["Nav"+N]._x = (N*11)+156;
        _root["Nav"+N].MyNumber = N;
    }
};
stop();
//
this.onEnterFrame = function() {
    if (C<6) {
        C++;
        // Replicate
        Clip.duplicateMovieClip("Clip"+C,C);
        Clip1._alpha = 25;
        _root["Clip"+C]._x=(C*5)+186;
        _root["Clip"+C]._y=200;
    } else {
        C = 0;
    };
};
```

Now the MC we just made will duplicate across the screen to form six buttons. The key here is `_root["Nav"+N].MyNumber = N`. This tells each duplicate, as it is created, what number it is. Remember on the button when we wrote `loadMovieNum("audio/0"+MyNumber+".swf", 10)`? This makes each button load a different audio clip because each button's host movie clip knows itself to be a different number than the rest.

Save a new version as 'A_05.fla' and export. (or refer to the file `A_05.fla`). All this did was give us a more versatile equalizer because we can now test different audio clips on the fly.

Project B (The enhanced Engine)

For the next project, we are going to take a look into the intro toy that I built for www.cymbalbranding.com. It utilizes audio reactivity in a bit more of a unique and interactive way. What is interesting about this is that it reacts to *both* the audio *and* to the user.

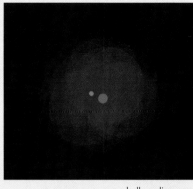

www.cymbalbranding.com

This project will go in a different direction from that which Project A did, but we will be using a lot of the same setup and a lot of the same code as Project A. If anything that follows is confusing, refer back to Project A.

To get set up, keep the same stage settings as Project A, Save a new file called 'B_01.fla'. Create another instance of the movie clip Clip. Now we should have two movie clips on the stage, both instances of Clip. Rename one of them 'Origin' and the other 'Drag'. Place Drag at x=200, y=100 and place Origin at x=300 and y=200.

Then, in the Actions layer, change the script to read as so.

```
_quality = "low";
fscommand(allowscale="false");
loadMovieNum("audio/03.swf", 10);
stop();

this.onEnterFrame = function() {
    // Dragger
    if (MD) {
        _root.Drag._x = _root._xmouse;
    }
    // Elastic Engine
    TXn = (TXn*.95)+(_root.Drag._x-_root.Origin._x)*.025;
    _root.Origin._x += TXn;
    _root.Origin._y = _root.Drag._y + (_level10.amp[_level10._currentframe]*2)+TXn;
    // Draw Lines
    this.createEmptyMovieClip("Draw", C+100000);
    Draw.lineStyle(.25, 0xFF3399, 25);
    Draw.moveTo(_root.Origin._x, _root.Origin._y);
    Draw.lineTo(_root.Drag._x, _root.Drag._y);
};
this.onMouseDown = function() {
    MD = 1;
};
this.onMouseUp = function() {
    MD = 0;
};
```

This is what all of the setup code looks like for Project B. If we look this over a bit, we will see some new things that we haven't talked about yet. We will also see some familiar code, so let's look more closely at this.

The first thing that is different is that we are loading in a different audio clip. We can change this to any value from 01 to 06 to try our different audio clips.

The next thing that is different is that we have completely removed the `C` counter variable from Project A. This project will be using just one instance of Clip so we do not need any duplication (yet).

If we look down to the end of the code, we will see the addition of two new event functions. We are setting a variable called `MD` based on the behavior of the mouse. When the left mouse button is down, `MD = 1`, when it's up, `MD = 0`. Basically, this gives us a conditional situation that will allow us to tell if the mouse is pressed or not by looking to `MD`. Now if we look to the top again (under the comment `//Dragger`), we see how and why we use this. The line `_root.Drag._x = _root._xmouse` is triggered when `MD` is true. Any value (including 1) will read as true, so when the mouse is down, `MD = 1` and therefore, `_root.Drag._x = _root._xmouse`. So, when the mouse is pressed, the movie clip Drag will follow the mouse on the x axis.

Now that we have this dragging mechanism in place, we need to use it to affect something else. The next part of the code does just that (under the comment `//Elastic Engine`). For this, we are going to make Origin follow Drag by controlling the y axis with the audio and the x axis with this code.

Let's look into the x axis first. We see two lines that control the x axis. We have a variable and a property being set. `TXn=(TXn*.95)+(_root.Drag._x-_root.Origin._x)*.025` is probably the most complex single line of code in here. This is what gives us the calculation for the elastic motion.

We could also write `TXn=(TXn*F)+(_root.Drag._x-_root.Origin._x)*V`. This might help keep track of what the decimal values do. Think of `F` as *friction*, or how long the MC will take to come to rest after it is agitated. Think of `V` as *velocity*, or how fast the MC moves. Then we would need to declare `F = .95` and `D = .025` in the code. The closer to 1 each value gets, the faster (in the case of `V`) and longer (in the case of `F`) it will be. It takes more lines of code this way, but it might be easier to track. Also, try playing with these values. There's nothing like experimentation to aid learning!

It is easier to understand this if we break it into manageable parts. `_root.Drag._x-_root.Origin._x` is merely the distance between the two movie clips. This distance can be positive or negative, but at this point, that is what we need. If "Origin" is at 20 and "Drag" is at 100, then we are left with this simplified equation:

`TXn = (TXn*.95)+(100-20)*.025` or `TXn = (TXn*.95)+(80)*.025`

Flash uses the same rules that govern any math equation; calculations in parentheses come first. Now let's look at the `TXn*.95` part. This is really just a way to shave a bit off of the current value of `TXn`. Variables default to 0, so the first time we use it without setting it, `TXn` equals 0. So if `TXn` was 0, then 0 * .95 is 0. So now we have `TXn = (0)+(80)*.025`. The next calculation will be 80 * .025, resulting in 2. `TXn = (0)+2` is what is left and we can see that `TXn` will equal 2. `_root.Origin._x += TXn` just adds `TXn` to the x location of Origin. So 2 will be added to Origin thereby making its new x location 22.

Now, to see the behavior in action, let's run it through again. Now `TXn` is 2, so 2 * .95 is 1.9, and the new locations are 22 and 100, so now we have `TXn = (1.9)+(78)*.025`. The next calculation will be 78 * .025, resulting in 1.95. `TXn = (1.9)+1.95` is what is left and we can see that `TXn` will equal 3.85. Now Origin is at 25.85 and `TXn` is at 3.85

Let's run it through one more time. Now `TXn` is 3.85, so 3.85 * .95 is 3.65, and the new locations are 25.85 and 100, so now we have `TXn = (3.85)+(74.15)*.025`. The next calculation will be 74.15 x .025, resulting in about 1.85. `TXn = (3.85)+ 1.85` is what is left and we can see that `TXn` will equal around 5.7.

After three iterations, we can start to see the behavior. The closer the two MCs get, the larger the distance that "Origin" will move each "frame". This is why, as they get farther away from one another, "Origin" goes less distance each "frame" and appears to slow down. They do this until the distance that they jump becomes opposite (like positive to negative), at which point, "Origin" starts to come back toward "Drag".

The next step is to set the y location. `_root.Origin._y = _root.Drag._y+(_level10.amp[_level10._currentframe]*2)+TXn` simply sets the y location of Origin to whatever y location Drag is at, then adds the level of the audio times two and then adds `TXn`. The addition of `TXn` is merely to add a bit of imperfection into the movement.

Finally, we apply the line drawing code the same as in Project A.

Save this and export (or refer to the file `B_01.fla`). We can see that we have two connected points and one reacts to the audio while the other can be dragged.

Circles in the sound

For the next addition, we are going to make another movie clip. This is going to be a rather complex clip, so let's do it one step at a time. Make a circle with no fill and a hairline stroke. Create a movie clip out of this and set the registration point to center, and name it 'Node3'. Now, select this clip. It does not need an instance name, so leave that blank. Make this movie clip into another and again set the registration point to center, and this time name it 'Node2'. Select this clip. It too, needs no instance name. Double-click into Node2 (which now has Node3 inside of it). Select Node3 and move it up 10 pixels. Click back out to the root level. Now select Node2 and make it into yet another movie clip. Set the registration point again to center and name this one 'Node1'. Select it and give it an instance name of 'Node'. Now double-click into Node1. Duplicate the keyframe at frame 1 to frame 12. Select frame 1 and set it to a motion tween with a clockwise rotation of 1. The reason why we moved Node3 up 10 pixels inside of Node2 was so that when we tween Node2 inside of Node1 and install the rotation, it will wobble.

Now that our movie clip is ready, add a few lines (which will look familiar) to the code on the root in the layer "Actions".

```
_quality = "low";
fscommand(allowscale="false");
loadMovieNum("audio/03.swf", 10);
stop();

this.onEnterFrame = function() {
    // Replicate
    if (C<59) {
        _root.Node.duplicateMovieClip("Node"+C, C);
        C++;
    }
    // Dragger
    if (MD) {
        _root.Drag._x = _root._xmouse;
    }
    // Elastic Engine
    TXn = (TXn*.95)+(_root.Drag._x-_root.Origin._x)*.025;
    _root.Origin._x += TXn;
    _root.Origin._y = _root.Drag._y +
                      (_level10.amp[_level10._currentframe]*2)+TXn;
    // Draw Lines
    this.createEmptyMovieClip("Draw", C+100000);
    Draw.lineStyle(.25, 0xFF3399, 25);
    Draw.moveTo(_root.Origin._x, _root.Origin._y);
    Draw.lineTo(_root.Drag._x, _root.Drag._y);
};
this.onMouseDown = function() {
    MD = 1;
};
this.onMouseUp = function() {
    MD = 0;
};
```

We should remember this from before. If not, look back to Project A. The only difference is that we aren't resetting C, so this loop happens only once.

Lastly, to make this iteration complete, we need to apply a few actions to the "Node" MC.

```
onClipEvent (load) {
    _x = _root.Origin._x;
    _y = _root.Origin._y;
}
onClipEvent (enterFrame) {
    _x -= (_x-_root.Origin._x)/(random(20)+1);
    _y -= (_y-_root.Origin._y)/(random(20)+1);
    _rotation++;
    _yscale = _xscale = Math.abs(_x-_root.Origin._x)-100;
}
```

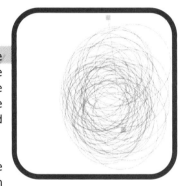

One of the greatest things about Flash MX is the ability to target `clipEvents` *remotely*. We could write these `clipEvents` on the root, but we don't. The reason why is that when we create the duplicates, we want them *all* to have these actions. If the actions are on the movie clip and then it's duplicated, they will all carry onto the duplicate. But, if we try to target, we need to write a `for` statement to send the actions 60 times to each movie clip. This would not work very well, so we use old style `clipEvent` locations.

As for the actual code, we have nothing too complex here. We initialize the locations to the location of Origin (which is moving about), as in `_x = _root.Origin._x`. Then, on each frame passage, we set properties. We start with the x and the y again by subtracting the distance from themselves to the Origin MC. To that we then divide by a random value. This all looks like: `_x -= (_x-_root.Origin._x)/(Math.random(20)+1)`. Next, we set the rotation to continually count incrementally. Lastly, we again use the distance, but this time we use `Math.abs` to make sure that the value is a positive value. Then we minus 100. This becomes the scale.

Save this as a new version named 'B_02.fla' and export (or refer to the file `B_02.fla`). We get a much more dynamic engine now.

As an interesting variation here, we can try adding a fill in Node3.

For the next iteration, we will make one small change to make the entire thing fully interactive. We can make it drag on both axes by writing this:

```
_quality = "low";
fscommand(allowscale="false");
loadMovieNum("audio/03.swf", 10);
stop();

this.onEnterFrame = function() {
    // Replicate
    if (C<59) {
        _root.Node.duplicateMovieClip("Node"+C, C);
        C++;
    }
    // Dragger
    if (MD) {
        _root.Drag._x = _root._xmouse;
    }
    // Elastic Engine
    TXn = (TXn*.96)+(_root.Drag._x-_root.Origin._x)*.05;
    TYn = (TYn*.96)+(_root.Drag._y-_root.Origin._y)*.05;
    _root.Origin._x += (TXn+(_level10.amp[_level10._currentframe]*.5));
    _root.Origin._y += (TYn+(_level10.amp[_level10._currentframe]*.5));
    // Draw Lines
    this.createEmptyMovieClip("Draw", C+100000);
    Draw.lineStyle(.25, 0xFF3399, 25);
    Draw.moveTo(_root.Origin._x, _root.Origin._y);
    Draw.lineTo(_root.Drag._x, _root.Drag._y);
};
this.onMouseDown = function() {
    MD = 1;
};
this.onMouseUp = function() {
    MD = 0;
};
```

Here we have simply created elasticity code for the y axis also. We changed a few values; like the .96 (which was .95) and the .05 (which was .025). Also, we have added the "amp" audio values to the x and y so that the audio makes the entire thing "bounce". What we get as a result is a much more interactive toy. We can now drag it around in any direction and do what we want with it.

Save this as a new version named 'B_03.fla' and export (or refer to the file B_03.fla).

Project C (A playful application)...

The last thing we are going to look into is a playful little toy that I have begun working on. This is not done, and truthfully, I'm not even sure where I want to go with it. But, nonetheless, I thought it would be a good thing to share. I am not going to go into a lot of detail on how this actually works because the difficult parts have been covered already. My advice is to look into this file and see what makes it tick. This is actually quite an easy file to understand without guidance because most of it is hard-coded (meaning that it isn't dynamic or in built on-the-fly).

Basically, Project C is a stickman that dances. We use the audio in pretty much the same way as we have in the last two projects, only this time we make something a bit different. The only real trick here is that we need to establish the rules and relationships that govern the body structure of the figure. Once the figure knows how it is assembled, we can let it dance.

The following goes on the root:

```
_quality = "low";
fscommand(allowscale="false");
loadMovieNum("audio/05.swf", 10);
F = .5;
V = .5;
Range = 40;
this.onLoad = function() {
    for (N-1; N<7; N++) {
        // Replicate
        Nav.duplicateMovieClip("Nav"+N, N);
        _root["Nav"+N]._x = (N*11)+156;
        _root["Nav"+N].MyNumber = N;
    }
};
stop();
//
this.onEnterFrame = function() {
    LineWidth = .25;
    LineAlpha = 25;
    LineColor = 0xFF3399;
    // LeftLeg
    this.createEmptyMovieClip("LeftTibia", 101);
    LeftTibia.lineStyle(LineWidth, LineColor, LineAlpha);
    LeftTibia.moveTo(this.AnkleLeft._x, this.AnkleLeft._y);
    LeftTibia.lineTo(this.KneeLeft._x, this.KneeLeft._y);
    this.createEmptyMovieClip("LeftFemur", 102);
    LeftFemur.lineStyle(LineWidth, LineColor, LineAlpha);
    LeftFemur.moveTo(this.KneeLeft._x, this.KneeLeft._y);
    LeftFemur.lineTo((this.Hips._x-(this.Hips._width/2)), this.Hips._y);
    // RightLeg
    this.createEmptyMovieClip("RightTibia", 103);
    RightTibia.lineStyle(LineWidth, LineColor, LineAlpha);
```

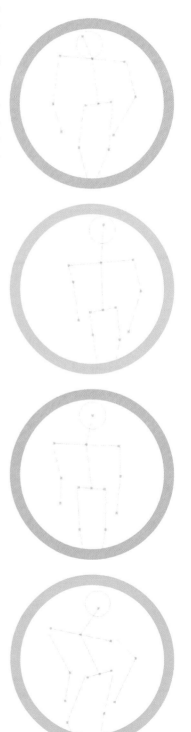

```
    RightTibia.moveTo(this.AnkleRight._x, this.AnkleRight._y);
    RightTibia.lineTo(this.KneeRight._x, this.KneeRight._y);
    this.createEmptyMovieClip("RightFemur", 104);
    RightFemur.lineStyle(LineWidth, LineColor, LineAlpha);
    RightFemur.moveTo(this.KneeRight._x, this.KneeRight._y);
    RightFemur.lineTo((this.Hips._x+(this.Hips._width/2)),  this.Hips._y);
    // LeftArm
    this.createEmptyMovieClip("LeftRadius", 105);
    LeftRadius.lineStyle(LineWidth, LineColor, LineAlpha);
    LeftRadius.moveTo(this.WristLeft._x, this.WristLeft._y);
    LeftRadius.lineTo(this.ElbowLeft._x, this.ElbowLeft._y);
    this.createEmptyMovieClip("LeftHumerous", 106);
    LeftHumerous.lineStyle(LineWidth, LineColor, LineAlpha);
    LeftHumerous.moveTo(this.ElbowLeft._x, this.ElbowLeft._y);
    LeftHumerous.lineTo((this.Shoulders._x-(this.Shoulders._width/2)), this.Shoulders._y);
    // RightArm
    this.createEmptyMovieClip("RightRadius", 107);
    RightRadius.lineStyle(LineWidth, LineColor, LineAlpha);
    RightRadius.moveTo(this.WristRight._x, this.WristRight._y);
    RightRadius.lineTo(this.ElbowRight._x, this.ElbowRight._y);
    this.createEmptyMovieClip("RightHumerous", 108);
    RightHumerous.lineStyle(LineWidth, LineColor, LineAlpha);
    RightHumerous.moveTo(this.ElbowRight._x, this.ElbowRight._y);
    RightHumerous.lineTo((this.Shoulders._x+(this.Shoulders._width/2)), this.Shoulders._y);
    // Spine
    this.createEmptyMovieClip("Spine", 109);
    Spine.lineStyle(LineWidth, LineColor, LineAlpha);
    Spine.moveTo(this.Shoulders._x, this.Shoulders._y);
    Spine.lineTo(this.Hips._x, this.Hips._y);
    // Head
    this.createEmptyMovieClip("Skull", 110);
    Skull.lineStyle(LineWidth, LineColor, LineAlpha);
    Skull.moveTo(this.Shoulders._x, this.Shoulders._y);
    Skull.lineTo(this.Head._x, this.Head._y);
};
```

And, the following goes on each joint movie clip:

```
onClipEvent (load) {
    XD = _x;
    YD = _y;
}
onClipEvent (enterFrame) {
    TXn = (TXn*_root.F)+(XD-_x)*_root.V;
    _x += TXn;
    TYn = (TYn*_root.F)+(YD-_y)*_root.V;
    _y += TYn;
    TRn = (TRn*_root.F)+(0-_rotation)*_root.V;
```

```
    _rotation += TRn;
    if (_level10.amp[_level10._currentframe]>40) {
        TXn += (random(_root.Range)-(_root.Range/2));
        TYn += (random(_root.Range)-(_root.Range/2));
        TRn += (random(_root.Range)-(_root.Range/2));
    }
}
```

A lot of this will look familiar, some will not. All in all, it is pretty simple to dissect.

If we refer to the file B_03.fla, we see the figure assemble and the figure reacting...

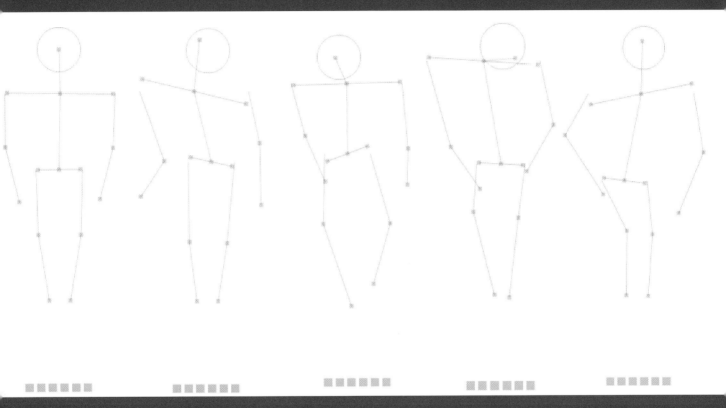

All this really consists of is a bunch of movie clips arranged as the joints (Head, Neck, Shoulders, Elbows, Wrists, Hips, Knees and Ankles) of a human body. We connect the joints with lines as we handled the lines in Project A and B. Then we make each joint react to the audio stream... and that's really all there is to this. The joints use the same elasticity code as Project B did, so really, *nothing* here is new. Even the movie clips are the same.

And that's it. Explore this file. Figure it out. Change it. Break it. Fix it. Rebuild it. Whatever. The best thing to do is to just get into it. As long as you are exploring, you are learning.

If you have any questions or need assistance with any of this code, you may e-mail me at support@soundofdesign.com with a subject line of "Sound Re-Activity".

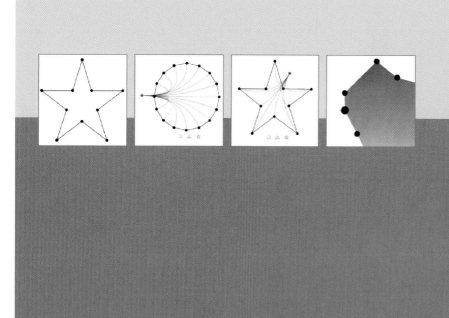

points, lines, and movement
jd hooge

There are a lot of ways to achieve the same goal using Flash. I try to keep my code as streamlined as possible. There are many ways to refine your code and your files, such as using loops, functions, and few graphics on the stage. Also, it is very important to limit how many operations are running constantly...

This project is simply an experiment that dives into several new Flash MX techniques and methods. Our main goal in this project is to plot out the lines and points of specific shapes, I'm going to use a circle, a triangle and a star. This example uses points (movie clips attached from the Library) and lines (drawn with the drawing API methods) to draw our shapes. After we have achieved that goal, we'll start to explore a few other techniques to enhance the result.

We build an '**Array Recorder**', which allows us to click several points to make a shape. The points' coordinates are recorded into arrays. Then, we take those arrays into a new FLA, and loop through the coordinates placing a movie clip at each point. Lastly, we connect the points with lines. This is done using the moveTo and lineTo methods.

After we have created our shape, we'll experiment with a few other techniques.

The first is to add another line to each point, which curves to a central point or hub. This is done using the moveTo and curveTo methods.

The second step will be to experiment with applying different types of programmatic motion to our points.

Third, we'll add an element of interactivity by allowing the user to change from one shape to the next, creating a morphing effect.

Fourth, we'll play around with the new dynamic masking feature (the setMask method).

Lastly, we will add a final touch by applying elastic scaling motion to the points, creating a bouncing effect.

Typically, I like to run my Flash files on LOW quality. However, in this project, I am using a lot of circles that don't render well when aliased, so I have kept all of the files on HIGH quality. Feel free to switch the quality to LOW during the tutorial to see the performance difference. Let's dive in and get Flashing!

The array recorder

Our array recorder is a separate Flash file that allows us to click several points to form a shape. The points' coordinates are recorded into arrays so we can use them in our design:

Start a new movie and set the movie size to 400 x 600 and the Frame Rate to 40 fps. The first thing you want to create is the grid that you'll use as your drawing area. My grid is set to 380 x 380. The grid is made up of vertical and horizontal lines that are 20 pixels apart. Before you move on, turn your grid into a movie clip, name it Grid, place it on the stage at (10, 10) and give it the instance name Grid.

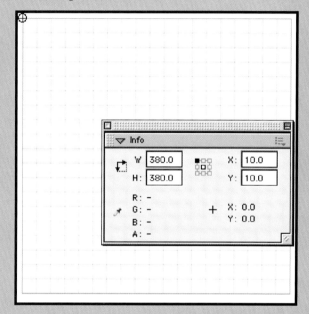

Below your grid, you'll have some space left over, which we'll use to display the coordinates. Create two dynamic text fields and give them variable names display_x and display_y respectively.

Now you are going to create your point. Create a new movie clip and name it Point. Make sure you use the advanced settings and check the box that reads Export for ActionScript. This allows you to attach that clip from the Library by referring to that name. Now go into the empty movie clip and create a small circle with the dimensions 8 x 8, making sure that the zero point is centered.

Now you have all the elements you need to begin building the engine for the recorder.

In the first frame of the main timeline, add this line to start off with:

```
fscommand ("allowscale", "false");
```

This line makes sure that the user cannot scale the movie up or down.

Now, we are going to start a function that will be executed onMouseDown. For now, the function is going to simply attach and position a point (movie clip Point) each time the user clicks the mouse.

```
Grid.onMouseDown = function () {
if (_ymouse < Grid._y + Grid._height) {   // If the mouse is within the grid
d++;   // create a variable d and increment it by one
   Grid.attachMovie("Point", "p"+d, d+3000);   // attach a point
   Point = Grid["p"+d];   // Use Point as a shortcut name for Grid["p"+d]
   Point._x = Grid._xmouse;   // Place the Point._x pos at the _xmouse pos
   Point._y = Grid._ymouse;   // Place the Point._y pos at the _ymouse pos
}
}
```

Test your movie. You'll be able to click around the grid, creating a point with each click. Now we want to record the positions you select into arrays, so we're going to establish a few arrays right away.

```
Coords = new Array();
XPos = new Array();
YPos = new Array();
```

Now we'll add a couple lines to the if statement that will record the coordinates of the mouse each time the user clicks on the grid.

```
Grid.onMouseDown = function() {
if (_ymouse < Grid._y + Grid._height) {
d++;
   Grid.attachMovie("Point", "p"+d, d+3000);
   Point = Grid["p"+d];
   Point._x = Grid._xmouse;
   Point._y = Grid._ymouse;
Coords [d] = new Array(Grid._xmouse, Grid._ymouse);   // * Look below
      xPos.push(Coords[d][0]);   // Add the new _x coordinate to the xPos array
      yPos.push(Coords[d][1]);   // Add the new _y coordinate to the yPos array
display_x = xPos;   // Assign the xPos array to the first text field
display_y = yPos;   // Assign the yPos array to the Second text field
}
}
```

Let's look at these new lines.

```
Coords [d] = new Array(Grid._xmouse, Grid._ymouse);
```

The first new line creates an array with 2 values (x and y) nested within `Coords`.

```
xPos.push(Coords[d][0]);
```

This line adds the new _x value to the `xPos` array.

```
yPos.push(Coords[d][1]);
```

This line adds the new _y value to the `yPos` array.

```
display_x = xPos;
display_y = yPos;
```

These two lines simply assign the `xPos` and `yPos` arrays to the text fields that you created before. As long as you have given the text fields the proper variable names, the coordinates should appear in the text boxes below your grid as you click.

Test your movie again. Now you can click around the grid and the text fields below are recording each click. The top text field records each _x value and the bottom field records each _y value. To make it a bit easier to see the shape you are creating when clicking points on the grid, we'll now connect the points and fill the shape.

To do this, the first thing you need to do is create an empty movie clip. This is so you can reference your line (and fill) by a name. Add this line after the above function:

```
Grid.createEmptyMovieClip("Line", 2000);
```

Now we will create another function that runs constantly (`onEnterFrame`).

```
this.onEnterFrame = function() {
  Grid.Line.clear();
  Grid.Line.beginFill(0x31424D, 30);
  Grid.Line.lineStyle(1, 0x999999, 30);
  Grid.Line.moveTo(Point._x, Point._y);
  for (i=1; i<=d; i++) {
    Grid.Line.lineTo(Coords[i][0], Coords[i][1], Coords[i][0], Coords[i][1]);
  }
  Grid.Line.endFill();
}
```

It simply starts the fill, sets the line styles, and then we loop through the next line, `lineTo`:

```
for (i=1; i<=d; i++) {
  Grid.Line.lineTo(Coords[i][0], Coords[i][1];
}
```

So, for each time `i` is less than or equal to `d`, the following statement executes:

```
Grid.Line.lineTo(Coords[i][0], Coords[i][1]);
```

Each time this statement is run, it defines a new end point for the line. Remember that each time you click, you are incrementing `d` by 1. So, each time you click, the statement extends the line to the new point you create.

The last line,

```
Grid.Line.endFill();
```

...applies the fill (specified previously by `beginFill`) to the lines added since the call to `beginFill`.

This completes the array recorder! You can check that your script matches this:

```
fscommand ("allowscale", "false");
//
Coords=new Array(), xPos=new Array(), yPos=new Array();
//
Grid.onMouseDown = function() {
  if (_ymouse < Grid._y + Grid._height) {
    d++;
    Grid.attachMovie("Point", "p"+d, d+3000);
    Point = Grid["p"+d];
    Point._x = Grid._xmouse;
    Point._y = Grid._ymouse;
    Coords[d] = new Array(Grid._xmouse, Grid._ymouse);
    xPos.push(Coords[d][0]);
    yPos.push(Coords[d][1]);
    display_x = xPos;
    display_y = yPos;
  }
};
//
Grid.createEmptyMovieClip("Line", 2000);
//
this.onEnterFrame = function() {
  Grid.Line.clear();
  Grid.Line.beginFill(0x31424D, 30);
  Grid.Line.lineStyle(1, 0x999999, 30);
  Grid.Line.moveTo(Point._x, Point._y);
  for (i=1; i<=d; i++) {
    Grid.Line.lineTo(Coords[i][0], Coords[i][1]);
  }
  Grid.Line.endFill();
};
};};
```

I have added a lot more functionality to my array recorder (`Part01.fla`, which you can download from www.friendsofED.com), which I suggest you do as well. Some ideas are:

Create shapes with evenly spaced-apart points (ahead of time) in a vector program. Then bring them into your array recorder file. When you run your SWF in the Flash player, you can simply trace over the shape, clicking on each point. This will simplify the process and allow you to create perfect shapes.

Once you have created several different shapes in a vector program, bring them all in to your array recorder, create a movie clip, put them on different frames with stops, then on the root level, create icons for each type of shape. Put `mouseDown` actions on each icon to switch the shape that you want to trace. If you do this, you will also want a RESET feature that will remove all your lines and clear your arrays (in case you mess up or want to switch shapes without having to close the file and open it again). Here is a little RESET function that you could call from your icons:

```
function reset() {
   Grid.Line.removeMovieClip();
   for (j=d; j>0; j—) {
     Grid["p"+j].removeMovieClip();
   }
   d = 0;
   xPos.splice(0);
   yPos.splice(0);
   Grid.createEmptyMovieClip("Line", 2000);
}
```

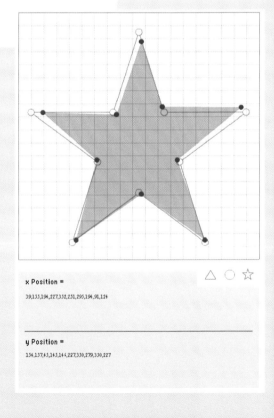

x Position =

39,155,194,227,332,231,295,194,91,124

y Position =

154,157,43,143,144,227,330,279,330,227

Plotting the points

We are going to start out slowly and build this experiment in four parts. The first part is plotting the points (which will be quite easy). What we are going to do is take the coordinates for a shape that we've created using the array recorder and plot them out. We'll use a star that I drew with my array recorder. Here are the coordinates for my star:

```
shape_x = [20, 149, 190, 229, 359, 255, 295, 189, 84, 125, 20];
shape_y = [152, 152, 27, 152, 152, 229, 352, 276, 352, 229, 152];
```

There are a number of very involved ways of getting these values into our new FLA, but by far the simplest is to run your array recorder and copy and paste the values into your new file. Let's begin:

Start a new movie; the movie size should be 400 x 440 and the Frame Rate 40 fps as before. Also add the same `allowscale` line.

```
fscommand("allowscale", "false");
```

We need to create our Point movie clip that we will use to plot the coordinates. So, create a circle with a 10 pixel width and height. Make the circle into a movie clip, name it `Point` and make sure you use the advanced settings and check the Export for ActionScript box. Now, go into the clip and make sure that the registration point of the shape is in the center.

As I mentioned, we're going to use a star shape that I created with my array recorder. So, first of all, we need to bring in those coordinates. Below the `allowscale` line, add these two lines:

```
shape_x = [20, 149, 190, 229, 359, 255, 295, 189, 84, 125, 20];
shape_y = [152, 152, 27, 152, 152, 229, 352, 276, 352, 229, 152];
```

You might be used to creating arrays like this:

```
shape_x = new Array(20, 149, 190, 229, 359, 255, 295, 189, 84, 125,
20);
```

But this is a little bit quicker and easier if you want to give the array a value right away:

```
shape_x = [20, 149, 190, 229, 359, 255, 295, 189, 84, 125, 20];
```

Now we just need to loop through these arrays and place points in the right places. We'll add a new function that runs `onEnterFrame`:

```
this.onEnterFrame = function() {
if (i<=shape_x.length-2) {
    i++;
    this.attachMovie("Point", "m"+i, 1000+i);
    this["m"+i]._x = shape_x[i]+10;
    this["m"+i]._y = shape_y[i]+10;
  }
};
```

This should be look pretty familiar, we are just attaching a Point for each coordinate and then moving it to the appropriate spot. The +10 makes up for the 10 pixel margin around the grid in the array recorder file.

Yes, we could have done this with a for loop but I chose to use an if statement so we see the progression (This will be important later when we give them motion).

That's it! Test your movie. You will see the points snap into place, one by one, although very quickly.

Here's the complete code, which is `part02.fla` in the download:

```
fscommand ("allowscale", "false");
//
shape_x = [20, 149, 190, 229, 359, 255, 295, 189, 84, 125, 20];
shape_y = [152, 152, 27, 151, 153, 228, 352, 276, 352, 229, 152];
//
this.onEnterFrame = function() {
   if (i<=shape_x.length-2) {
      i++;
      this.attachMovie("Point", "m"+i, 1000+i);
      this["m"+i]._x = shape_x[i]+10;
      this["m"+i]._y = shape_y[i]+10;
   }
};
```

Join the dots

Now that we have plotted the points, we can easily connect them. All we're going to do is create an empty movie clip to reference our line and add an else statement to our existing if statement.

First, after the two arrays and above the if statement, add this line:

```
this.createEmptyMovieClip("l1", 100);   // l1 stands for Line One
```

We have just created an empty movie clip so we can reference our line by a name. We put the line on level 100. Let's also create a shortcut name (Point) that we can use to reference `["m"+i]`. This makes it easier on the processor because it only has to make that calculation once `["m"+i]` rather that each time we want to reference a property or variable of `["m"+i]`. So add this line to the if statement right after the `attachMovie` line:

```
Point = this["m"+i];
```

138

Then we can substitute `Point` for `this["m"+i]` in the next two lines. So, this is what we have now:

```
if (i<=shape_x.length-2) {
    i++;
    this.attachMovie("Point", "m"+i, 1000+i);
Point = this["m"+i];
    Point._x = shape_x[i]+10;
    Point._y = shape_y[i]+10;
}
```

Here are the new lines we need to add as an `else` statement:

```
this.l1.clear();  // Clear Line 1 each time the frame loops
this.l1.lineStyle(1, 0x555555);  // Define Line 1 thickness and color
this.l1.moveTo(Point._x, Point._y);  // Define starting point for Line 1
```

Then we'll add a for loop inside the `else` statement for the `lineTo` statement:

```
for (j=0; j<=shape_x.length-2; j++) {
    this.lb.lineTo(this["m"+(j+1)]._x, this["m"+(j+1)]._y);
}
```

This statement just sets an end point for the line over and over until it gets to the end of the loop. That's it. Test your movie again and watch the star take shape as the points are connected one by one. Here is the complete code so far (`part03.fla`):

```
fscommand("allowscale", "false");
//
shape_x = [20, 150, 190, 230, 360, 255, 295, 190, 85, 125, 20];
shape_y = [152, 152, 27, 152, 152, 230, 352, 276, 352, 230, 152];
//
this.createEmptyMovieClip("l1", 200);
//
this.onEnterFrame = function() {
    if (i<=shape_x.length-2) {
        i++;
        this.attachMovie("Point", "m"+i, 1000+i);
        Point = this["m"+i];
        Point._x = shape_x[i]+10;
        Point._y = shape_y[i]+10;
        else {
        this.l1.clear();
        this.l1.lineStyle(.25, 0x555555);
        this.l1.moveTo(Point._x, Point._y);
        for (j=0; j<=shape_x.length-2; j++) {
          this.l1.lineTo(this["m"+(j+1)]._x, this["m"+(j+1)]._y);
        }
    }
};
```

Adding curves

We're going to add an apex point right in the middle of our shape. Then we will draw a curved line from each shape point to the apex. We'll make the apex moveable so you can see the curved lines in action.

Before we do any of that, let's fill our shape with a color. In the else statement, between this line:

```
this.l1.clear();
```

...and this line:

```
this.l1.lineStyle(.1, 0x555555);
```

...add this new line:

```
this.l1.beginFill(0xf8f8f8);
```

Then we have to apply the fill. At the bottom of the else statement, after the for loop, add this line:

```
this.l1.endFill();
```

Now your statement looks like this:

```
if (i<=shape_x.length-2) {
    i++;
    this.attachMovie("Point", "m"+i, 1000+i);
    Point = this["m"+i];
    Point._x = shape_x[i]+10;
    Point._y = shape_y[i]+10;
} else {
    this.l1.clear();
    this.l1.beginFill(0xf8f8f8);
    this.l1.lineStyle(.25, 0x555555);
    this.l1.moveTo(Point._x, Point._y);
    for (j=0; j<=shape_x.length-2; j++) {
        this.l1.lineTo(this["m"+(j+1)]._x, this["m"+(j+1)]._y);
    }
    this.l1.endFill();
}
```

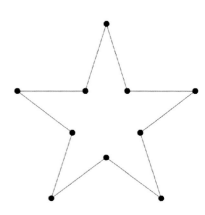

Now let's create our apex point. Since we want to be able to move the apex point around, we'll make it a button within a movie clip. First, go into your Library and duplicate your Point movie clip that already exists. Give it a new name – Apex – and make sure you check the box that reads Export for ActionScript as well as Export in First Frame. Also, make sure the new identifier name is Apex as well. Now go into the Apex movie clip.

First of all, change the color of the circle in this movie clip so you can identify the apex from the other points.

While you are still editing the movie clip, select the circle and convert it to a button. Simply name it Button. Now go into the button, add an Over frame (Change the color of the circle again for the Over state), and a Hit frame (Make the circle a few pixels larger in the Hit state so that it's easier to grab).

OK, so you have created a button within a movie clip. Now let's make it draggable. Go into the Edit Mode of the Apex movie clip. Click once on the button and pull up your ActionScript window. Add the following lines of code to the button:

```
on (press) {
    startDrag(this, true);
}
on (release) {
    stopDrag();
}
```

This will allow us to click and drag the Apex movie clip. Let's look at the first line to clarify exactly what we are doing:

```
startDrag(this, true);
```

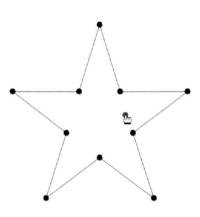

The first parameter, this, is the target path of the movie clip to drag. The second parameter, true, specifies that the draggable movie clip should lock to the center of the mouse position.

Now, to test this draggable movie clip, you simply attach it from the Library and position it. Go back to your code on the main timeline. Near the top of the script, right after your arrays (shape_x and shape_y), add these lines:

```
this.attachMovie("Apex", "Apex", 20000);   // Attach the Apex
Apex._x = 200; // Position the Apex _x
Apex._y = 200; // Position the Apex _y
```

We want this point to be on top of all other elements to we put it on level 20000, just to be safe. Then we center the clip at 200, 200.

Now you can test your movie. You will see your Apex Point right there in the center. Make sure that you can click and drag it around. Nice.

The last step of here is quite simple. We are just going to add another line, which we'll call l2, and then define all the properties of the line including thickness, color, alpha, starting points and ending points.

So, the first thing we need to do is create another empty movie clip called l2. Add this line right after the first createEmptyMovieClip line:

```
this.createEmptyMovieClip("l2", 200);
```

Your entire main stage code should now look like this:

```
fscommand("allowscale", "false");
//
shape_x = [20, 150, 190, 230, 360, 255, 295, 190, 85, 125, 20];
shape_y = [152, 152, 27, 152, 152, 230, 352, 276, 352, 230, 152];
//

this.attachMovie("Apex", "Apex", 20000);  // Attach the Apex
Apex._x = 200; // Position the Apex _x
Apex._y = 200; // Position the Apex _y

this.createEmptyMovieClip("l1", 200);
this.createEmptyMovieClip("l2", 200);
//
this.onEnterFrame = function() {
   if (i<=shape_x.length-2) {
      i++;
      this.attachMovie("Point", "m"+i, 1000+i);
      Point = this["m"+i];
      Point._x = shape_x[i]+10;
      Point._y = shape_y[i]+10;
   } else {
      this.l1.clear();
      this.l1.beginFill(0xf8f8f8);
      this.l1.lineStyle(.25, 0x555555);
      this.l1.moveTo(Point._x, Point._y);
      for (j=0; j<=shape_x.length-2; j++) {
         this.l1.lineTo(this["m"+(j+1)]._x, this["m"+(j+1)]._y);
      }
      this.l1.endFill();
   }
};
```

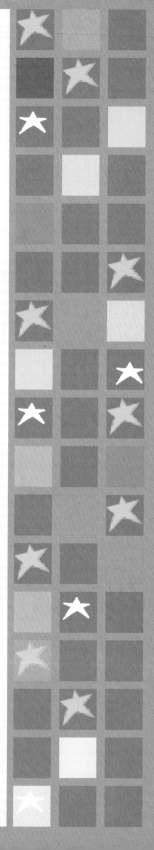

Now let's add the line properties for l2 to the else statement. After the l1.moveTo line, add the following lines:

```
this.l2.clear();  // Clear each time the frame loops
this.l2.lineStyle(.1, 0x444444, 40);  // Define thickness, color and
alpha
```

Now we'll add the following moveTo and curveTo lines to the for loop:

```
this.l2.moveTo(Apex._x, Apex._y);
this.l2.curveTo(200, 200, this["m"+(j+1)]._x, this["m"+(j+1)]._y);
```

Let's look at those two lines in detail:

```
this.l2.moveTo(Apex._x, Apex._y);
```

The reason why we are putting the moveTo line for l2 inside the loop is because we want the line to start at the apex each time and then branch out to one of the points. So each time the frame loops and j is incremented by 1, the starting point for the line is reset back to the apex. Now, let's look at the curveTo line:

```
this.l2.curveTo(200, 200, this["m"+(j+1)]._x, this["m"+(j+1)]._y);
```

So, here are our arguments for the curveTo line:

- For the controlX argument, we have 200. We want the line to curve towards the middle.

- For the controlY argument, we have 200. We want the line to curve towards the middle.

- For the anchorX argument, we have this["m"+(j+1)]._x. We want the line to end at the next point.

- For the anchorY argument, we have this["m"+(j+1)]._y. We want the line to end at the next point.

Now test your movie! You won't be able to see the curves until you drag the Apex Point. Now you see the power of the API drawing methods in Flash MX!

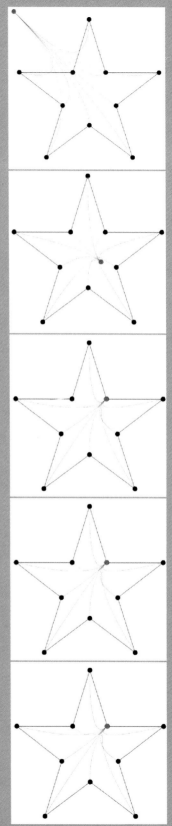

Your complete code for part04.fla looks like this:

```
fscommand ("allowscale", "false");
//
shape_x = [20, 150, 190, 230, 360, 255, 295, 190, 85, 125, 20];
shape_y = [152, 152, 27, 152, 152, 230, 352, 276, 352, 230, 152];
//
this.attachMovie("Apex", "Apex", 20000);
Apex._x = 200;
Apex._y = 200;
//
this.createEmptyMovieClip("l1", 100);
this.createEmptyMovieClip("l2", 200);
//
this.onEnterFrame = function() {
  if (i<=shape_x.length-2) {
    i++;
    this.attachMovie("Point", "m"+i, 1000+i);
    Point = this["m"+i];
    Point._x = shape_x[i]+10;
    Point._y = shape_y[i]+10;
  } else {
    this.l1.clear();
    this.l1.lineStyle(.25, 0x555555);
    this.l1.beginFill(0xf8f8f8);
    this.l1.moveTo(Point._x, Point._y);
    this.l2.clear();
    this.l2.lineStyle(.1, 0x444444, 40);
    for (j=0; j<=shape_x.length-2; j++) {
  this.l1.lineTo(this["m"+(j+1)]._x,
this["m"+(j+1)]._y);
      this.l2.moveTo(Apex._x, Apex._y);
this.l2.curveTo(200, 200, this["m"+(j+1)]._x,
this["m"+(j+1)]._y);
    }
    this.l1.endFill();
  }
};
```

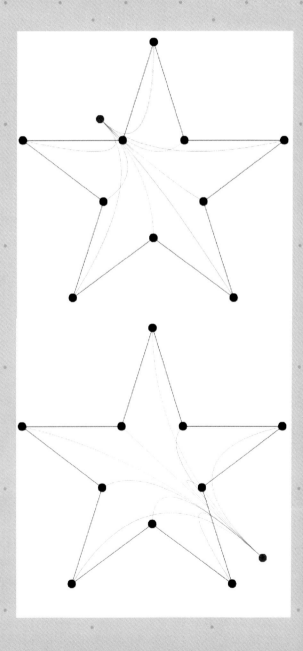

Adding motion

We're going to learn a bit of programmatic motion to give our shape some life. First of all, I want to show you the general equations that I use for *easing* motion and *elastic* motion.

Easing

```
_x -= (_x-xn)*friction;
_y -= (_y-yn)*friction;
```

With the easing equations, you simply need to set a variable named `friction` to something like .1, .2, or .3. Then you set the `xn` and `yn` variables. If the equations are looping constantly, `_x` will ease towards `xn` and `_y` will ease towards `yn`. (If you don't set a starting point for `_x` and `_y`, they will start at 0) If we apply the equations to a movie clip (`Mc`), they will look like this:

```
Mc._x -= (Mc._x-Mc.xn)*friction;
Mc._y -= (Mc._y-Mc.yn)*friction;
```

Recap:

```
Mc._x = Starting point for x
Mc._y = Starting point for y
Mc.xn = Destination for x
Mc.xn = Destination for y
friction = Friction (self explanitory)
```

Elastic

```
_x -= x=(x+(_x-xn)*friction)*elast;
_y -= y=(y+(_y-yn)* friction)*elast;
```

As you can see with the elastic equations, you only have one extra variable to set. That variable is `elast`. You want to set this variable to something like .7. You can try different combinations of friction and elasticity. I try to make sure that together, they equal 1. Again, if you don't set a starting point for `_x` and `_y`, they will start at 0. If we apply the equations to a movie clip (Mc), they will look like this:

```
Mc._x -= x=(x+(Mc._x-Mc.xn)*friction)*elast;
Mc._y -= y=(y+(Mc._y-Mc.yn)* friction)*elast;
```

Now let's apply the elastic motion to our star. More specifically, let's add the elasticity to each of our points. If you want, you can try the easing motion as well. I'll leave that up to you.

We need to do four things:

- Set the `_x` and `_y` of each point (we'll do this in our `if` statement)

- Set the `xn` and `yn` of each point (we'll do this in our `if` statement also)

- Apply the equation to each point (we'll do this with a separate `for` loop)

- Set the `friction` and `elast` variables

We'll do them in that order. First, change the following lines in your `if` statement (Copy these lines before you change them because we'll use them in the next step):

```
Point._x = shape_x[i]+10;
Point._y = shape_y[i]+10;
```

...to the following:

```
Point._x = this["m"+(i-1)]._x;
Point._y = this["m"+(i-1)]._y;
```

These two lines are setting the starting coordinates for each point. Notice that instead of using `Point` in the second part of the equation, we are using this: `["m"+(i-1)]._x`. This is because we want to assign each point to start where the last point is located now. This creates a bit of a trailing effect rather than having them all start off at 0.

Now we'll reuse the lines from before. Paste the following lines:

```
Point._x = shape_x[i]+10;
Point._y = shape_y[i]+10;
```

...and change them to the following:

```
Point.xn = shape_x[i]+10;
Point.yn = shape_y[i]+10;
```

Next, we'll apply the equation to each point. To do this, we'll create a new `for` loop that will go before the `if` statement. So, before the `if` statement, add the following `for` loop:

```
for (c=1; c<=shape_x.length-1; c++) {
    Point = this["m"+c];
    Point._x -= x=(x+(Point._x-Point.xn)*accel)*elast;
    Point._y -= y=(y+(Point._y-Point.yn)*accel)*elast;
}
```

Once again, we create a shortcut name `Point` to simplify our equation. Then we simply apply the elasticity equation to each point.

Lastly, we need to set the `friction` and `elast` variables. Do this just below the arrays are set at the very top of your code:

```
friction = .3;
elast = .7;
```

That's it! Now test your movie and watch it spring into action!

These programmatic motion equations can be extremely helpful. I find myself using one or the other (easing or elasticity) somehow in every Flash web site or experiment that I build. As I mentioned before, you can experiment with different levels of friction and elasticity to get the effect that you want.

Next, we're going to add a few more arrays and allow the user to morph the shape from one set of coordinated to another. Once we accomplish that, you will see the affect of the elastic motion much more clearly.

Your complete code should now look like this (part05.fla):

```
fscommand ("allowscale", "false");
//
shape_x = [20, 150, 190, 230, 360, 255, 295, 190, 85, 125, 20];
shape_y = [152, 152, 27, 152, 152, 230, 352, 276, 352, 230, 152];
//
friction = .3;
elast = .7;
//
this.attachMovie("Apex", "Apex", 20000);
Apex._x = 200;
Apex._y = 200;
//
this.createEmptyMovieClip("l1", 100);
this.createEmptyMovieClip("l2", 200);
//
this.onEnterFrame = function() {
   for (c=1; c<=shape_x.length-1; c++) {
      Point = this["m"+c];
      Point._x -= x=(x+(Point._x-Point.xn)*friction)*elast;
      Point._y -= y=(y+(Point._y-Point.yn)*friction)*elast;
   }
   if (i<=shape_x.length-2) {
      i++;
      this.attachMovie("Point", "m"+i, 1000+i);
      Point = this["m"+i];
      Point._x = this["m"+(i-1)]._x;
      Point._y = this["m"+(i-1)]._y;
      Point.xn = shape_x[i]+10;
      Point.yn = shape_y[i]+10;
   } else {
      this.l1.clear();
      this.l1.lineStyle(.25, 0x555555);
      this.l1.beginFill(0xf8f8f8);
      this.l1.moveTo(Point._x, Point._y);
      this.l2.clear();
```

147

```
        this.l2.lineStyle(.1, 0x444444, 40);
        for (j=0; j<=shape_x.length-2; j++) {
           this.l1.lineTo(this["m"+(j+1)]._x, this["m"+(j+1)]._y);
           this.l2.moveTo(Apex._x, Apex._y);
           this.l2.curveTo(200, 200, this["m"+(j+1)]._x,
    this["m"+(j+1)]._y);
        }
        this.l1.endFill();
     }
  };
```

Try altering the `elast` and `friction` values to see what happens!

Morphing shapes

Now that we've spent plenty of time with the star shape, I think it's about time we change things up a bit. What we're going to do here is add a little interactivity. We are going to bring in a few more arrays (shape coordinates) and allow the user to switch from one shape to the next... Since we have already applied motion properties to the points, they will bounce from one shape to the next.

Just to keep it simple, we will use three shapes. Of course, you could use as many shapes as you want. Right away, let's replace your two arrays at the top of your code with these six arrays:

```
shape_x_1 = [40, 51, 83, 131, 190, 247, 296, 328, 340, 328, 296,
247, 189, 132, 83, 50, 40];
shape_y_1 = [190, 132, 84, 51, 40, 52, 84, 133, 191, 248, 297, 329,
341, 329, 297, 247, 190];
//
shape_x_2 = [52, 86, 120, 155, 192, 226, 260, 295, 330, 260, 190,
120, 52];
shape_y_2 = [280, 230, 180, 130, 74, 130, 180, 230, 281, 281, 281,
281, 280];
//
shape_x_3 = [20, 149, 190, 229, 359, 255, 295, 189, 84, 125, 20];
shape_y_3 = [152, 152, 27, 151, 153, 228, 352, 276, 352, 229, 152];
```

Notice that they are named `shape_x_1`, `shape_x_2`, etc. This is going to change a few things throughout our code considering we were referencing arrays `shape_x` and `shape_y` before. We'll get to that in a minute. But first let me explain how this is going to work:

We're going to create a variable called `active` that will refer to the active shape. That's easy right? So each time we want to switch to a different shape, we're going to change the value of active. Right below the `friction` and `elast` value setting, add this line:

```
active = 1;
```

As I mentioned above, we changed the names of our arrays so we are going to have to address this in the places in which we reference the arrays. Also, we have more than one array, so in those places, we are going to create expressions that makes sure we reference the active array. So, each time we've used an `if` statement or `for` loop, we must change the conditional argument. For example, change this line:

```
for (c=1; c<=shape_x.length-1; c++) {
}
```

...to this:

```
for (c=1; c<=this["shape_x_"+active].length-1; c++) {
}
```

Do this for each `if` statement or `for` loop. Also, there is one other small part that you must address:

change:

```
Point.xn = shape_x[i]+10;
Point.yn = shape_y[i]+10;
```

...to:

```
Point.xn = this["shape_x_"+active][i]+10;
Point.yn = this["shape_y_"+active][i]+10;
```

You might also notice that some of the shapes have more points than others. Taking this into account, we are going to create a function that gets rid of extra points or creates more, depending on which shape we are switching to and from. This function will have a `for` loop and a `while` loop. The `for` loop re-sets the `xn` and **yn** values of all the points to their new coordinates. The `while` loop removes any extra points. Add this function before all other functions.

```
function changeShape() {
  for (k=0; k<=this["shape_x_"+active].length-1; k++) {
    this["m"+k].xn = this["shape_x_"+active][k]+10;
    this["m"+k].yn = this["shape_y_"+active][k]+10;
  }
  while (i>=this["shape_x_"+active].length-1) {
    this["m"+i].removeMovieClip();
    i--;
  }
}
```

The last step is to create a way to switch from one shape to the next. I have chosen to create three buttons. Each button is a small icon of the shape that it will trigger. They are a circle, triangle and star respectively.

On the first button, I have added the following code:

```
on (release) {
  active = 1;
  changeShape()
}
```

This simply changes the variable active to 1 and calls the changeShape function. The second button has the same code, on it except that it sets active to 2. The third button has the same code, except it sets active to 3. This is downloadable as part06.fla.

That's it! Test your movie now and watch the shape change from one to the next!

Your code should now look like this:

```
fscommand ("allowscale", "false");
//
shape_x_1 = [40, 51, 83, 131, 190, 247, 296, 328, 340, 328, 296, 247,
189, 132, 83, 50, 40];
shape_y_1 = [190, 132, 84, 51, 40, 52, 84, 133, 191, 248, 297, 329, 341,
329, 297, 247, 190];
//
shape_x_2 = [52, 86, 120, 155, 192, 226, 260, 295, 330, 260, 190, 120, 52];
shape_y_2 = [280, 230, 180, 130, 74, 130, 180, 230, 281, 281, 281, 281, 280];
//
shape_x_3 = [20, 149, 190, 229, 359, 255, 295, 189, 84, 125, 20];
shape_y_3 = [152, 152, 27, 151, 153, 228, 352, 276, 352, 229, 152];
//
this.attachMovie("Apex", "Apex", 20000);
Apex._x = 200;
Apex._y = 200;
//
```

```
friction = .3;
elast = .7;
active = 1;
//
this.createEmptyMovieClip("l1", 100);
this.createEmptyMovieClip("l2", 200);
//
function changeShape() {
  for (k=0; k<=this["shape_x_"+active].length-1; k++) {
    this["m"+k].xn = this["shape_x_"+active][k]+10;
    this["m"+k].yn = this["shape_y_"+active][k]+10;
  }
  while (i>=this["shape_x_"+active].length-1) {
    this["m"+i].removeMovieClip();
    i--;
  }
}
//
this.onEnterFrame = function() {
  for (c=1; c<=this["shape_x_"+active].length-1; c++) {
    Point = this["m"+c];
    Point._x -= x=(x+(Point._x-Point.xn)*friction)*elast;
    Point._y -= y=(y+(Point._y-Point.yn)*friction)*elast;
  }
  if (i<=this["shape_x_"+active].length-2) {
    i++;
    this.attachMovie("Point", "m"+i, 1000+i);
    Point = this["m"+i];
    Point._x = this["m"+(i-1)]._x;
    Point._y = this["m"+(i-1)]._y;
    Point.xn = this["shape_x_"+active][i]+10;
    Point.yn = this["shape_y_"+active][i]+10;
  } else {
    this.l1.clear();
    this.l1.lineStyle(.25, 0x555555);
    this.l1.beginFill(0xf8f8f8);
    this.l1.moveTo(Point._x, Point._y);
    this.l2.clear();
    this.l2.lineStyle(.1, 0x444444, 40);
    for (j=0; j<=this["shape_x_"+active].length-2; j++) {
     this.l1.lineTo(this["m"+(j+1)]._x, this["m"+(j+1)]._y);
      this.l2.moveTo(Apex._x, Apex._y);
      this.l2.curveTo(200, 200, this["m"+(j+1)]._x, this["m"+(j+1)]._y);
    }
    this.l1.endFill();
  }
};
```

Dynamic masking

Another fundamental feature new with Flash MX is the `setMask` method, it allows you to assign a movie clip to mask another movie clip with ActionScript. I put together a couple of examples that utilize this method.

The first example will make each Point into a `maskMovieClip`. We just need to create a new movie clip with an image in it and then add a couple of lines to our main code.

Make a new movie clip. Name it 'img' and make sure you give it the identifier 'img' as well so we can attach it from the Library. Now, inside the img movie clip, you need to import an image. Any image will do as long as it is at least 400 pixels wide by 400 pixels tall. Put the image on the first frame of the clip and make sure the registration point is at the top-left corner.

Now go back to your main code. The first line to add is the line that attaches the img movie clip. Find the line inside your `if` statement that attaches the Points:

```
this.attachMovie("Point", "m"+i, 1000+i);
```

Right, after this line, add:

```
this.attachMovie("img", "img"+i, 500+i);
```

So, we are attaching an `img` for each `Point`. Now, at the bottom of your `if` statement, just before the `else`, add this line:

```
this["img"+i].setMask(Point);
```

This assigns the first `Point` to mask the first `img`, and so on...

Lastly, we need to remove any extra `img` movie clips in the `changeShape` function, just like we do for any extra points. So, in that function, after this line:

```
this["m"+i].removeMovieClip();
```

...add this line:

```
this["img"+i].removeMovieClip();
```

Now test your movie, you will see that each point is filled with an image as it moves about. Feel free to make the points bigger or change the shape entirely.

Your code for `Part07.01.fla` should now look like this:

```
fscommand ("allowscale", "false");
//
shape_x_1 = [40, 51, 83, 131, 190, 247, 296, 328, 340, 328, 296, 247, 189, 132, 83, 50, 40];
shape_y_1 = [190, 132, 84, 51, 40, 52, 84, 133, 191, 248, 297, 329, 341, 329, 297, 247, 190];
//
shape_x_2 = [52, 86, 120, 155, 192, 226, 260, 295, 330, 260, 190, 120, 52];
shape_y_2 = [280, 230, 180, 130, 74, 130, 180, 230, 281, 281, 281, 281, 280];
//
shape_x_3 = [20, 149, 190, 229, 359, 255, 295, 189, 84, 125, 20];
shape_y_3 = [152, 152, 27, 151, 153, 228, 352, 276, 352, 229, 152];
//
this.attachMovie("Apex", "Apex", 20000);
Apex._x = 200;
Apex._y = 200;
//
friction = .3;
elast = .7;
active = 1;
//
this.createEmptyMovieClip("l1", 100);
this.createEmptyMovieClip("l2", 200);
//
function changeShape() {
    for (k=0; k<=this["shape_x_"+active].length-1; k++) {
        this["m"+k].xn = this["shape_x_"+active][k]+10;
        this["m"+k].yn = this["shape_y_"+active][k]+10;
    }
    while (i>=this["shape_x_"+active].length-1) {
        this["m"+i].removeMovieClip();
        this["img"+i].removeMovieClip();
        i—;
    }
}
//
this.onEnterFrame = function() {
    for (c=1; c<=this["shape_x_"+active].length-1; c++) {
        Point = this["m"+c];
        Point._x -= x=(x+(Point._x-Point.xn)*friction)*elast;
        Point._y -= y=(y+(Point._y-Point.yn)*friction)*elast;
    }
    if (i<=this["shape_x_"+active].length-2) {
        i++;
        this.attachMovie("Point", "m"+i, 1000+i);
        this.attachMovie("img", "img"+i, 500+i);
        Point = this["m"+i];
        Point._x = this["m"+(i-1)]._x;
        Point._y = this["m"+(i-1)]._y;
        Point.xn = this["shape_x_"+active][i]+10;
```

153

```
        Point.yn = this["shape_y_"+active][i]+10;
        this["img"+i].setMask(Point);
    } else {
      this.l1.clear();
      this.l1.lineStyle(.25, 0x555555);
      this.l1.beginFill(0xf8f8f8);
      this.l1.moveTo(Point._x, Point._y);
      this.l2.clear();
      this.l2.lineStyle(.1, 0x444444, 40);
      for (j=0; j<=this["shape_x_"+active].length-2; j++) {
          this.l1.lineTo(this["m"+(j+1)]._x, this["m"+(j+1)]._y);
          this.l2.moveTo(Apex._x, Apex._y);
          this.l2.curveTo(200, 200, this["m"+(j+1)]._x,
➡this["m"+(j+1)]._y);
      }
      this.l1.endFill();
    }
};
```

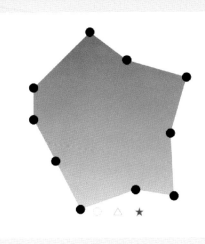

The second example will make our entire shape (l1) into the maskMovieClip.

First let's simplify things and get rid of l2 and the apex. Just delete all the code that pertains to both of them. Now that's out of the way, we'll just take the lines that we added in the later iteration, move them, and modify them a bit.

In your `if` statement, you just added 2 lines:

```
this.attachMovie("img", "img"+i, 500+i);
```

and

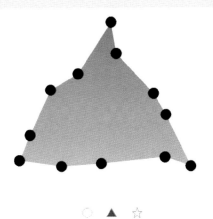

```
this["img"+i].setMask(Point);
```

Take both of these lines and move them up above all the functions, right underneath your `createEmptyMovieClip` line. Change them to look like this:

```
this.attachMovie("img", "img", 500);
img.setMask(l1);
```

OK, now we just have one `img` clip and it is masked by l1.

That's it! (If you feel the need to check your movie at this point - part07.02.fla.)

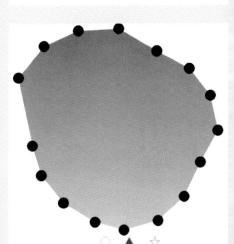

154

One more thing

I thought I would add one last modification to give you an idea of how versatile and useful the elastic motion equation is. All were going to do is put a function inside the Point clip that controls its _xscale and _yscale.

Copy part07.01.fla and save it as a new file (in the download part08.fla), add this script on the first frame of the Point movie clip:

```
_xscale = 250; // Start _xscale at 250
_yscale = 250; // Start _yscale at 250
//
xsn = 100; // End _xscale at 100
ysn = 100; // end _yscale at 100
//
this.onEnterFrame = function() {
  // Run scale function until my _xscale and _yscale reach 100
  if (_xscale and _yscale>100) {
    _xscale -= xs=(xs+(_xscale-xsn)*_parent.friction)*_parent.elast;
    _yscale -= ys=(ys+(_yscale-ysn)*_parent.friction)*_parent.elast;
          }
};
```

Test your movie one last time to see the points bounce before they rest at 100% scale. These are the kinds of simple touches that you can use to make your Flash interfaces or experiments a bit more natural. I enjoy creating living, breathing animals that have emotions and reactions. This leads to intuitive user interaction.

You have now completed the tutorial. I hope that you are beginning to see the potential of the new Flash MX method. Also, I hope you appreciate and adopt some of my tendencies to simplify code. Notice that the entire SWF file (without the JPG) is only 4k!

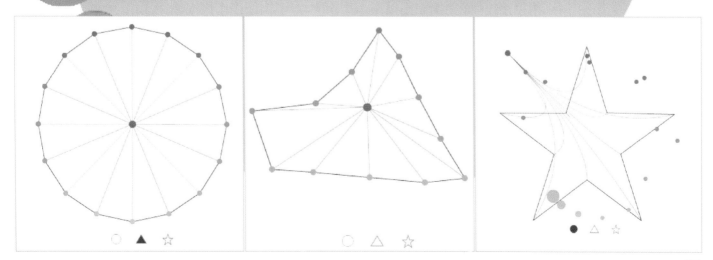

bezier curve creatures
lifaros

I find that very few interesting things in life are perfectly straight, most are curvy, and in order to make pretty, bouncy, wiggly things that move with fluidity we need to be able to draw and animate smooth curves.

As you already know, Flash MX includes the very useful `curveTo` function within the Drawing API. I introduced some Bezier concepts within my earlier **Scriptable Masks** chapter, so we're ready to leap straight in. Hopefully you shouldn't find this too complex...

Drawing API and Quadratic Bezier Splines

First of all open `mx_cs_000.fla`, test the movie, and investigate how dragging the blue dots changes the shape of the curve.

The parametric equation of the quadratic Bezier spline is as follows:

```
x(t)= x1(1-t)(1-t)+2x2(1-t)t+x3*t*t
y(t)= y1(1-t)(1-t)+2y2(1-t)t+y3*t*t
```

...where:

`x1,y1` are the coordinates of the first anchor point
`x2,y2` are the coordinates of the control point
`x3,y3` are the coordinates of the second anchor point

Moving the slider changes the value of `t`. When `t` equals 0, the red dot is over the first anchor point and when `t` equals 1, the red dot is over the second anchor point.

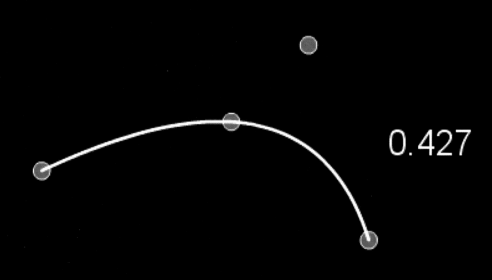

0.427

I'll now run through and explain the Bezier prototypes that will be used in most of this chapter's experiments. These live on the actions layer on the first frame of the FLA.

bezierPoints: This prototype sets the three couples of coordinates of the Bezier control points. We usually use the coordinates of the draggable dots as the parameters of this method. The prototype property, used this way, means that all instances of the bezierPoints class inherit the function.

```
MovieClip.prototype.bezierPoints = function(x1, y1, x2, y2, x3, y3) {
    this.x1=x1, this.y1=y1;
    this.x2=x2, this.y2=y2;
    this.x3=x3, this.y3=y3;
};
```

bezierDraw: This method draws a Bezier spline curve using the Drawing API functions.

```
MovieClip.prototype.bezierDraw = function(strokewidth, strokecolor, strokealpha) {
    this.clear();
    this.lineStyle(strokewidth, strokecolor, strokealpha);
    this.moveTo(this.x1, this.y1);
    this.curveTo(this.x2, this.y2, this.x3, this.y3);
};
```

bezierQuadratic: This method calculates the coordinates of a point within the curve, given t and the coordinates of the three control points (a,b,c) as parameters.

```
MovieClip.prototype.bezierQuadratic = function(t, a, b, c) {
    return (1-t)*(1-t)*a+2*(1-t)*t*b+t*t*c;
};
```

...and finally we create our Bezier movie clip. This script is on the second frame of our FLA:

```
bez = [];
bez[0] = createEmptyMovieClip("body", 1);
t=.5;
this.onEnterFrame = function() {
    bez[0].bezierPoints(dot1._x, dot1._y, dot2._x, dot2._y, dot3._x, dot3._y);
    bez[0].bezierSegment(0, 1);
    bez[0].bezierDraw(2, 0xffffff, 100);
    red._x = bezierQuadratic(t, dot1._x, dot2._x, dot3._x);
    red._y = bezierQuadratic(t, dot1._y, dot2._y, dot3._y);
};
stop();
```

0.2045

The Bezier derivative

Another important parametric equation that we should investigate is the Bezier first derivative. It allows us to obtain the slope and the angle on any point of the Bezier curve - so we could draw a tangent if we so wished:

$$x'(t) = 2x1(t-1)+2x2(1-2t)+2x3t$$
$$y'(t) = 2y1(t-1)+2y2(1-2t)+2y3t$$

I've coded a little movie that uses this equation in order to draw perpendicular lines over the curve; it's fairly similar to the last FLA we created. Open up `mx_cs_000b.fla` and test the movie.

This ActionScript is on the first frame of the FLA:

bezierAngle: This method calculates the angle:

```
MovieClip.prototype.bezierAngle = function(t) {
    return (Math.atan2(this.bezierDerivative(t, this.y1, this.y2, this.y3),
this.bezierDerivative(t, this.x1, this.x2, this.x3)));
};
```

bezierDerivative: This method returns the Bezier first derivative:

```
MovieClip.prototype.bezierDerivative = function(t, a, b, c) {
    return 2*a*(t-1)+2*b*(1-2*t)+2*c*t;
};
```

And this method draws the perpendicular lines:

```
MovieClip.prototype.bezierPerpendiculars = function(delta, radius, strokewidth, strokecolor,
➥strokealpha) {
    var t = 0, x, y, angle;
    this.lineStyle(strokewidth, strokecolor, strokealpha);
    for (t=0; t<=1.001; t += delta) {
      angle = this.bezierAngle(t);
      x = bezierQuadratic(t, this.x1, this.x2, this.x3);
      y = bezierQuadratic(t, this.y1, this.y2, this.y3);
      this.moveTo(x+radius*Math.cos(angle-.5*Math.PI), y+radius*Math.sin(angle-.5*Math.PI));
      this.lineTo(x+radius*Math.cos(angle+.5*Math.PI), y+radius*Math.sin(angle+.5*Math.PI));
    }
};
```

Finally we create the Bezier curve with the following code on the second frame:

```
bez = [];
bez[0] = createEmptyMovieClip("body", 1);
this.onEnterFrame = function() {
    bez[0].bezierPoints(dot1._x, dot1._y, dot2._x, dot2._y, dot3._x,
➡dot3._y);
    bez[0].bezierDraw(2, 0xffffff, 100);
    bez[0].bezierPerpendiculars(.025, 20, 2, 0xffffff, 100);
};
stop();
```

The Bezier segment

I've developed an easy method for drawing a segment of the Bezier curve between two given values of t. We know that each Bezier segment is another Bezier curve, but this segment has three new control points b1, b2, and b3. Take a look at mx_cs_001.fla to see it in action.

bezierSegment: This movieclip method calculates the new control points:

```
MovieClip.prototype.bezierSegment = function(t1, t2) {
    this.bx1 = this.bezierQuadratic(t1, this.x1, this.x2, this.x3);
    this.by1 = this.bezierQuadratic(t1, this.y1, this.y2, this.y3);
    this.bx3 = this.bezierQuadratic(t2, this.x1, this.x2, this.x3);
    this.by3 = this.bezierQuadratic(t2, this.y1, this.y2, this.y3);
    this.bx2 = this.bezierControl(t1, t2, this.x1, this.x2, this.x3);
    this.by2 = this.bezierControl(t1, t2, this.y1, this.y2, this.y3);
};
```

bezierControl: This method is used by the bezierSegment method to perform its calculations.

```
MovieClip.prototype.bezierControl = function(t1, t2, a, b, c) {
    return a+(t1+t2)*(b-a)+t1*t2*(c-2*b+a);
};
```

bezierDraw: This method has been adapted from the previous FLAs to now draw a Bezier segment.

```
MovieClip.prototype.bezierDraw = function(strokewidth, strokecolor,
➡strokealpha) {
    this.clear();
    this.lineStyle(strokewidth, strokecolor, strokealpha);
    this.moveTo(this.bx1, this.by1);
    this.curveTo(this.bx2, this.by2, this.bx3, this.by3);
};
```

t1   t2

0.647   0.38

t1   t2

0.2   0.8

t1   t2

0.647   0

t1   t2

0.74   0.8

show dots
hide lines

161

The following methods are used to draw the auxiliary dots and lines involved in Bezier curves:

```
MovieClip.prototype.bezierLine = function(t, a, b) {
    return a*(1-t)+b*t;
};
MovieClip.prototype.drawLine = function(x1, y1, x2, y2, strokewidth, strokecolor, strokealpha) {
    this.lineStyle(strokewidth, strokecolor, strokealpha);
    this.moveTo(x1, y1);
    this.lineTo(x2, y2);
};
MovieClip.prototype.calculateAuxPoints = function(t1, t2) {
    this.sx1 = bezierLine(t1, this.x1, this.x2);
    this.sy1 = bezierLine(t1, this.y1, this.y2);
    this.sx2 = bezierLine(t1, this.x2, this.x3);
    this.sy2 = bezierLine(t1, this.y2, this.y3);
    this.sx3 = bezierLine(t2, this.x1, this.x2);
    this.sy3 = bezierLine(t2, this.y1, this.y2);
    this.sx4 = bezierLine(t2, this.x2, this.x3);
    this.sy4 = bezierLine(t2, this.y2, this.y3);
};
MovieClip.prototype.drawAuxLines = function() {
    this.drawLine(this.x1, this.y1, this.x2, this.y2, 2, 0x6699ff, 100);
    this.drawLine(this.x2, this.y2, this.x3, this.y3, 2, 0x6699ff, 100);
    this.drawLine(this.sx1, this.sy1, this.sx2, this.sy2, 2, 0x6699ff, 100);
    this.drawLine(this.sx3, this.sy3, this.sx4, this.sy4, 2, 0x6699ff, 100);
};
MovieClip.prototype.drawAuxPoints = function() {
    this.drawDot(this.bx1, this.by1, 5, 1, 0xff3366, 100);
    this.drawDot(this.bx2, this.by2, 5, 1, 0xff3366, 100);
    this.drawDot(this.bx3, this.by3, 5, 1, 0xff3366, 100);
    this.drawDot(this.sx1, this.sy1, 5, 1, 0x6699ff, 100);
    this.drawDot(this.sx2, this.sy2, 5, 1, 0x6699ff, 100);
    this.drawDot(this.sx3, this.sy3, 5, 1, 0x6699ff, 100);
    this.drawDot(this.sx4, this.sy4, 5, 1, 0x6699ff, 100);
};
MovieClip.prototype.drawDot = function(x, y, w, strokewidth, strokecolor, strokealpha) {
    this.lineStyle(strokewidth, strokecolor, strokealpha);
    this.moveTo(x+w, y+w);
    this.lineTo(x-w, y+w);
    this.lineTo(x-w, y-w);
    this.lineTo(x+w, y-w);
    this.lineTo(x+w, y+w);
};
```

...and finally we create the movieclip:

```
bez = [];
bez[0] = createEmptyMovieClip("body", 1);
t1 = .2,t2 = .8;
lines=1, dots=1;
this.onEnterFrame = function() {
    bez[0].bezierPoints(dot1._x, dot1._y, dot2._x, dot2._y, dot3._x, dot3._y);
    bez[0].bezierSegment(t1, t2);
    bez[0].bezierDraw(3, 0xffffff, 100);
    bez[0].calculateAuxPoints(t1, t2);
    lines ? bez[0].drawAuxLines() : null;
    dots ? bez[0].drawAuxPoints() : null;
};
stop();
```

Move both sliders to change the value of t1 and t2. If you press the buttons you can turn the auxiliary dots and lines on or off.

mx_cs_002.fla

When the button is pressed in this next file, the Bezier segment will start growing. You can also set the speed at which it grows.

```
bez = [];
bez[0] = createEmptyMovieClip("body", 1);
speed = .02;
but.onPress = function() {
    t = 0;
    this.onEnterFrame = function() {
        t += speed;
        if (t>1) {
          t = 1;
          this.onEnterFrame = null;
        }
        bez[0].bezierPoints(dot1._x, dot1._y, dot2._x, dot2._y, dot3._x, dot3._y);
        bez[0].bezierSegment(0, t);
        bez[0].bezierDraw(2, 0xffffff, 100);
    };
};
stop();
```

Building a Bezier Random Path Generator

Time to develop an interesting application. This feisty little app draws Bezier splines, one by one, perfectly joined, generating a continuous path without corners. We are using the "divide and conquer" smoothing method explained within my **Scriptable Masks** chapter.. This file is `mx_cs_003.fla`.

First of all, we need to add some of the methods that we've used in previous FLAs. The following methods go in frame 1: `bezierQuadratic`, `bezierDraw`, `bezierSegment`, `bezierControl` and `bezierPoints`. We also need to add another large method to generate the Bezier path:

```
MovieClip.prototype.bezierPath = function(xpos, ypos, boxw, boxh, speed, curves, jump, fangle,
➥vangle, strokewidth, strokecolor, strokealpha) {
    this.bez = [];
    this.index = 0;
    this.t = 0;
    var x1, y1, x2, y2, x3, y3, x4, y4, x4z, y4z, angle, anglez, r, q, speed, k;
    var top = ypos-.5*boxh, bottom = ypos+.5*boxh, left = xpos-.5*boxw, right = xpos+.5*boxw;
    angle = 360*Math.random();
    r = jump+jump*(Math.random()-.5);
    x2=xpos+r*Math.cos(angle*dtr), y2=ypos+r*Math.sin(angle*dtr);
    angle += (random(2) ? 1 : -1)*(90+90*(Math.random()-.5));
    r = jump+jump*(Math.random()-.5);
    x4=x2+r*Math.cos(angle*dtr), y4=y2+r*Math.sin(angle*dtr);
    x3=.5*(x2+x4), y3=.5*(y2+y4);
    this.bez[this.index] = this.createEmptyMovieClip("body"+this.index, this.index+1);
    this.bez[this.index].bezierPoints(xpos, ypos, x2, y2, x3, y3);
    this.onEnterFrame = function() {
      this.t += speed;
      if (this.t>1) {
        this.bez[this.index-curves].removeMovieClip();
        r = jump+jump*(Math.random()-.5);
        anglez = angle+(random(2) ? 1 : -1)*(fangle+2*vangle*(Math.random()-.5));
        k = 0;
        do {
          anglez = anglez+15*k++*Math.pow(-1, k);
          x4z = x4+r*Math.cos(anglez*dtr);
          y4z = y4+r*Math.sin(anglez*dtr);
        } while (x4z<left or x4z>right or y4z<top or y4z>bottom);
        angle = anglez;
        x1=x3, y1=y3;
        x2=x4, y2=y4;
        x4=x4z, y4=y4z;
        x3=.5*(x2+x4), y3=.5*(y2+y4);
        this.t = 0;
        this.index++;
        this.bez[this.index] = this.createEmptyMovieClip("body"+this.index, this.index+1);
        this.bez[this.index].bezierPoints(x1, y1, x2, y2, x3, y3);
      }
      this.bez[this.index].clear();
      this.bez[this.index].bezierSegment(0, this.t);
      this.bez[this.index].bezierDraw(strokewidth, strokecolor, strokealpha);
      this.bez[this.index-curves].clear();
      this.bez[this.index-curves].bezierSegment(this.t, 1);
      this.bez[this.index-curves].bezierDraw(strokewidth, strokecolor, strokealpha);
    };
  };
```

Once a new Bezier path is created, the method generates the first bezier curve (bez[0]), and its three control points. Each Bezier segment grows within the onEnterFrame event handler. When the Bezier curve is complete (when t equals 1), an if statement creates a new curve, and the cycle continues.

I have also included another effect, while bez[index] grows, the last Bezier curve (bez [index-curves]) decreases, meaning that the lines get to a certain length and then appear to move around almost like snakes. I have also included a do{}while statement in order to detect if the curve goes beyond the boundaries of the box – if so, the angle is changed until a valid position is achieved.

This method receives the following variables as parameters:

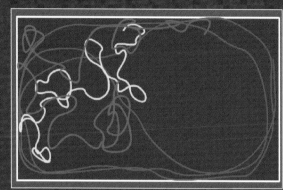

xpos, ypos: Bezier path origin
boxw, boxh: size of the path box
speed: t parameter speed
curves: number of Bezier curves within the trail
jump: value that controls the distance between control points
fangle, vangle: fixed and variable angles
strokewidth, strokecolor, strokealpha: self explanatory

Finally we create the objects and set the parameters:

```
dtr = Math.PI/180;     // degrees to radians conversion factor
sw=550, sh=400, sx=.5*sw, sy=.5*sh;     // stage boundaries and center coordinates
boxheight=300, boxwidth=500;     // box size
drawBox(sx, sy, boxwidth, boxheight, 3, 0xffffff, 100, .2, 30);
spline = [];
spline[1] = createEmptyMovieClip("sp2", 1);
spline[2] = createEmptyMovieClip("sp3", 2);
spline[3] = createEmptyMovieClip("sp4", 3);
spline[1].bezierPath(sx, sy, boxwidth, boxheight, .2, 55, 70, 30, 10, 3, 0xff0099, 100);
spline[2].bezierPath(sx, sy, boxwidth, boxheight, .2, 55, 30, 90, 45, 3, 0xffff00, 100);
spline[3].bezierPath(sx, sy, boxwidth, boxheight, .2, 55, 50, 90, 70, 3, 0x6666ff, 100);
stop();
```

As you can see, I have created three independent Bezier paths: A yellow (spline[1]), a red (spline[2]), and a blue (spline[3]). I have also included a movieclip method to draw a box, given its position, size, and colors. This box can be used to show the boundaries of our Bezier paths.

```
MovieClip.prototype.drawBox = function(xpos, ypos, mywidth, myheight, strokewidth, strokecolor,
➥strokealpha, fillcolor, fillalpha) {
    this.beginFill(fillcolor, fillalpha);
    this.lineStyle(strokewidth, strokecolor, strokealpha);
    this.moveTo(xpos-mywidth/2, ypos+myheight/2);
    this.lineTo(xpos-mywidth/2, ypos-myheight/2);
    this.lineTo(xpos+mywidth/2, ypos-myheight/2);
    this.lineTo(xpos+mywidth/2, ypos+myheight/2);
    this.endFill();
};
```

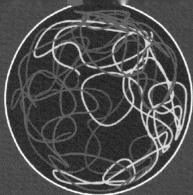

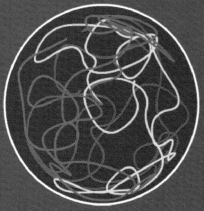

mx_cs_004.fla

In this next FLA we have modified the code in order to obtain a circular boundary.

```
dtr = Math.PI/180;// degrees to radians conversion factor
// stage boundaries and center coordinates
sw=550, sh=400, sx=.5*sw, sy=.5*sh;radius = 150;
drawCircle(sx, sy, radius, 8, 3, 0xffffff, 100, .2, 30);
spline = [];
spline[1] = createEmptyMovieClip("sp1", 1);
spline[2] = createEmptyMovieClip("sp2", 2);
spline[3] = createEmptyMovieClip("sp3", 3);
spline[1].bezierPath(sx, sy, radius, .1, 55, 70, 90,45,3, 0xff0099, 100);
spline[2].bezierPath(sx, sy, radius, .1, 55, 70, 90,45,3, 0xffff00, 100);
spline[3].bezierPath(sx, sy, radius, .1, 55, 70, 90,45,3, 0x6666ff, 100);
stop();
```

We have also modified the parameters of the bezierPath method to receive a radius rather than a box size:

```
MovieClip.prototype.bezierPath = function(xpos, ypos,
➥radius, speed, curves, jump, fangle, vangle, strokewidth,
➥strokecolor, strokealpha) {
```

The last thing that we've done is to change the do{}while loop...

```
do {
    anglez = anglez+25*k++*Math.pow(-1, k);
   x4z = x4+r*Math.cos(anglez*dtr);
   y4z = y4+r*Math.sin(anglez*dtr);
   } while (distance(x4z, y4z, xpos, ypos)>radius);
```

...and added a distance function to the very end of the code to keep the curves within the boundary:

```
function distance(x1, y1, x2, y2) {
   dx = x2-x1;
   dy = y2-y1;
   return (Math.sqrt(dx*dx+dy*dy));
}
```

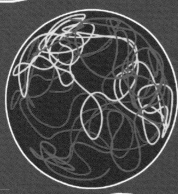

...as you can see, it creates some truly beautiful effects.

mx_cs_005.fla

This FLA is a great candidate for experimentaion, for instance I'm going to create three Bezier paths, with each one enclosed within a different circle.

```
dtr = Math.PI/180; // degrees to radians conversion factor
// stage boundaries and center coordinates
sw=550, sh=400, sx=.5*sw, sy=.5*sh;
```

```
radius = 100;
e = 120;
drawCircle(sx+e*Math.cos(-.5*Math.PI), sy+e*Math.sin(-.5*Math.PI),
  ➥radius, 8, 3, 0xffffff, 100,.2, 30);
drawCircle(sx+e*Math.cos(-.5*Math.PI+120*dtr), sy+e*Math.sin(-.5*Math.PI+120*dtr),
  ➥ radius, 8, 3, 0xffffff, 100, .2, 30);
drawCircle(sx+e*Math.cos(-.5*Math.PI+240*dtr), sy+e*Math.sin(-.5*Math.PI+240*dtr),
  ➥ radius, 8, 3,0xffffff, 100, .2, 30);
spline = [];
spline[1] = createEmptyMovieClip("sp1", 1);
spline[2] = createEmptyMovieClip("sp2", 2);
spline[3] = createEmptyMovieClip("sp3", 3);
spline[1].bezierPath(sx+e*Math.cos(-.5*Math.PI), sy+e*Math.sin(-.5*Math.PI), radius,
  ➥.1, 5, 50,90, 45, 3, 0x6666ff, 100);
spline[2].bezierPath(sx+e*Math.cos(-.5*Math.PI+120*dtr), sy+e*Math.sin(-
  ➥.5*Math.PI+120*dtr),radius, .1, 5, 50, 45, 20, 3, 0xffff00, 100);
spline[3].bezierPath(sx+e*Math.cos(-.5*Math.PI+240*dtr), sy+e*Math.sin(-
  ➥.5*Math.PI+240*dtr),radius, .1, 5, 50, 90, 90, 3, 0xff0099, 100);
stop();
```

mx_cs_006.fla

Finally, we're going to code a "follow the leader" Flash movie. We'll have a single line being drawn with four arrows following it – one at the very tip of the line, and three following at different speeds depending on their distance from the leader.

Start with the usual boundaries and conversions:

```
dtr = Math.PI/180;     // degrees to radians conversion factor
sw=550, sh=400, sx=.5*sw, sy=.5*sh;     // stage boundaries and center coordinates
```

We then create the four arrows using the `drawarrow` method. This method just contains instructions for the Drawing API and can be found in the FLA. Next, we create the spline:

```
spline = [];
spline[1] = createEmptyMovieClip("sp", 5);
spline[1].bezierPath(sx, sy, sw-50, sh-50, .2, 75, 70, 90, 45, 3, 0xffff00, 100);
```

Following this, we open an `onEnterFrame` event handler and calculate the position of the arrows:

```
this.onEnterFrame = function() {
    ff = spline[1].bez[spline[1].index];
```

Next we calculate the angles between the three following arrows and the leader arrow:

```
a1z = myangle(arrow1._x, arrow1._y, ff.bx3, ff.by3);
a2z = myangle(arrow2._x, arrow2._y, ff.bx3, ff.by3);
a3z = myangle(arrow3._x, arrow3._y, ff.bx3, ff.by3);
```

The next three lines make sure that the trailing arrows are attracted to the leader arrow:

```
arrow1._x += (ff.bx3-arrow1._x)/10, arrow1._y += (ff.by3-arrow1._y)/10;
arrow2._x += (ff.bx3-arrow2._x)/20, arrow2._y += (ff.by3-arrow2._y)/20;
arrow3._x += (ff.bx3-arrow3._x)/30, arrow3._y += (ff.by3-arrow3._y)/30;
```

Following that, we calculate the angle, distance, and repulsive force between the arrows:

```
d12 = mydistance(arrow1._x, arrow1._y, arrow2._x, arrow2._y);
a12 = myangle(arrow1._x, arrow1._y, arrow2._x, arrow2._y);
f12x=15*Math.exp(-d12/20)*Math.cos(a12), f12y=15*Math.exp(-d12/20)*Math.sin(a12);
f21x=15*Math.exp(-d12/20)*Math.cos(a12+Math.PI), f21y=15*Math.exp(-d12/20)*Math.sin(a12+Math.PI);
d13 = mydistance(arrow1._x, arrow1._y, arrow3._x, arrow3._y);
a13 = myangle(arrow1._x, arrow1._y, arrow3._x, arrow3._y);
f13x=15*Math.exp(-d13/20)*Math.cos(a13), f13y=15*Math.exp(-d13/20)*Math.sin(a13);
f31x=15*Math.exp(-d13/20)*Math.cos(a13+Math.PI), f31y=15*Math.exp(-d13/20)*Math.sin(a13+Math.PI);
d23 = mydistance(arrow2._x, arrow2._y, arrow3._x, arrow3._y);
a23 = myangle(arrow2._x, arrow2._y, arrow3._x, arrow3._y);
f23x=15*Math.exp(-d23/20)*Math.cos(a23), f23y=15*Math.exp(-d23/20)*Math.sin(a23);
f32x=15*Math.exp(-d23/20)*Math.cos(a23+Math.PI), f32y=15*Math.exp(-d23/20)*Math.sin(a23+Math.PI);
```

And finally each arrow is correctly located and rotated on the stage:

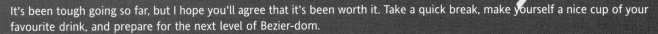

```
    arrow1._x += f21x+f31x;
    arrow1._y += f21y+f31y;
    arrow1._rotation = a1z/dtr;
    arrow2._x += f12x+f32x;
    arrow2._y += f12y+f32y;
    arrow2._rotation = a2z/dtr;
    arrow3._x += f13x+f23y;
    arrow3._y += f13y+f23x;
    arrow3._rotation = a3z/dtr;
    arrow0._x = ff.bx3;
    arrow0._y = ff.by3;
    arrow0._rotation = ff.bezierAngle(spline[1].t)/dtr;
};
stop();
```

It's been tough going so far, but I hope you'll agree that it's been worth it. Take a quick break, make yourself a nice cup of your favourite drink, and prepare for the next level of Bezier-dom.

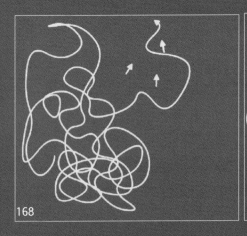
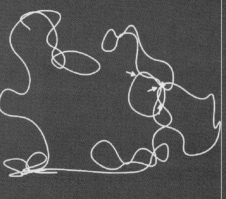
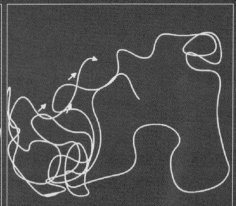

The Bezier Vertex, Symmetry Axis, Directrix, Focal Length, Focus, Latus Rectum, Area and Arc Length

The purpose of this experiment is to show that we can use the Drawing API to develop advanced geometry applications. In the first example, I'm going to use some methods to calculate and draw the important parameters of the quadratic Bezier curve. As I have already commented, a quadratic Bezier spline is a parabolic segment, so this curve has a vertex, a symmetry axis, a directrix, a focus, and so on.

Most of these Bezier formulas aren't common knowledge among ActionScripters, so I hope you'll find them useful.

mx_bezier_vertex.fla

First of all we create all the methods and functions that we need to calculate the parameters, and to draw the lines and curves. The method's names are self-explanatory.

drawLine: This method draws a line between two given points:

```
MovieClip.prototype.drawLine = function(x1, y1, x2, y2, strokewidth, strokecolor, strokealpha) {
    this.lineStyle(strokewidth, strokecolor, strokealpha);
    this.moveTo(x1, y1);
    this.lineTo(x2, y2);
};
```

bezierQuadratic: This method calculates the quadratic Bezier value given t and the coordinates of the control points as parameters:

```
MovieClip.prototype.bezierQuadratic = function(t, a, b, c) {
    return (1-t)*(1-t)*a+2*(1-t)*t*b+t*t*c;
};
```

bezierPoints: This method sets the control points given three points (draggable blue dots) as parameters:

```
MovieClip.prototype.bezierPoints = function(x1, y1, x2, y2, x3, y3) {
    this.bx1=this.x1=x1, this.by1=this.y1=y1;
    this.bx2=this.x2=x2, this.by2=this.y2=y2;
    this.bx3=this.x3=x3, this.by3=this.y3=y3;
};
```

bezierSegment: This method calculates the new control points given t1 and t2 as parameters:

```
MovieClip.prototype.bezierSegment = function(t1, t2) {
    this.bx1 = this.bezierQuadratic(t1, this.x1, this.x2, this.x3);
    this.by1 = this.bezierQuadratic(t1, this.y1, this.y2, this.y3);
    this.bx3 = this.bezierQuadratic(t2, this.x1, this.x2, this.x3);
    this.by3 = this.bezierQuadratic(t2, this.y1, this.y2, this.y3);
    this.bx2 = this.bezierControl(t1, t2, this.x1, this.x2, this.x3);
    this.by2 = this.bezierControl(t1, t2, this.y1, this.y2, this.y3);
};
```

169

bezierControl: This method is called from the `bezierSegment` method, and it's used to calculate the control point of a Bezier segment:

```
MovieClip.prototype.bezierControl = function(t1, t2, a, b, c) {
    return a+(t1+t2)*(b-a)+t1*t2*(c-2*b+a);
};
```

bezierDraw: This method draws a Bezier curve:

```
MovieClip.prototype.bezierDraw = function(strokewidth, strokecolor, strokealpha) {
    this.clear();
    this.lineStyle(strokewidth, strokecolor, strokealpha);
    this.moveTo(this.bx1, this.by1);
    this.curveTo(this.bx2, this.by2, this.bx3, this.by3);
};
```

bezierVertex: This method calculates the value of t (vt) and the coordinates (vx, vy) of the quadratic Bezier's vertex. I'm also calculating the slope (vm) and the angle (va) at this point, because we need these values to calculate other parameters:

```
MovieClip.prototype.bezierVertex = function() {
    this.vm = -(this.x2-.5*this.x3-.5*this.x1)/(this.y2-.5*this.y3-.5*this.y1);
    this.vt = (-this.vm*(this.x2-this.x1)+(this.y2-this.y1))/(this.vm*
➡(this.x1-2*this.x2+this.x3)-(this.y1-2*this.y2+this.y3));
    this.vx = this.bezierQuadratic(this.vt, this.x1, this.x2, this.x3);
    this.vy = this.bezierQuadratic(this.vt, this.y1, this.y2, this.y3);
    this.va = this.bezierAngle(this.vt);
};
```

bezierSymmetryAxis: This method calculates and draws the symmetry axis (red line) of the parabola. This line passes through the vertex and the focus:

```
MovieClip.prototype.bezierSymmetryAxis = function() {
    var ax, ay, bx, by, r = 700;
    ax = this.vx+r*Math.cos(Math.atan(this.vm)-.5*Math.PI);
    ay = this.vy+r*Math.sin(Math.atan(this.vm)-.5*Math.PI);
    bx = this.vx+r*Math.cos(Math.atan(this.vm)+.5*Math.PI);
    by = this.vy+r*Math.sin(Math.atan(this.vm)+.5*Math.PI);
    this.drawLine(ax, ay, bx, by, 2, 0xff3300, 100);
};
```

bezierAngle: This method calculates the angle of the Bezier curve given t as a parameter:

```
MovieClip.prototype.bezierAngle = function(t) {
    return (Math.atan2(this.bezierDerivative(t, this.y1, this.y2, this.y3),
➡this.bezierDerivative(t, this.x1, this.x2, this.x3)));
};
```

bezierDerivative: This method calculates the first derivative of the Bezier curve given `t` and the control points as parameters. This method is called from the `bezierAngle` method to calculate the angle:

```
MovieClip.prototype.bezierDerivative = function(t, a, b, c) {
    return 2*a*(t-1)+2*b*(1-2*t)+2*c*t;
};
```

bezierProjection: This method calculates and draws the projections (blue lines) of the anchor points in the parabola axis. These values will be used to calculate the focal length:

```
MovieClip.prototype.bezierProjection = function() {
    this.ra = distance(this.x1, this.y1, this.vx, this.vy);
    this.rb = distance(this.vx, this.vy, this.x3, this.y3);
    this.alfa = this.va-angle(this.x1, this.y1, this.vx, this.vy);
    this.beta = angle(this.vx, this.vy, this.x3, this.y3)-this.va;
    this.rax=this.ra*Math.cos(this.alfa), this.ray=this.ra*Math.sin(this.alfa);
    this.ax=this.vx+this.rax*Math.cos(this.va+Math.PI),
    ➥ this.ay=this.vy+this.rax*Math.sin(this.va+Math.PI);
    this.rbx=this.rb*Math.cos(this.beta), this.rby=this.rb*Math.sin(this.beta);
    this.bx=this.vx+this.rbx*Math.cos(this.va),
    ➥this.by=this.vy+this.rbx*Math.sin(this.va);
    this.drawLine(this.ax, this.ay, this.x1, this.y1, 2, 0x6600ff, 100);
    this.drawLine(this.ax, this.ay, this.vx, this.vy, 2, 0x6600ff, 100);
    this.drawLine(this.bx, this.by, this.x3, this.y3, 2, 0x6600ff, 100);
    this.drawLine(this.bx, this.by, this.vx, this.vy, 2, 0x6600ff, 100);
};
```

bezierFocalLength: This method calculates the focal length or distance from the vertex to the focus:

```
MovieClip.prototype.bezierFocalLength = function() {
    this.a = .25*this.ra*Math.cos(this.alfa)/Math.tan(this.alfa);
};
```

bezierFocus: This method calculates the coordinates of the quadratic Bezier's focus:

```
MovieClip.prototype.bezierFocus = function() {
    this.fx = this.vx+this.a*Math.cos(this.va+.5*Math.PI);
    this.fy = this.vy+this.a*Math.sin(this.va+.5*Math.PI);
};
```

bezierLatusRectum: This method calculates and draws (the white line) the **latus rectum** of the parabola. This is a line that passes through the focus, and is perpendicular to the symmetry axis. The length of the latus rectum equals four times the focal length:

```
MovieClip.prototype.bezierLatusRectum = function() {
    var lax, lay, lbx, lby;
    lax = this.fx+2*this.a*Math.cos(this.va-Math.PI);
    lay = this.fy+2*this.a*Math.sin(this.va-Math.PI);
    lbx = this.fx+2*this.a*Math.cos(this.va);
    lby = this.fy+2*this.a*Math.sin(this.va);
    this.drawLine(lax, lay, lbx, lby, 2, 0xffffff, 100);
};
```

bezierDirectrix: This method calculates and draws (the yellow line) the **directrix** of the parabola. The distance from any given point of the parabola to the directrix equals the distance from the point to the focus:

```
MovieClip.prototype.bezierDirectrix = function() {
    var ax, ay, bx, by, dx, dy, r = 400;
    dx = this.vx+this.a*Math.cos(this.va-.5*Math.PI);
    dy = this.vy+this.a*Math.sin(this.va-.5*Math.PI);
    ax = dx+r*Math.cos(this.va);
    ay = dy+r*Math.sin(this.va);
    bx = dx-r*Math.cos(this.va);
    by = dy-r*Math.sin(this.va);
    this.drawLine(ax, ay, bx, by, 2, 0xffff00, 100);
};
```

distance: This function calculates the distance between two points given their coordinates as parameters:

```
function distance(x1, y1, x2, y2) {
    return Math.sqrt(x2*x2+x1*x1-2*x1*x2+y2*y2+y1*y1-2*y1*y2);
}
```

angle: This function calculates the angle between two points given their coordinates as parameters:

```
function angle(x1, y1, x2, y2) {
    return Math.atan2(y2-y1, x2-x1);
}
```

parabolaArcLength: This function calculates the length of a parabola, and is used to calculate the Bezier arc length:

```
function parabolaArcLength(a, b) {
    return .5*Math.sqrt(b*b+16*a*a)+((b*b)/(8*a))*Math.log((4*a+Math.sqrt(b*b+16*a*a))/b);
}
```

bezierArcLength: This method calculates the length of a Bezier curve:

```
MovieClip.prototype.bezierArcLength = function() {
    this.l1 = .5*parabolaArcLength(this.ray, 2*Math.abs(this.rax));
    this.l2 = .5*parabolaArcLength(this.rby, 2*Math.abs(this.rbx));
    this.arc = this.rax<0 or this.rbx<0 ? Math.abs(this.l2-this.l1) : this.l1+this.l2;
};
```

triangleArea: This function calculates the area of a triangle given the coordinates of its vertices as parameters, and is used to calculate the Bezier area:

```
function triangleArea(x1, y1, x2, y2, x3, y3) {
    return .5*Math.abs(x1*y2+y1*x3+y3*x2-y2*x3-y1*x2-x1*y3);
}
```

bezierArea: This method calculates the area of a Bezier curve. It uses the "Quadrature of Parabola" formula discovered by Archimedes:

```
MovieClip.prototype.bezierArea = function() {
    this.area = (2/3)*triangleArea(this.x1, this.y1, this.x2, this.y2, this.x3, this.y3);
};
```

We're finally ready to create our Bezier spline (bez[1]) and set up the onEnterFrame loop. Remember to include three
blue draggable dots on the stage named dot1, dot2, and dot3, a white dot named "focus" and a red dot named
"vertex". I have also included two dynamic text boxes in order to show the value of the bezier area and arc length.

Lifaros Bezier Curve Creatures

```
bez = [];
bez[0] = this.createEmptyMovieClip("body1", 1);
bez[1] = this.createEmptyMovieClip("body2", 2);
focus.swapDepths(100), vertex.swapDepths(101), dot1.swapDepths(102), dot2.swapDepths(103),
➡dot3.swapDepths(104);
this.onEnterFrame = function() {
    bez[0].bezierPoints(dot1._x, dot1._y, dot2._x, dot2._y, dot3._x, dot3._y);
    bez[0].bezierSegment(-3, 3);
    bez[0].bezierDraw(2, 0xff0000, 100);
    bez[1].bezierPoints(dot1._x, dot1._y, dot2._x, dot2._y, dot3._x, dot3._y);
    bez[1].bezierDraw(2, 0xffffff, 100);
    bez[1].bezierVertex();
    bez[1].bezierSymmetryAxis();
    bez[1].bezierProjection();
    bez[1].bezierFocalLength();
    bez[1].bezierFocus();
    bez[1].bezierLatusRectum();
    bez[1].bezierDirectrix();
    bez[1].bezierArcLength();
    bez[1].bezierArea();
    arc = "Bezier Arc Length = "+(Math.floor(100*bez[1].arc))/100;
    area = "Bezier Area = "+(Math.floor(100*bez[1].area))/100;
    vertex._x = bez[1].vx;
    vertex._y = bez[1].vy;
    focus._x = bez[1].fx;
    focus._y = bez[1].fy;
};
stop();
```

As you can see, these are neither complex data structures nor nested loops, I'm just calling all the methods that were previously explained one by one. I'll run through what each of the colored lines represents:

White Bezier spline = parabolic segment
Red Bezier spline = auxiliary parabolic segment
Straight red line = parabola's symmetry axis
Straight yellow line = parabola's directrix
Blue lines = parabola's projections
White dot = parabola's focus
Red dot = parabola's vertex
Blue dots = Bezier's control points

This Bezier demonstration is a good example of Flash applied to educational purposes, and there are many other examples that you can develop using this foundation. For instance, this can be used to simulate the behaviour of incident rays in a parabolic dish.

I have already explained the "divide and conquer" smoothing method for drawing soft curves in my earlier **Scriptable Masks** chapter. This time I'm going to show you another more complex method that can be used to draw Bezier splines through all given points. This is a special kind of Bezier spline. We are also going to use this formula to draw closed Bezier shapes.

Bezier Area = 41148.42
Bezier Arc Length = 535.17

Bezier Area = 21252.33
Bezier Arc Length = 443.2

Bezier Area = 18569.33
Bezier Arc Length = 429.44

Bezier Splines

Our first experiment will be to find a Bezier spline that passes through four points and features two Bezier curves.

mx_spline_000.fla

Open up the FLA and run it. As you can see, we have four draggable blue dots, named `p1`, `p2`, `p3`, and `p4`. The task is to define and display the Bezier control points `c2` and `c3` (the red dots).

First of all, let `m23` be the midpoint between `c2` and `c3`, let `m2` be the midpoint between `m23` and `p1`, and let `p2` be the midpoint between `m2` and `c2`.

Hence:

```
m23x  =  .5(c2x+c3x)
m2x   =  .5(p1x+m23x)
p2x   =  .5(c2x+m2x)
```

So our first equation is this: `p2x = .5(c2x+.5(p1x+.5(c2x+c3x)))`

...and let `m3` be the midpoint between `m23` and `p4`, and let `p3` be the midpoint between `m3` and `c3`.

```
m3x  =  .5(p4x+m23x)
p3x  =  .5(c3x+m3x)
```

So our second equation is: `p3x = .5(c3x+.5(p4x+.5(c2x+c3x)))` Then from equations 1 and 2:

5c2x+c3x = 8(p2x-p1x/4)
c2x+5c3x = 8(p3x-p4x/4)

This system of equations can be expressed as a matrix multiplication:

$$\begin{bmatrix} 5 & 1 \\ 1 & 5 \end{bmatrix} \begin{bmatrix} C2x \\ C3x \end{bmatrix} = \begin{bmatrix} 8(p2x-p1x/4) \\ 8(p3x-p4x/4) \end{bmatrix}$$

...so we can use determinants to solve this system. Once solved for x and y we get:

```
c3x  =  (1/3)(5p3x-p2x-(5/4)p4x+(1/4)p1x);
c3y  =  (1/3)(5p3y-p2y-(5/4)p4y+(1/4)p1y);
c2x  =  (1/3)(5p2x-p3x-(5/4)p1x+(1/4)p4x);
c2y  =  (1/3)(5p2y-p3y-(5/4)p1y+(1/4)p4y);
```

We are now ready to code this spline. First of all, we need to include the following methods:

drawLines: This method is used to draw lines:

```
MovieClip.prototype.drawLine = function(x1, y1, x2, y2, strokewidth,
➥strokecolor, strokealpha) {
    this.lineStyle(strokewidth, strokecolor, strokealpha);
    this.moveTo(x1, y1);
    this.lineTo(x2, y2);
};
```

bezierDraw: This method is used to draw Bezier curves:

```
MovieClip.prototype.bezierDraw = function(x1, y1, x2, y2, x3, y3,
➥strokewidth, strokecolor, strokealpha) {
    this.lineStyle(strokewidth, strokecolor, strokealpha);
    this.moveTo(x1, y1);
    this.curveTo(x2, y2, x3, y3);
};
```

Then we create the Bezier spline, calculate the control points, and draw the Bezier curves:

```
fscommand("showmenu", false);
createEmptyMovieClip("spline", 1);
c2.swapDepths(100), c3.swapDepths(101);
dot1.swapDepths(103), dot2.swapDepths(104), dot3.swapDepths(105),
➥dot4.swapDepths(106);
lines = 1;
this.onEnterFrame = function() {
    p1x=dot1._x, p1y=dot1._y;
    p2x=dot2._x, p2y=dot2._y;
    p3x=dot3._x, p3y=dot3._y;
    p4x=dot4._x, p4y=dot4._y;
    c3x = (1/3)*(5*p3x-p2x-(5/4)*p4x+(1/4)*p1x);
    c3y = (1/3)*(5*p3y-p2y-(5/4)*p4y+(1/4)*p1y);
    c2x = (1/3)*(5*p2x-p3x-(5/4)*p1x+(1/4)*p4x);
    c2y = (1/3)*(5*p2y-p3y-(5/4)*p1y+(1/4)*p4y);
    m23x=.5*(c2x+c3x), m23y=.5*(c2y+c3y);
    m2x=.5*(m23x+p1x), m2y=.5*(m23y+p1y);
    m3x=.5*(m23x+p4x), m3y=.5*(m23y+p4y);
    this.spline.clear();
    this.spline.bezierDraw(p1x, p1y, c2x, c2y, m23x, m23y, 2, 0xffffff, 100);
    this.spline.bezierDraw(p4x, p4y, c3x, c3y, m23x, m23y, 2, 0xffffff, 100);
    if (lines) {
        c2._visible = 1;
        c3._visible = 1;
        m23._visible = 1;
        m2._visible = 1;
        m3._visible = 1;
        c2._x=c2x, c2._y=c2y;
        c3._x=c3x, c3._y=c3y;
        m23._x=m23x, m23._y=m23y;
        m2._x=m2x, m2._y=m2y;
        m3._x=m3x, m3._y=m3y;
        this.spline.drawLine(c2x, c2y, c3x, c3y, 2, 0xff0000, 100);
        this.spline.drawLine(p1x, p1y, c2x, c2y, 2, 0xff0000, 100);
        this.spline.drawLine(p4x, p4y, c3x, c3y, 2, 0xff0000, 100);
        this.spline.drawLine(p4x, p4y, m23x, m23y, 2, 0xffff00, 100);
        this.spline.drawLine(p1x, p1y, m23x, m23y, 2, 0xffff00, 100);
        this.spline.drawLine(c2x, c2y, m2x, m2y, 2, 0x6666ff, 100);
        this.spline.drawLine(c3x, c3y, m3x, m3y, 2, 0x6666ff, 100);
    } else {
        c2._visible = 0;
```

show aux lines

show aux lines

show aux lines

hide aux lines

175

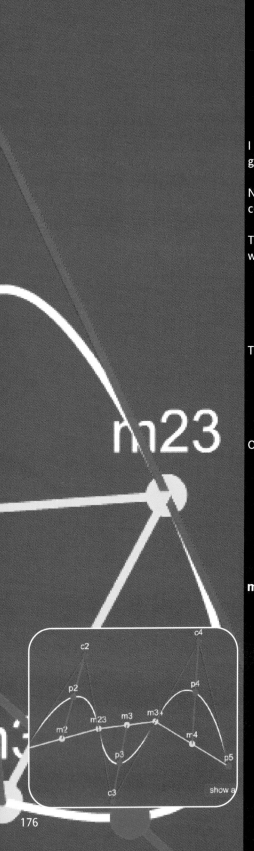

```
            c3._visible = 0;
            m23._visible = 0;
            m2._visible = 0;
            m3._visible = 0;
        }
    };
    stop();
```

I have included a button to turn the auxiliary lines and dots on and off. These auxiliary graphic elements are just for learning, so remove them if they're not necessary.

Now we're going to find a Bezier spline that passes through five points and features three curves. The task is to define the external control dots c2, c3, and c4.

The procedure is the same as in the previous example, so we don't need to repeat the whole algebraic processes:

```
5c2x+c3x  = 8(p2x-p1x/4)
c3x+5c4x  = 8(p4x-p5x/4)
c2x+ 6c3x+c4x = 8p3
```

This system of equations can be expressed as a matrix multiplication:

$$\begin{bmatrix} 5 & 1 & 0 \\ 0 & 1 & 5 \\ 1 & 6 & 1 \end{bmatrix} \begin{bmatrix} C2x \\ C3x \\ C4x \end{bmatrix} = \begin{bmatrix} 8(p2x-p1x/4) \\ 8(p4x-p5x/4) \\ 8p3 \end{bmatrix}$$

Once solved for x and y we get:

```
c2x = (1/70)(116p2x-29p1x+4p4x-p5x-20p3x);
c2y = (1/70)(116p2y-29p1y+4p4y-p5y-20p3y);
c3x = (5/70)(-4p4x+p5x-4p2x+p1x+20p3x);
c3y = (5/70)(-4p4y+p5y-4p2y+p1y+20p3y);
c4x = (1/70)(116p4x-29p5x+4p2x-p1x-20p3x);
c4y = (1/70)(116p4y-29p5y+4p2y-p1y-20p3y);
```

mx_spline_001.fla

```
fscommand("showmenu", false);
createEmptyMovieClip("spline", 1);
c2.swapDepths(100), c3.swapDepths(101), c4.swapDepths(102);
dot1.swapDepths(103), dot2.swapDepths(104), dot3.swapDepths(105),
dot4.swapDepths(106), dot5.swapDepths(107);
lines = 1;
this.onEnterFrame = function() {
    p1x=dot1._x, p1y=dot1._y;
    p2x=dot2._x, p2y=dot2._y;
    p3x=dot3._x, p3y=dot3._y;
    p4x=dot4._x, p4y=dot4._y;
    p5x=dot5._x, p5y=dot5._y;
    c2x = (1/70)*(116*p2x-29*p1x+4*p4x-p5x-20*p3x);
    c2y = (1/70)*(116*p2y-29*p1y+4*p4y-p5y-20*p3y);
    c3x = (5/70)*(-4*p4x+p5x-4*p2x+p1x+20*p3x);
```

```
    c3y = (5/70)*(-4*p4y+p5y-4*p2y+p1y+20*p3y);
    c4x = (1/70)*(116*p4x-29*p5x+4*p2x-p1x-20*p3x);
    c4y = (1/70)*(116*p4y-29*p5y+4*p2y-p1y-20*p3y);
    m23x=.5*(c2x+c3x), m23y=.5*(c2y+c3y);
    m34x=.5*(c3x+c4x), m34y=.5*(c3y+c4y);
    m2x=.5*(m23x+p1x), m2y=.5*(m23y+p1y);
    m3x=.5*(m23x+m34x), m3y=.5*(m23y+m34y);
    m4x=.5*(m34x+p5x), m4y=.5*(m34y+p5y);
    this.spline.clear();
    this.spline.bezierDraw(p1x, p1y, c2x, c2y, m23x, m23y, 2, 0xffffff, 100);
    this.spline.bezierDraw(p5x, p5y, c4x, c4y, m34x, m34y, 2, 0xffffff, 100);
    this.spline.bezierDraw(m23x, m23y, c3x, c3y, m34x, m34y, 2, 0xffffff, 100);
    if (lines) {
      c2._visible = 1;
      c3._visible = 1;
      c4._visible = 1;
      m23._visible = 1;
      m34._visible = 1;
      m2._visible = 1;
      m3._visible = 1;
      m4._visible = 1;
      c2._x=c2x, c2._y=c2y;
      c3._x=c3x, c3._y=c3y;
      c4._x=c4x, c4._y=c4y;
      m23._x=m23x, m23._y=m23y;
      m34._x=m34x, m34._y=m34y;
      m2._x=m2x, m2._y=m2y;
      m3._x=m3x, m3._y=m3y;
      m4._x=m4x, m4._y=m4y;
      this.spline.drawLine(c2x, c2y, c3x, c3y, 2, 0xff0000, 100);
      this.spline.drawLine(c3x, c3y, c4x, c4y, 2, 0xff0000, 100);
      this.spline.drawLine(p1x, p1y, c2x, c2y, 2, 0xff0000, 100);
      this.spline.drawLine(p5x, p5y, c4x, c4y, 2, 0xff0000, 100);
      this.spline.drawLine(p5x, p5y, m34x, m34y, 2, 0xffff00, 100);
      this.spline.drawLine(p1x, p1y, m23x, m23y, 2, 0xffff00, 100);
      this.spline.drawLine(m34x, m34y, m23x, m23y, 2, 0xffff00, 100);
      this.spline.drawLine(c2x, c2y, m2x, m2y, 2, 0x6666ff, 100);
      this.spline.drawLine(c3x, c3y, m3x, m3y, 2, 0x6666ff, 100);
      this.spline.drawLine(c4x, c4y, m4x, m4y, 2, 0x6666ff, 100);
    } else {
      c2._visible = 0;
      c3._visible = 0;
      c4._visible = 0;
      m23._visible = 0;
      m34._visible = 0;
      m2._visible = 0;
      m3._visible = 0;
      m4._visible = 0;
    }
  }
};
stop();
```

You can calculate the equations to solve Bezier splines for more than five points using the same procedure. I won't do it here, but I'd be interested in seeing the results if anyone attempts it.

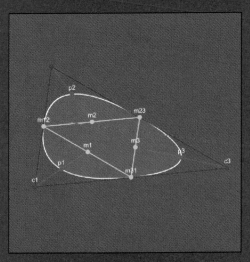

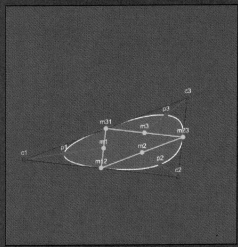

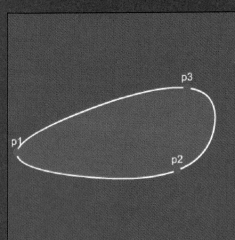

Bezier Shapes

We can use the same procedure to solve the equations for closed shapes, starting with a closed shape with three points.

mx_shape_001.fla

Open up and run the FLA. As you can see, we have three draggable blue dots named p1, p2, and p3. The task is to find the Bezier control points c1, c2, and c3 (red dots).

First of all, let m12 be the midpoint between c1 and c2, let m23 be the midpoint between c2 and c3, and let m31 be the midpoint between c3 and c1:

```
m12x = .5(c1x+c2x)
m23x = .5(c2x+c3x)
m31x = .5(c3x+c1x)
```

Let m1 be the midpoint between m31 and m12, let m2 be the midpoint between m12 and m23, and let m3 be the midpoint between m23 and m31:

```
m1x = .5(m31x+m12x)
m2x = .5(m12x+m23x)
m3x = .5(m23x+m31x)
```

Let p1 be the midpoint between c1 and m1, let p2 be the midpoint between c2 and m2, and let p3 be the midpoint between c3 and m3:

```
p1x = .5(c1x+m1x)
p2x = .5(c2x+m2x)
p3x = .5(c3x+m3x)
```

Hence:

```
p1x = .5(c1x+.5(.5(c3x+c1x)+.5(c1x+c2x)))    equation 1
p2x = .5(c2x+.5(.5(c1x+c2x)+.5(c2x+c3x)))    equation 2
p3x = .5(c3x+.5(.5(c2x+c3x)+.5(c3x+c1x)))    equation 3
```

Then from equations 1, 2 and 3:

```
6c1x+c2x+c3x = 8p1x
c1x+6c2x+c3x = 8p2x
c1x+c2x+6c3x = 8p3x
```

This system of equations can be expressed as a matrix multiplication:

$$
\begin{bmatrix} 6 & 1 & 1 \\ 1 & 6 & 1 \\ 1 & 1 & 6 \end{bmatrix} \begin{bmatrix} C1x \\ C2x \\ C3x \end{bmatrix} = \begin{bmatrix} 8p1x \\ 8p2x \\ 8p3x \end{bmatrix}
$$

Once solved for x and y, we get:

```
c1x = (1/5)(7p1x-p2x-p3x);
c1y = (1/5)(7p1y-p2y-p3y);
c2x = (1/5)(7p2x-p1x-p3x);
c2y = (1/5)(7p2y-p1y-p3y);
c3x = (1/5)(7p3x-p1x-p2x);
c3y = (1/5)(7p3y-p1y-p2y);
```

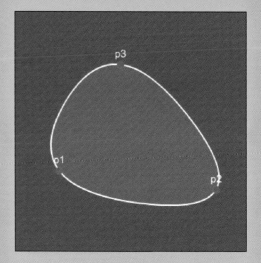

We are now ready to write the code for our closed Bezier shape:

```
fscommand("showmenu", false);
this.createEmptyMovieClip("shape", 1);
dot1.swapDepths(2), dot2.swapDepths(3), dot3.swapDepths(4);
m1.swapDepths(5), m2.swapDepths(6), m3.swapDepths(7);
m12.swapDepths(8), m23.swapDepths(9), m31.swapDepths(10);
c1.swapDepths(11), c2.swapDepths(12), c3.swapDepths(13);
lines = 1;
this.onEnterFrame = function() {
    p1x=dot1._x, p1y=dot1._y;
    p2x=dot2._x, p2y=dot2._y;
    p3x=dot3._x, p3y=dot3._y;
    c1x = (1/5)*(7*p1x-p2x-p3x);
    c1y = (1/5)*(7*p1y-p2y-p3y);
    c2x = (1/5)*(7*p2x-p1x-p3x);
    c2y = (1/5)*(7*p2y-p1y-p3y);
    c3x = (1/5)*(7*p3x-p1x-p2x);
    c3y = (1/5)*(7*p3y-p1y-p2y);
    m12x=.5*(c1x+c2x), m12y=.5*(c1y+c2y);
    m23x=.5*(c2x+c3x), m23y=.5*(c2y+c3y);
    m31x=.5*(c3x+c1x), m31y=.5*(c3y+c1y);
    m1x=.5*(m12x+m31x), m1y=.5*(m12y+m31y);
    m2x=.5*(m12x+m23x), m2y=.5*(m12y+m23y);
    m3x=.5*(m23x+m31x), m3y=.5*(m23y+m31y);
    this.shape.clear();
    this.shape.beginFill(0x777777, 100);
    this.shape.lineStyle(2, 0xffffff, 100);
    this.shape.moveTo(m31x, m31y);
    this.shape.curveTo(c1x, c1y, m12x, m12y);
    this.shape.curveTo(c2x, c2y, m23x, m23y);
    this.shape.curveTo(c3x, c3y, m31x, m31y);
    this.shape.endFill();
    if (lines) {
      c1._visible = 1;
      c2._visible = 1;
      c3._visible = 1;
      m12._visible = 1;
      m23._visible = 1;
```

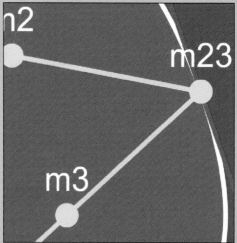

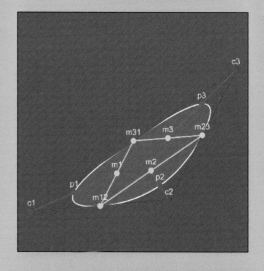

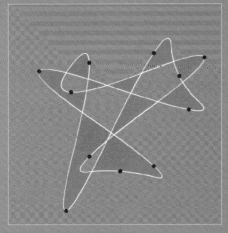

```
                              m31._visible = 1;
                              m2._visible = 1;
                              m3._visible = 1;
                              m1._visible = 1;
                              c2._x=c2x, c2._y=c2y;
                              c3._x=c3x, c3._y=c3y;
                              c1._x=c1x, c1._y=c1y;
                              m12._x=m12x, m12._y=m12y;
                              m23._x=m23x, m23._y=m23y;
                              m31._x=m31x, m31._y=m31y;
                              m2._x=m2x, m2._y=m2y;
                              m3._x=m3x, m3._y=m3y;
                              m1._x=m1x, m1._y=m1y;
                              this.shape.drawLine(c1x, c1y, c2x, c2y, 2, 0xff0000, 100);
                              this.shape.drawLine(c2x, c2y, c3x, c3y, 2, 0xff0000, 100);
                              this.shape.drawLine(c3x, c3y, c1x, c1y, 2, 0xff0000, 100);
                              this.shape.drawLine(m23x, m23y, m31x, m31y, 2, 0xffff00, 100);
                              this.shape.drawLine(m31x, m31y, m12x, m12y, 2, 0xffff00, 100);
                              this.shape.drawLine(m12x, m12y, m23x, m23y, 2, 0xffff00, 100);
                              this.shape.drawLine(c2x, c2y, m2x, m2y, 2, 0x6666ff, 100);
                              this.shape.drawLine(c3x, c3y, m3x, m3y, 2, 0x6666ff, 100);
                              this.shape.drawLine(c1x, c1y, m1x, m1y, 2, 0x6666ff, 100);
                           } else {
                           c1._visible = 0;
                           c2._visible = 0;
                           c3._visible = 0;
                           m12._visible = 0;
                           m23._visible = 0;
                           m31._visible = 0;
                           m2._visible = 0;
                           m3._visible = 0;
                           m1._visible = 0;
                           }
                        };
                        stop();
```

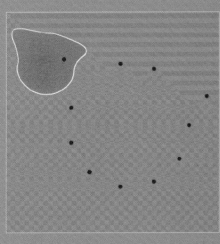

mx_shape_002.fla

This is an automatic version of the Bezier shape method. I have calculated the solution for all the equation systems for n = 3 up to 14.

This application needs the following methods:

drawShape: This method draws all the Bezier curves of the closed shape, given all the control points' coordinates:

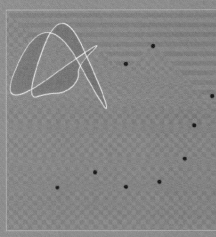

```
MovieClip.prototype.drawShape = function(sx, sy, nn, fillwidth,
➥fillcolor, fillalpha) {
```

```
      this.clear();
      this.beginFill(fillcolor, fillalpha);
      this.lineStyle(fillwidth, 0xffffff, fillalpha);
      this.moveTo((sx[nn-1]+sx[0])/2, (sy[nn-1]+sy[0])/2);
      for (var i = 0; i<(nn-1); i++) {
        this.curveTo(sx[i], sy[i], (sx[i]+sx[i+1])/2, (sy[i]+sy[i+1])/2);
      }
      this.curveTo(sx[nn-1], sy[nn-1], (sx[nn-1]+sx[0])/2, (sy[nn-1]+sy[0])/2);
      this.endFill();
    };
```

matrixGenerator: This function generates the coefficients matrix (the solution of the equation systems):

```
  function matrixGenerator(aux, n) {
    z = aux.slice(0);
    var b = [];
    b[0] = z.slice(0);
    for (i=1; i<n; i++) {
      z.unshift(z.pop());
      b[i] = z.slice(0);
    }
    return (b);
  }
```

createV: This function creates the equation system vector:

```
  function createV(n) {
    v = [];
    v[0] = 6;
    v[1] = 1;
    for (i=2; i<n-1; i++) {
      v[i] = 0;
    }
    v[n-1] = 1;
  }
```

duplicateDots: This function generates all the necessary draggable blue dots:

```
  function duplicateDots(dots) {
    for (var i = 0; i<dots; i++) {
      dot.duplicateMovieClip("dot"+i, 100+i);
      this["dot"+i]._x = 275+100*Math.cos((2*Math.PI/dots)*i);
      this["dot"+i]._y = 200+100*Math.sin((2*Math.PI/dots)*i);
    }
    dot._visible = 0;
  }
```

Then we are ready to create the "shape" movieclip, generate vectors and the solution matrix, and draw the Bezier shape.

```
this.createEmptyMovieClip("shape", 1);
max = 5;
vector = [];
vector[3] = [35, -5, -5];
vector[4] = [204, -36, 12, -36];
vector[5] = [1189, -203, 29, 29, -203];
vector[6] = [6930, -1190, 210, -70, 210, -1190];
vector[7] = [40391, -6929, 1183, -169, -169, 1183, -6929];
vector[8] = [235416, -40392, 6936, -1224, 408, 1224, 6936, -40392];
vector[9] = [1372105, -235415, 40385, -6895, 985, 985, -6895, 40385, -235415];
vector[10] = [7997214, -1372106, 235422, -40426, 7134, -2378, 7134, -40426, 235422, -1372106];
vector[11] = [46611179, -7997213, 1372099, -235381, 40187, -5741, -5741, 40187, -235381,
➡1372099, -7997213];
vector[12] = [271669860, -46611180, 7997220, -1372140, 235620, -41580, 13860, -41580, 235620,
➡-1372140, 7997220, -46611180];
vector[13] = [1583407981, -271669859, 46611173, -7997179, 1371901, -234227, 33461, 33461,
➡-234227, 1371901, -7997179, 46611173, -271669859];
vector[14] = [9228778026, -1583407982, 271669866, -46611214, 7997418, -1373294, 242346, -80782,
➡242346, -1373294, 7997418, -46611214, 271669866, -1583407982];
duplicateDots(max);
createV(max);
dm = matrixGenerator(vector[max], max);
for (i=0, j=0; i<max; i++) {
    den += v[i]*dm[i][0];
}
cx=[], cy=[];
this.onEnterFrame = function() {
    for (kk=0, i=0; i<max; i++) {
        for (cx[i]=0, cy[i]=0, j=0; j<max; j++) {
            cx[i] += (8/den)*this["dot"+j]._x*dm[i][j];
            cy[i] += (8/den)*this["dot"+j]._y*dm[i][j];
        }
    }
    this.shape.drawShape(cx, cy, max, 0, 0xff6666, 100);
};
stop();
```

The solution for all the equation systems for n = 3 to 14 were included as vectors (vector[3] to vector[14]).

The key variable here is **max**, which represents the number of points of the Bezier closed shape. We have also generated the solution coefficients matrix (dm) in order to calculate all the control points (cx[] and cy[])

I hope all this advanced math has given you some ideas and you have learned a lot. If you need ideas on where to go from here, try solving these kinds of closed splines in a 3D environment. Hint: use the xyz parametric Bezier equations. I find this kind of thing really amazing, and I hope it has a similar effect on you.

Bezier Tentacles

We're now ready to draw complex filled lines and curves, so it's time to have some fun! I'm going to try and simulate the soft, organic, hypnotic movement of tentacles.

mx_tentacles_00.fla

This is an OOP application so the first step is to create the constructor function:

tentacle: This function receives all the necessary parameters to create a tentacle object. Each tentacle needs some variables that control its shape. The most important are the number of segments, the radius, and the compression factor. Other parameters control the modulated movement: angle and da (delta angle).

```
function tentacle(segments, radius, thick, comp, xpos, ypos, angle, da, strokewidth,
➥strokecolor, strokealpha, fillcolor, fillalpha) {
    this.body = createEmptyMovieClip("bodyholder"+k, k++);
    this.x=[], this.y=[], this.a=[], this.mx=[], this.my=[];
    this.rx=[], this.ry=[], this.rmx=[], this.rmy=[];
    this.lx=[], this.ly=[], this.lmx=[], this.lmy=[];
    this.da = da;
    this.r = [];
    this.frec = [];
    this.thick = [];
    this.segments = segments;
    this.strokewidth = strokewidth;
    this.strokecolor = strokecolor;
    this.strokealpha = strokealpha;
    this.fillcolor = fillcolor;
    this.fillalpha = fillalpha;
    this.thick[0] = thick;
    this.r[0] = radius;
    this.a[0] = angle;
    this.x[0] = xpos;
    this.y[0] = ypos;
    this.f = 1;
    for (var i = 1; i<=this.segments; i++) {
      this.frec[i] = 3*(Math.random()-.5);
      this.r[i] = this.r[i-1]*comp;
      this.thick[i] = this.thick[i-1]*comp;
    }
}
```

`modulateTentacles`: This method modulates the position of every point, so we generate the tentacle's movement:

```
this.tentacle.prototype.modulateTentacles = function(t) {
    var i = 1;
    this.a[i] = this.a[i-1];
    this.x[i] = this.x[i-1]+this.r[i]*Math.cos(this.a[i]*dtr);
    this.y[i] = this.y[i-1]+this.r[i]*Math.sin(this.a[i]*dtr);
    for (var i = 2; i<=this.seqments; i++) {
      this.a[i] = this.a[i-1]+this.da*Math.sin(this.frec[i]*t*dtr);
      this.x[i] = this.x[i-1]+this.r[i]*Math.cos(this.a[i]*dtr);
      this.y[i] = this.y[i-1]+this.r[i]*Math.sin(this.a[i]*dtr);
    }
    this.rx[0] = this.x[0]-this.thick[0]*Math.sin(this.a[1]*dtr);
    this.ry[0] = this.y[0]+this.thick[0]*Math.cos(this.a[1]*dtr);
    this.lx[0] = this.x[0]+this.thick[0]*Math.sin(this.a[1]*dtr);
    this.ly[0] = this.y[0]-this.thick[0]*Math.cos(this.a[1]*dtr);
    for (var i = 1; i<this.segments; i++) {
      this.rx[i] = this.x[i]-(this.thick[i]/Math.cos(.5*(this.a[i+1]-
➡this.a[i])*dtr))*Math.sin(.5*(this.a[i+1]+this.a[i])*dtr);
      this.ry[i] = this.y[i]+(this.thick[i]/Math.cos(.5*(this.a[i+1]-
➡this.a[i])*dtr))*Math.cos(.5*(this.a[i+1]+this.a[i])*dtr);
      this.lx[i] = this.x[i]+(this.thick[i]/Math.cos(.5*(this.a[i+1]-
➡this.a[i])*dtr))*Math.sin(.5*(this.a[i+1]+this.a[i])*dtr);
      this.ly[i] = this.y[i]-(this.thick[i]/Math.cos(.5*(this.a[i+1]-
➡this.a[i])*dtr))*Math.cos(.5*(this.a[i+1]+this.a[i])*dtr);
    }
    this.rx[this.segments] = this.x[i]-this.thick[i]*Math.sin(this.a[i]*dtr);
    this.ry[this.segments] = this.y[i]+this.thick[i]*Math.cos(this.a[i]*dtr);
    this.lx[this.segments] = this.x[i]+this.thick[i]*Math.sin(this.a[i]*dtr);
    this.ly[this.segments] = this.y[i]-this.thick[i]*Math.cos(this.a[i]*dtr);
};
```

`drawLines`: This method draws all the lines between the tentacle's points:

```
this.tentacle.prototype.drawLines = function() {
    this.body.clear();
    this.body.lineStyle(this.strokewidth, this.strokecolor, this.strokealpha);
    this.body.moveTo(this.lx[0], this.ly[0]);
    this.body.lineTo(this.rx[0], this.ry[0]);
    for (var i = 1; i<=this.segments-1; i++) {
      this.body.lineTo(this.rx[i], this.ry[i]);
    }
    this.body.lineTo(this.lx [this.segments-1], this.ly[this.segments-1]);
    for (var i = (this.segments-2); i>=1; i--) {
      this.body.lineTo(this.lx[i], this.ly[i]);
    }
    this.body.lineTo(this.lx[0], this.ly[0]);
```

```
    this.body.moveTo(this.x[0], this.y[0]);
    for (var i = 1; i<=this.segments-1; i++) {
        this.body.lineTo(this.x[i], this.y[i]);
    }
};
```

Next, on the second frame, we create the tentacle:

```
dtr = Math.PI/180;
tentacle1 = new tentacle(20, 100, 20, .85, 550*.5, 400, -90, 90, 2, 0xff3366, 100, 0xff3333,
➡100);
speed = 15;
this.onEnterFrame = function() {
    this.tentacle1.modulateTentacles(speed*t++);
    this.tentacle1.drawLines();
};
stop();
```

Just change these parameters to create other weird creatures.

Key Variables:

segments: the number of segments on each tentacle
radius: the length of the first segment
thick: the thickness of the first segment
comp: the compression factor between adjacent segments
xpos,ypos: the x,y coordinates of the first segment
angle: the fixed angle of the first segment
da: variable modulation angle
strokewidth, strokecolor, strokealpha, fillcolor, fillalpha: these parameters are self explanatory
speed: this is the modulation speed of the tentacle

Now we are going to add a method to draw curves instead of straight lines, so we'll get some soft, organic shapes.

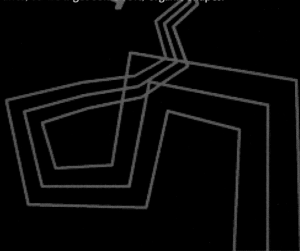

mx_tentacles_01.fla

`drawTentacles`: This method draws Bezier curves between the points of the tentacle:

```
this.tentacle.prototype.drawTentacles = function() {
    this.body.clear();
    this.body.beginFill(this.fillcolor, this.fillalpha);
    this.body.lineStyle(this.strokewidth, this.strokecolor, this.strokealpha);
    this.body.moveTo(this.lx[0], this.ly[0]);
    this.body.lineTo(this.rx[0], this.ry[0]);
    this.body.curveTo(this.rx[1], this.ry[1], this.rmx[2], this.rmy[2]);
    for (var i = 2; i<this.segments-1; i++) {
      this.body.curveTo(this.rx[i], this.ry[i], this.rmx[i+1], this.rmy[i+1]);
    }
    this.body.curveTo(this.rx[this.segments-1], this.ry[this.segments-1], this.rx[this.segments],
➥this.ry[this.segments]);
    this.body.lineTo(this.lx[this.segments], this.ly[this.segments]);
    this.body.curveTo(this.lx[this.segments-1], this.ly[this.segments-1],
➥this.lmx[this.segments-1], this.lmy[this.segments-1]);
    for (var i = (this.segments-2); i>=2; i--) {
      this.body.curveTo(this.lx[i], this.ly[i], this.lmx[i], this.lmy[i]);
    }
    this.body.curveTo(this.lx[1], this.ly[1], this.lx[0], this.ly[0]);
    this.body.endFill();
};
```

And then we generate five tentacles, so we got a nice Bezier anemone.

```
dtr = Math.PI/180;
tentacle1 = new tentacle(10, 80, 10, .8, 550*.618, 400, -90, 90, 2, 0xffffff, 100, 0xff3333, 100);
tentacle2 = new tentacle(10, 80, 10, .8, 550*.618, 400, -90, 90, 2, 0xffffff, 100, 0xff3355, 100);
tentacle3 = new tentacle(10, 80, 10, .8, 550*.618, 400, -90, 90, 2, 0xffffff, 100, 0xff3377, 100);
tentacle4 = new tentacle(10, 80, 10, .8, 550*.618, 400, -90, 90, 2, 0xffffff, 100, 0xff3399, 100);
tentacle5 = new tentacle(10, 80, 10, .8, 550*.618, 400, -90, 90, 2, 0xffffff, 100, 0xff33bb, 100);
speed = 1;
this.onEnterFrame = function() {
    this.tentacle1.modulateTentacles(speed*t++);
    this.tentacle1.drawTentacles();
    this.tentacle2.modulateTentacles(speed*t++);
    this.tentacle2.drawTentacles();
    this.tentacle3.modulateTentacles(speed*t++);
    this.tentacle3.drawTentacles();
    this.tentacle4.modulateTentacles(speed*t++);
    this.tentacle4.drawTentacles();
    this.tentacle5.modulateTentacles(speed*t++);
    this.tentacle5.drawTentacles();
};
stop();
```

Finally, let's look at different kinds of tentacles. I've changed a few of the parameers to alter the color and shape of the tentacles:

mx_tentacles_02.fla

```
dtr = Math.PI/180;
tentacle1 = new tentacle(7, 20, 20, 1.2, 220, 400, -90, 30, 2, 0xffffff, 100, 0x6633ff, 100);
tentacle2 = new tentacle(5, 80, 15, 1, 275, 400, -90, 60, 2, 0xffffff, 100, 0xff3366, 100);
tentacle3 = new tentacle(20, 80, 10, .9, 320, 400, -90, 90, 2, 0xffffff, 100, 0xffcc00, 100);
speed = 3;
this.onEnterFrame = function() {
    this.tentacle1.modulateTentacles(speed*t++);
    this.tentacle1.drawTentacles();
    this.tentacle2.modulateTentacles(speed*t++);
    this.tentacle2.drawTentacles();
    this.tentacle3.modulateTentacles(speed*t++);
    this.tentacle3.drawTentacles();
};
stop();
```

There are loads of places you can take this now. Modify, experiment, and make it your own. I hope you manage to make it do things I've never even considered, and I hope you let me know when you do. I'd love to see what you make of it.

runtime 3D

brandon
williams

The discovery of 3D has a long history. The Greek mathe-matician Euclid wrote the first geometry book of its kind called *The Elements*. In two of the thirteen chapters the foundation of three-dimensional geometry was laid in a series of postulates and definitions. Nearly two millennia later, Alexis Clairaut, a child prodigy in mathematics, wrote the first treatise on three-dimensional analytic geometry at the age of 18. Then 100 years later a Russian mathematician, Nikolai Lobatchewsky, completed a controversial paper stating that Euclid's geometry was only one specific case of a more general geometry, non-Euclidean geometry. His ideas were as ground breaking as Copernicus and Newton, and played a key role in Einstein's relativity. The third dimension has been rigorously studied by some of the most brilliant and creative mathematicians in history. This chapter will re-discover some of the creativity in order to create amazing Flash MX demonstrations.

3D and Flash MX

Creating 3D has become more of a possibility in Macromedia's new version of Flash. Now Flash 5 can natively draw geometric primitives such as lines and curves, and the ability to fill shapes with solid colors. Only one of these drawing methods was easily accessible in Flash making most 3D experiments either wire frame or static. Also with the support of classes and development of events in Flash MX creating 3D entirely through ActionScript can be more organized.

Ways of Creating 3D in Flash

There are many ways of controlling 3D environments in Flash. Suppose that there is a field of randomly distributed points, and that their position is held relative to a universal point, the origin. From the origin are three mutually perpendicular axes, the x, y, z axes. Any point in the field can be represented by an ordered triplet (a, b, c) denoting the distance to travel along each axis to get to the point.

To perform a translation, simply add a small value to the x-, y-, or z-coordinate of all points. Rotating the field of points is trickier. There are three ways of rotating the field that will be shown. The most basic method is to rotate the points about each of the coordinate axes. Give the point (x, y, z) and the rotation θ, you can find the rotated point (x', y', z') with the following equations

Rotation about the x-axis:
$$x' = x$$
$$y' = y \cos \theta - z \sin \theta$$
$$z' = y \sin \theta + z \cos \theta$$

Rotation about the y-axis:
$$x' = x \cos \theta + z \sin \theta$$
$$y' = y$$
$$z' = -x \sin \theta + z \cos \theta$$

Rotation abut the z-axis:
$$x' = x \cos \theta - y \sin \theta$$
$$y' = x \sin \theta + y \cos \theta$$
$$z' = z$$

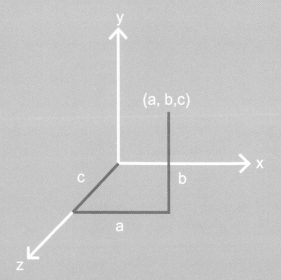

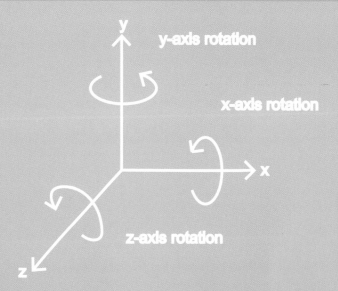

These equations can also be used in succession; you can rotate about one axis, take that new coordinate, and rotate about another axis.

Rather than being limited to only three axes to rotate about you can also rotate about any arbitrary axis. The axis is represented as an ordered triplet (a, b, c) with the requirement that its length must be one. You can pick any three real numbers for a, b, and c and make the axis unit length by dividing each coordinate by its length. Suppose that you choose an axis to go from the origin to the point (1, 1, 1). The length of this axis is $\sqrt{3}$, which is not one. Therefore an axis of unit length in the same direction as (1, 1, 1) would be $(1/\sqrt{3}, 1/\sqrt{3}, 1/\sqrt{3})$.

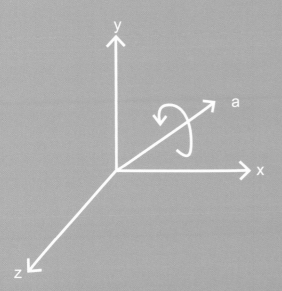

The equation for the rotation is too long to display just now, but will be given in the code later.

The final method of 3D uses a camera. Imagine you are a photographer taking pictures of the field of points. The pictures will look differently depending on the position of your camera and its orientation. We want a method to find the position of the points as they appear to the camera given the camera's position and orientation.

In order to completely describe the orientation of the camera you need three mutually perpendicular axes and they must all be of unit length. The axes are called side, up and out vectors and can be visualized as lines coming out of the side of the camera, the top, and out of the lens.

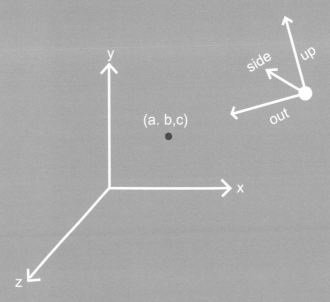

Once you have all of this information you can find what the point (x, y, z) looks like to the camera at (cx, cy, cz) with axes s, u, and o

$$x' = (x - cx) * s.x + (y - cy) * s.y + (z - cz) * s.z$$
$$y' = (x - cx) * u.x + (y - cy) * u.y + (z - cz) * u.z$$
$$z' = (x - cx) * o.x + (y - cy) * o.y + (z - cz) * o.z$$

All of these methods can also be combined. For example, if you are using a camera to view a field of points you can use the axis rotation equations to rotate the camera around.

Once you have performed all the necessary translations and rotations you are still left with a point somewhere at (x, y, z). However, Flash works only in (x, y). To change a point from (x, y, z) to (x, y) you must pick a value that represents the distance from your eye to the surface of the computer screen. There is no official or widely accepted name for this value, so it will simply be called perspective depth. Small values result in a fish-eye effect in your models where large values produce an isometric look.

The calculation from (x, y, z) to (x', y') is made with the following equations

```
perspective_ratio = perspective_depth / (z +
➡ perspective_depth)
x' = x * perspective_ratio
y' = y * perspective_ratio
```

The `perspective_ratio` value can also be used to scale movie clips that are being used to represent points. For example, say that you are making a 3D art gallery so that a user can walk around and look at the pictures. You would want the pictures to get smaller as you get farther. To do this set two variables to keep track of the width and height that you want the picture to be at the origin. Then, simply multiply those values by the `perspective_ratio` to get the width and height of the movie clip when it is in space

```
movie_clip._width  = origin_width *
➡ perspective_ratio;
movie_clip._height = origin_height *
➡ perspective_ratio;
```

You can also use the value of `perspective_depth` to determine when and when not to render images. If a point's z-position goes less than negative `perspective_depth` then you know the point has gone behind the user, and therefore does not need to be rendered. These exact equations are encapsulated in a custom movie clip method that can pass the 3D point of the movie clip, the original dimensions of the movie clip and the perspective depth of the environment and the function will render the movie clip on the stage as it appears with perspective.

The final step to rendering is setting the image's z-depth; this way images in the background are overlapped by images in the front. This is accomplished by swapping the depth of the image to the negative of the image's z-position. The negative is used because the larger the z-position of an object the farther it goes into the screen.

3D equations in Flash

The code supplied with this chapter consists of four classes for handling points, rotations, cameras and 3D objects, as well as a few addition methods and properties attached to the movie clip class and key object. The class for handling points is called `Vector3D`. A vector is a triplet of xyz-components, and is conceptually the same as a point. The class for handling rotations is called `Matrix3x3`. A matrix class was used because all rotations can be represented as matrices. Then, by multiplying a vector with a rotation matrix you get a rotated vector. Ultimately, a matrix class is more versatile and provides a better user-friendly interface to the library. The class for controlling a camera is simply `Camera3D`. The `Mesh` class holds a list of vertices, faces and lines that will make up a 3D object. You start by plotting all the vertices in the object through the `Mesh` class interface, and then connect vertices with lines and faces.

As a developer, all you need to know is what methods each class provides and how to use them. If you were to look through the code you would see that it closely resembles all the equations that were covered. The classes encapsulate all the functionality of a 3D engine, leaving a very simple interface for you to use. You have done this exact thing many times before. For example, using the Array class and its methods without ever seeing the code that is executed when you call the splice or push method. The library of code provided utilizes Flash MX's object-oriented programming language and Flash's new drawing methods.

Library classes, methods, properties and functions

A lot of the code that calculates the positions of our objects in the 3D world and then translates that to a position on our 2D screen, along with code that applies the math to those objects, will be used over and over again throughout this chapter. To that end, I've written a number of classes, which in true object oriented fashion, allow us to re-use the functions within different project – and of course for you to use afterwards in your own investigations. Before we start getting really creative, let's run through the functionality of these.

Need input

Most of the 3D samples made with the library of code must have the user press certain keys to navigate the environments. Some of the keys used were not predefined in the Key object like the shift, control, and arrow keys. The Flash manual provides key codes to all the keys, but it is cumbersome to look up codes constantly. Therefore a file was made that defined constants in the Key object for every key. You can use them the same way as you would the ones that Flash provides:

```
#include "Extra_Key_Properties.as"
trace (Key.isDown (Key.A)); // check if the A key is pressed
trace (Key.isDown (Key.F1));      // check if the Function One key is pressed
trace (Key.isDown (Key.QUOTE));   // check if the quote key is pressed
```

All the key codes were placed in the file named Extra_Key_Properties.as. The file should be included into all projects that require the user to provide some kind of input through the keyboard. This is a great way to save a lot of unnecessary typing, and also serves to keep your code ordered and makes the interesting bits easier to see.

Movie clip methods

While developing the samples for this chapter a certain block of code constantly came up. The most efficient method of doing 3D in Flash is to have movie clips represent the points and objects in your environment. This means for every file, after the final position of the points in 3D space have been calculated, the perspective ratio and perspective position would have to be calculated. It would be great if we could make one general method attached to the movie clip class, much like swapDepths, that would be passed a 3D point and then size and position the movie clip according to how it would look with perspective added. I created a file called Extra_MovieClip_Methods.as to hold this method. The method looks much like the equations we already covered:

```
MovieClip.prototype.render3D = function (point, center, origin_width,
origin_height, perspective_depth, alpha_plane)
{
  // calculate the perspective ratio
  var perspective_ratio = perspective_depth / (perspective_depth + point.z);

  // set the position and dimensions of this movie clip
  this._x = center.x + point.x * perspective_ratio;
  this._y = center.y - point.y * perspective_ratio;
  this._width  = origin_width  * perspective_ratio;
  this._height = origin_height * perspective_ratio;

  // set the movie clip's depth
  this.swapDepths (-point.z);

  // check if the user passed an alpha factor
  if (alpha_plane != undefined)
  {
    this._alpha = 100.0 * (alpha_plane - point.z - perspective_depth) / alpha_plane;
  }
}
```

The method takes quite a few parameters so it should be noted what they represent. The first two parameters must be of `Vector3D` type. The vector point is simply the position of the movie clip in 3D space. Because the origin on Flash's stage is in the upper-left corner the vector center allows you to define where you want the origin to be. The parameters `origin_width` and `origin_height` represent the movie clip's dimensions when it is at the origin. The movie clip is scaled larger or smaller than those two values depending on the movie clip's z-position. As discussed before, `perspective_depth` represents the distance from the viewer's eye to the screen. The last parameter, `alpha_plane`, is an optional parameter that when passed affects the alpha of the movie clip depending on its z-position. When you pass a value for `alpha_plane` the movie clip will have 100 alpha when its z-position is at the origin and 0 alpha when its z-position is equal to `alpha_plane`. This method allows you to have objects appear faint in the distance.

The vector

The vector class is the simplest of the four. It provides methods for settings its components, adding and subtracting vectors, find the length of a vector, multiplying vectors, and more. The following is a list and explanation of the most important methods:

addition (V)
Adds this vector and vector V together and stores the value in this vector.

dot_product (V)
Returns the dot product of this vector with vector V.

cross_product (V)
Returns a vector perpendicular to both this vector and V.

negate ( )
Reflects the Vector about the origin so that it points the opposite direction.

norm ( )
Returns the length of this vector.

normalize ( )
Sets the length of this vector to one.

return_addition (V)
Returns the addition of this vector and vector V.

return_subtraction (V)
Returns the vector made from subtracting V from this vector.

subtract (V)
Subtracts vector V from this vector and stores the value in this vector.

unit_vector ( )
Returns the unit vector of this vector.

render (line_color, line_thickness, timeline, tail, perspective_depth)
This method will draw a line in the timeline specified that represents this vector. The parameter tail is a Vector3D type that specifies where the vector's tail is placed. Since the vector is a 3D object you must also pass the perspective depth of the environment to project the vector onto a 2D screen.

The vector class provides the basis of the 3D engine, and is used thoroughly in the other classes; it is the only file included in every other file of the library. In a simple file, you will probably want to create an array of vectors to hold the position of the points in your environment. Then you can loop through the array and perform the necessary rotations and transformations, and render the movie clip that represents the point to the screen. The architecture of a simple 3D environment might look something like this:

```
points = Array of vectors
for (loop through all points)
{
   Attach movie clip to represent point
   points = Assign random point in space
}

for (loop through points every frame)
{
   Translate and rotate points
   Call the render3D method attached to the
point movie clip
}
```

The matrix

The matrix class is the next basic utility in the library. Every rotation can be represented as a matrix, whether it is about one of the x, y, z-axes or any arbitrary axis. One of the most important methods in the class load rotation matrices based on angles provided. However, to save computations, you must pass the sine and cosine of any rotation angles rather than the angles themselves. Given a matrix `R` and the sine and cosine of some rotation angle, this is how you would load rotation matrices:

```
R.load_rotation_x (sine, cosine);
R.load_rotation_y (sine, cosine);
R.load_rotation_z (sine, cosine);
```

You can even rotate about multiple axes by first representing each rotation with a separate matrix, and then multiplying the two together. For example, if you have a rotation matrix about the x-axis named A and a rotation matrix about the y-axis named B you can combine the two to a final rotation matrix with the following:

```
// rotation matrix about the x- and y-axis
R = A.matrix_multiplication (B);
```

The same operation can be done for three rotation matrices about each of the coordinate axes. However, if you wish to construct a rotation matrix about each axis a faster method to call is load_rotation_xyz. This method requires three pairs of sine and cosine values for the rotation angles about each axis. It will load a rotation matrix for a rotation about the xyz-axes.

You can also load a rotation matrix based off a rotation angle and an arbitrary axis, rather than only the coordinate axes. The axis must be of Vector3D type, and it must be of unit length. You may want to make it a habit to make a quick call to the normalize method from the axis vector before you ever pass it to a matrix. The method is used like this:

```
R.load_rotation_axis (axis, sine, cosine);
```

The most important method of the class is multiplying a matrix with a vector. This method is the entire point of having a matrix class. After you have loaded a rotation matrix you can rotate any vector by multiplying the vector with the matrix. If you had the rotation matrix R about the x-axis and the vector V, then you can rotate you can rotate the vector about the x-axis with the following:

```
V = R.vector_multiplication (V);
```

Take note that the vector_multiplication method returns the rotated vector instead of directly changing the vector. You can directly rotate the vector by simply assigning the vector to the return.

Here is a summary of the important methods in the Matrix3x3 class:

vector_multiplication (V)
Returns the vector made from multiplying this matrix with V.

matrix_multiplication (M)
Returns the matrix made from multiplying this matrix with M.

load_identity () Loads a matrix with no rotation.

load_rotation_x (sine, cosine)
Loads a rotation matrix about the x-axis.

load_rotation_y (sine, cosine)
Loads a rotation matrix about the y-axis.

load_rotation_z (sine, cosine)
Loads a rotation matrix about the z-axis.

load_rotation_xyz (sin_x, cos_x, sin_y, cos_y, sin_z, cos_z)
Loads a rotation matrix about the xyz-axes. You must pass the sine and cosine of each rotation angle.

load_rotation_axis (axis, sine, cosine)
Loads a rotation matrix about the vector axis. The vector must be of unit length.

The camera class provides an alternative to viewing a 3D environment. Before using the camera class you would probably first create an array of vectors for the positions of a field of points. Then you would create an instance of the camera class to view the points. Once created you can move and rotate the camera through various methods of the class. Some methods translate the camera along the x, y, z-axes, and others move the camera in the direction it is facing or any other direction. There are methods to rotate the camera about a coordinate axis, an arbitrary axis, or even one of its axes. Once you have the camera in its final position and orientation you then pass points to the method named transform_point, and it will return a vector that represents what the point looks like to the camera.

Since the camera class is more straightforward than the matrix class we can skip to the summary of the methods:

look_at_vector (P)
Makes the camera look at the point P.

look_at_triplet (x, y, z)
Same as look_at_vector except you can pass an ordered triplet.

move_sideways (d)
Translates the camera in the direction of its side vector.

move_upwards (d)
Translates the camera in the direction of its up vector.

move_forward (d)
Translates the camera in the direction of its out vector.

rotate_around_side (sine, cosine)
Rotates the camera about its side vector.

rotate_around_up (sine, cosine)
Rotates the camera about its up vector.

rotate_around_out (sine, cosine)
Rotates the camera about its out vector.

rotate_x (sine, cosine)
Rotates the camera about the x-axis.

rotate_y (sine, cosine)
Rotates the camera about the y-axis.

rotate_z (sine, cosine)
Rotates the camera about the z-axis.

rotate_axis (axis, sine, cosine)
Rotates the camera about the vector axis.

return_rotation_matrix ( )
Returns the camera's rotation matrix.

set_position (P)
Sets the position of the camera to the vector P.

set_position_x (x)
Sets the x-position of the camera.

set_position_y (y)
Sets the y-position of the camera.

set_position_z (z)
Sets the z-position of the camera.

translate (T)
Translates the camera by the vector T.

translate_x (tx)
Translates the camera along the x-axis.

translate_y (ty)
Translates the camera along the y-axis.

translate_z (tz)
Translates the camera along the z-axis.

transform_position (M)
Applies the rotation matrix M to the camera's position vector.

transform_point (P)
Returns a point that represents how point P looks to the camera.

The look_at and return_rotation_matrix methods may seem slightly ambiguous to the reader at first. The look_at methods are a very useful for keeping solid control over the camera. Sometimes by rotating about various axes you get the camera in a very weird orientation that is hard to navigate in. The look_at methods automatically make the camera look at a specific point, and fix the orientation of the camera to its most upright position. The return_rotation_matrix method returns a matrix that represents the orientation of the camera. This is useful for when you are rendering an object that you want to align with the camera. When you retrieve the rotation matrix you can apply it to any object and it will have the same orientation as the camera. This method is especially useful with the Mesh class.

The Mesh class provides a simple way of dealing with solid 3D objects. A mesh is a collection of vertices, lines and faces that make up a solid object.

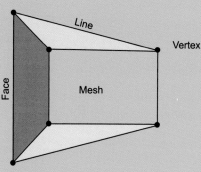

When you instantiate a mesh object, you must pass a reference to a timeline. The timeline is where the mesh object will render. To use the Mesh class you generally add the vertices of the object, and then add the lines and faces to the mesh. You can use the create_vertex_vector or create_vertex_triplet method to add a vertex to a mesh; the former takes a vector as its parameter where the latter takes an ordered triplet.

Once you have the vertices set for your mesh you can add lines and faces with the methods named create_line and create_face. Before you can understand how to use these methods you must understand a little of the class' architecture. When you call the methods to add a vertex you are pushing a vector into an array of vertices. Therefore each vertex can be associated with its index in the array. It is this index that you use to specify which vertices you want to connect with a line or face. The first two parameters in the create_line method are the indices to the vertices that you want to connect. The rest of the parameters are for specifying the color, thickness and alpha of the line. The create_face method is similar except you pass an array of indices representing all the vertices that the face is to fill.

Here is an example of a simple square mesh:

```
#include "Mesh.as"
square = new Mesh (_root);
square.create_vertex_triplet (-10.0, -10.0, 0.0);
square.create_vertex_triplet ( 10.0, -10.0, 0.0);
square.create_vertex_triplet ( 10.0,  10.0, 0.0);
square.create_vertex_triplet (-10.0,  10.0, 0.0);
square.create_face ( [0,1,2,3], 0xFFFFFF, 100.0);
```

Something very important to take note of is that vertices of a mesh are relative to the mesh's local origin. This means that the mesh as an entity has a central position (initially at the origin), which then has vertices position around it. Therefore you set the position of the vertices relative to (0, 0) to create the structure of the mesh, and the set the position of the mesh to wherever you want it in global coordinates.

There are two ways to rotate the mesh. You can rotate the vertices about the mesh's local origin, or you can rotate the mesh as a whole about the global origin. The former is done by passing a rotation matrix to the method `transform_vertices`, and the latter is done by passing a rotation matrix to the method `transform_position`.

Sometimes you do not want the mesh to be rendered in all areas of the screen; sometimes you want the mesh to be constrained to just a certain rectangular area of the screen. For example, say you want to have a split-screen interface – each side would render a different environment, but you would not want some of one side's graphics crossing over to the other side. To fix this, you clip all the meshes in each environment to a viewport. To do this, you call the method `clip_to_viewport` and pass the coordinates of the upper-left corner and the lower-right corner of the viewport. Those two parameters define a rectangle in which only objects in that window are rendered.

Here is a summary of the methods of the mesh object:

`camera_transformation (cam, perspective_depth)`
Calculates what the mesh looks like to the camera passed given the perspective depth of the environment.

`clip_to_viewport (left_x, left_y, right_x, right_y)`
Clips the mesh to the specified viewport so that any part of the mesh outside of the viewport is not rendered.

`create_face (vertices, color, alpha)`
Creates a face with the specified color and alpha that fills all the vertices in the array passed.

`create_line (j, k, color, thickness, alpha)`
Creates a line connecting the jth and kth vertices of the mesh with the specified color, thickness and alpha.

`create_vertex_vector (V)`
Creates a new vertex in the mesh at position V.

`create_vertex_triplet (x, y, z)`
Creates a new vertex in the mesh at the position of the ordered triplet passed

`num_vertices ( )`
Returns the number of vertices in the mesh.

`num_lines ( )`
Returns the number of lines in the mesh.

`num_faces ( )` Returns the number of faces in the mesh.

`render (center_x, center_y, perspective_depth)`
Renders the depth given the position of the origin on Flash's stage and the perspective depth of the environment.

`set_position_vector (V)`
Sets the position of the mesh to the vector V.

`set_position_triplet (x, y, z)`
Sets the position of the mesh to the ordered triplet passed.

`set_vertex_triplet (n, x, y, z)`
Sets the position of the nth vertex in the mesh to the ordered triplet passed.

`set_vertex_vector (n, V)`
Sets the position of the nth vertex in the mesh to V.

`set_vertex_x (n, x)`
Sets the x-position of the nth vertex.

`set_vertex_y (n, y)`
Sets the y-position of the nth vertex.

`set_vertex_z (n, z)`
Sets the z-position of the nth vertex.

`transform_position (M)`
Applies the rotation matrix M to the position of the mesh.

`transform_vertices (M)`
Applies the rotation matrix M to all the vertices in the mesh.

`unclip_to_viewport ( )`
Removes any clipping viewport that is intact.

There are a few idiosyncrasies with this class that you would not know unless you looked at the code. Firstly, you must always call the `transform_vertices` method before you can call the `camera_transformation` or `render` method. If you do not want to rotate the mesh in any way then call the method without passing a parameter and the method will take care of what needs to be done. Also, calling either `create_line` or `create_face` will undo a mesh's clipping viewport, if it has one.

All the samples in this chapter were created using this library of code provided.

Now for some fun!

File1

The first file, `file1.fla`, is so simple that it will only use the files `Vector3D.as` and `Extra_MovieClip_Methods.as`. It will simply take a collection of images and place them out randomly along the x and z-axis for the user to move through, without rotation. The user translates to the sides, backward and forward with the arrow keys. All the art is kept in a movie clip with the linkage name "art" and each frame contains a different piece of art. When the movies are attached to the stage each instance will go to a different frame so all the art is displayed. The initialization part of the code takes care of settings all the constants needed for rendering 3D, creating an array of vectors for the images' positions, and attach the images to the screen.

```
#include "Vector3D.as"
#include "Extra_MovieCLip_Methods.as"
// number of images that will be placed out
num_images = 15;
// perspective depth of the environment
perspective_depth = 400.0;
// original dimensions of the image
origin_width  = 60.0;
origin_height = 85.0;
// center of the screen
center = new Vector3D (275.0, 200.0);
// how much to translate the images when an arrow key is down
translation = 5.0;
// array of vectors that holds the position of each image
image_positions = new Array (num_images);
// attach all the images to the stage and give them a random position
for (var j = 0; j < num_images; j++)
{
  // attach an instance of the image on the stage
  _root.attachMovie ("art", "image" + j, j);
  // go to the image in the art collection
  _root["image" + j].gotoAndStop (j + 1);
  // assign the image a random position
  image_positions[j] = new Vector3D (Math.random () * 800.0 - 400.0,
0.0,Math.random ()  * 800.0 - 400.0);
}
```

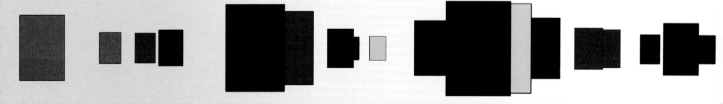

Now every frame you will first calculate by how much to translate each image. This is dependent on which keys the user is holding down. Once you have these values you loop through every image, translate it, and then render it. An extra conditional is added to check for any images that have gone behind the user. These images do not need to be rendered.

```
// function that handles rendering the images
_root.onEnterFrame = function ()
{
  // find out how much to translate the images by
  trans_x = translation * (Key.isDown (Key.LEFT) - Key.isDown (Key.RIGHT));
  trans_z = translation * (Key.isDown (Key.DOWN) - Key.isDown (Key.UP  ));
  // loop through each image to render it
  for (var j = 0; j < num_images; j++)
  {
    // translate the items
    image_positions[j].increment_x (trans_x);
    image_positions[j].increment_z (trans_z);
    // check if the image has gone behind the user
    if (image_positions[j].z < -perspective_depth)
    {
    // making the image invisble
    _root["image" + j]._visible = false;
    }
    else
    {
    // make the image visible
    _root["image" + j]._visible = true;
    // render the image
    _root["image" + j].render3D (image_positions[j], center, origin_width,
      ➡ origin_height, perspective_depth);
    }
  }
}
```

Our first file is done. Although simple, this file represents the basic architecture of every file to come. First, declare constants for the environment like the position of the origin and perspective depth. Second, attach all the objects that will be position in 3D space. Then, in an onEnterFrame event, capture the user's input as to how they want to rotate or translate, and finally render the environment. This simple architecture can also be encapsulated in a separate movie clip so that it does not interfere with your main movie.

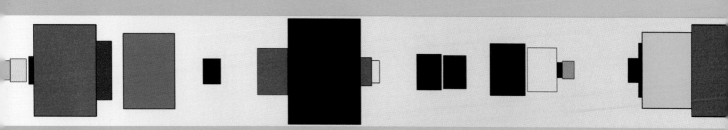

File2

The first iteration of this file is to add some rotation to the environment. I replaced the rectangular images with a graphic of a tree to give the feel that you are walking in a forest. The user can walk forward and backward with the up and down arrow keys, and turn to the sides with the side arrow keys. This file differs from the original quite a bit as far as methodology is concerned. The changes start after the line where the position of the center was declared. A more syntactically correct variable `num_trees` holds the number of trees in the environment. Since the movement the user is capable of now is more complicated the previous viewing system is replaced with an instance of the `Camera3D` class. A new variable is also created to measure how much the camera should translate and rotate when a key is pressed.

```
#include "Camera3D.as"
#include "Vector3D.as"
#include "Extra_MovieClip_Methods.as"
// ... same initializations and variables
// number of trees that will be placed out
num_trees = 15;
// how much to translate the camera when a key is pressed
translation = 5.0;
// how much to rotate when a key is pressed
rotation_inc = Math.PI / 50.0;
// camera that will move through the trees (give the camera some height so
// that it does not seem you are crawling on the forest floor)
cam = new Camera3D (0.0, (origin_height / 3.0), 0.0);
```

In the `onEnterFrame` function we take out the calculations of `trans_x` and `trans_z` to calculate the camera's position and orientation. To control the camera we first calculate how much the camera should translate and rotate, and then update the camera based on these values.

```
// find out how much to translate the camera by
trans_forward = translation * (Key.isDown (Key.UP) - Key.isDown (Key.DOWN));
// find out how much to rotate the camera
rotation = rotation_inc * (Key.isDown (Key.RIGHT) - Key.isDown (Key.LEFT));
// move and rotate the camera
cam.move_forward (trans_forward);
cam.rotate_y (Math.sin (rotation), Math.cos (rotation));
```

Now that we have the position and orientation of the camera, we do the same `for` loop from the previous file. In the previous file the first thing taken care of in the `for` loop was to find the newest position of the items by translating them along the x and y-axis. This is replaced with the calculation of the tree position by the camera transformation.

```
// find the position of the tree relative to the camera
tree_pos = cam.transform_point (tree_positions[j], perspective_depth);
```

After the final position of the tree is calculated, the code is the same for rendering. You now have a fully-grown forest to roam around in. Depending on how fast your computer is, you may want to add a few more trees by changing the variable `num_trees`.

File3

The next file breaks away from style of the previous two to develop another important way to do 3D. The next couple of iterations will plot a field of points and rotate them in various ways. `file3.fla` is initialized similar to the previous files except there are variables for tracking the rotation angles about all three coordinate axes, and the points are plotted randomly on all three axes.

The first few lines of the code are the same as before; initializing variables for the number of points in the field, the perspective depth of the environment, the original dimensions of the movie clips, and the position of the origin.

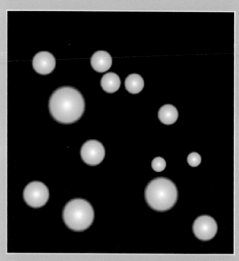

```
#include "Vector3D.as"
#include "Matrix3x3.as"
#include "Extra_MovieClip_Methods.as"
// number of points in the field
num_points = 20;
// perspective depth of the environment
perspective_depth = 400.0;
// original dimensions of the points
origin_width  = 20.0;
origin_height = 20.0;
// center of the screen
center = new Vector3D (275.0, 200.0);
```

The next lines set up the variables that will keep track of how fast the field rotates when a given key is pressed, the current angles the field is being rotated by, and the array that holds the position of the all the points. The variable `rotation` is a matrix type, and is the first use of the `Matrix` class so far. Remember that we can load a matrix with values that will represent a rotation given three rotation angles.

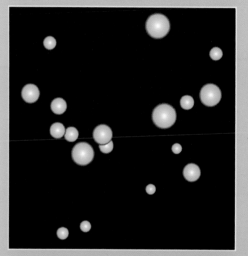

```
// how much to rotate when a key is pressed
rotation_inc = Math.PI / 50.0;
// array of vectors that holds the position of each point
point_positions = new Array (num_points);
// temporary point that holds the position of a point after it has
been rotated
point_pos = new Vector3D (0.0, 0.0, 0.0);
// rotation angles about the x, y and z-axis
angle_x = 0.0;
angle_y = 0.0;
angle_z = 0.0;
// rotation matrix about the xyz-axes
rotation = new Matrix3x3 ();
```

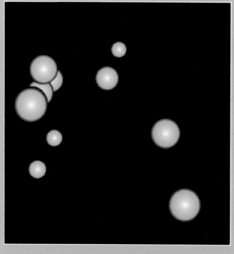

The final block of initialization code attaches the points to the stage and places them randomly in 3D space.

```
// attach all the points to the stage and give them a random position
for (var j = 0; j < num_points; j++)
{
    // attach an instance of the point to the stage
    _root.attachMovie ("point", "point" + j, j);

    // assign the point a random position
    point_positions[j] = new Vector3D (Math.random () * 300.0 - 150.0,
    ➡ Math.random () * 300.0 - 150.0, Math.random () * 300.0 - 150.0);
}
```

The onEnterFrame function is simpler in this file. We first calculate how much the points are rotated about the axes depending on which keys the user is pressing, and load the rotation matrix about the x, y, z-axes. Remember that the load_rotation_xyz method of the Matrix class must be passed the sine and cosine of the rotation angles.

```
// function that handles rendering the points
_root.onEnterFrame = function ()
{
// get the current rotation angles based on what keys the user is pressing
angle_x += rotation_inc *(Key.isDown (Key.UP) - Key.isDown (Key.DOWN));
angle_y += rotation_inc *(Key.isDown (Key.LEFT) - Key.isDown (Key.RIGHT));
angle_z += rotation_inc *(Key.isDown (Key.SHIFT) - Key.isDown (Key.CONTROL));
// load the rotation matrix about the xyz-axes
rotation.load_rotation_xyz (Math.sin (angle_x), Math.cos (angle_x),
➡ Math.sin (angle_y), Math.cos (angle_y), Math.sin (angle_z), Math.cos
➡ (angle_z));
```

Finally, a simple for loop can be done to find the position of the point after the necessary rotations have been performed, and render the movie clip that represents the point.

```
// loop through all the points and apply the rotation matrix
for (var j = 0; j < num_points; j++)
{
    // find the position of the point after the rotations
    point_pos = rotation.vector_multiplication (point_positions[j]);
    // render the point
    _root["point" + j].render3D (point_pos, center, origin_width,
    ➡ origin_height, perspective_depth);
    }
}
```

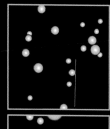

File4

The next iteration, `file4.fla`, replaces the rotation about the x, y, z-axes with a rotation about an arbitrary axis. The axis is chosen as the vector going from the center of the stage to the user's mouse. This file differs from the previous only in the `onEnterFrame` function. At the beginning of the function the rotation angle about the arbitrary axis is constantly incremented, the axis is calculated and drawn, and the rotation matrix is loaded. Everything after that is the same.

```
// increment the rotation angle
rotation_angle += rotation_inc;
// calculate the axis of rotation (the y-component is calculated differently
// because of the fact that Flash's positive y-axis runs down the screen)
axis.reset_components ((_root._xmouse - center.x), (center.y - _root._ymouse), 0.0);
// clear the previously draw axis
_root.clear ();
// draw the axis
axis.render (0xFFFFFF, 1.0, _root, center, perspective_depth);
// make sure the axis of rotation is of unit length
axis.normalize ();
// load the rotation matrix based on the rotation angle and axis
rotation.load_rotation_axis (axis, Math.sin (rotation_angle), Math.cos
➡ (rotation_angle));
```

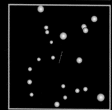

File5

The next iteration, `file5.fla`, uses a camera to navigate through the field of points. The camera rotates about its side vector and the global y-axis with the arrow keys, and translates in the direction of its out vector and side vector with the letter keys W, S, A and D. As you will see in iterations to come there are other ways to control the camera's orientation other than rotating about the side vector and y-axis.

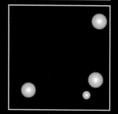

The good news about this file is that the initialization is nearly identical to the previous. Everything between including the libraries and the declaration of the angle variables is the same. Instead of variables holding the rotation angles of the points about some axes there will be rotation angles for the camera about the y-axis and side vector. We will also instantiate an object from the camera class.

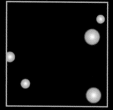

```
#include "Vector3D.as"
#include "Camera3D.as"
#include "Extra_Key_Properties.as"
#include "Extra_MovieClip_Methods.as"
// same variables declared in last file …
// rotation angle of the camera about its side vector and the global y-axis
rotation_side = 0.0;
rotation_y   = 0.0;
// camera that will move through the field of points
cam = new Camera3D (0.0, 0.0, 0.0);
```

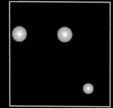

After the above line is the exact same `for` loop that attaches the point movie clips to the stage. The `onEnterFrame` function is also similar. It calculates the rotation and translation values, updates the camera's position and orientation, loops through every point, finds the point's position relative to the camera, and renders the point.

```
// function that handles rendering the points
_root.onEnterFrame = function ()
{
    // move the camera
    cam.move_forward (translation_inc*(Key.isDown (Key.W)-Key.isDown (Key.S)));
    cam.move_sideways (translation_inc*(Key.isDown (Key.D)-Key.isDown (Key.A)));
    // calculate the rotation angles of the camera
    rotation_y = rotation_inc * (Key.isDown (Key.RIGHT)-Key.isDown (Key.LEFT));
    rotation_side = rotation_inc * (Key.isDown (Key.DOWN) - Key.isDown (Key.UP ));
    // rotate the camera
    cam.rotate_around_side (Math.sin (rotation_side), Math.cos (rotation_side));
    cam.rotate_y (Math.sin (rotation_y), Math.cos (rotation_y));
    // loop through each point to render it
    for (var j = 0; j < num_points; j++)
    {
        // find the position of the point relative to the camera
        point_pos = cam.transform_point (point_positions[j], perspective_depth);
        // check if the point has gone behind the user
        if (point_pos.z <= -perspective_depth)
        {
            // making the point invisble
            _root["point" + j]._visible = false;
        }
        else
        {
            // make the point visible
            _root["point" + j]._visible = true;
            // render the point
            _root["point" + j].render3D (point_pos, center, origin_width,
            ➥ origin_height, perspective_depth);
        }
    }
}
```

To visualize the way the camera rotates when you press the arrow keys imagine you are film cameraman on a platform that spins. The side arrow keys would control the spinning of the platform. Also image that the only movement that you can make with the camera itself is rotating up and down. The up and down arrow keys would control that movement. The only way to face a certain direction is to spin and rotate up and down.

File6

In the next iteration, `file6.fla`, we change the control of the camera's orientation. This time when you press the side arrow keys the camera will rotate about its up vector. There are only a few lines to change to make this new file, and it happens at the beginning of the `onEnterFrame` function.

```
// move the camera
cam.move_forward (translation_inc * (Key.isDown (Key.W) - Key.isDown (Key.S)));
cam.move_sideways (translation_inc * (Key.isDown (Key.D) - Key.isDown (Key.A)));
// calculate the rotation angles of the camera
rotation_up   = rotation_inc * (Key.isDown (Key.RIGHT) - Key.isDown (Key.LEFT));
rotation_side = rotation_inc * (Key.isDown (Key.DOWN ) - Key.isDown (Key.UP ));
// rotate the camera
cam.rotate_around_side (Math.sin (rotation_side), Math.cos (rotation_side));
cam.rotate_around_up (Math.sin (rotation_up), Math.cos (rotation_up));
```

The camera now has a completely different feel when you are navigating through the field of points.

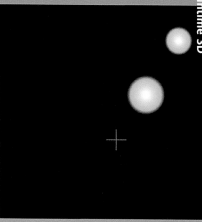

File7

You can make the field of points more interactive by having the camera's orientation based off of the user's mouse position. This is done in the next iteration, `file7.fla`, and the file behaves more as a game. The file's only difference from `file6.fla` is in the calculation of `rotation_up` and `rotation_side` in the `onEnterFrame` function.

```
// calculate the rotation angles based on the mouse position
// relative to the center of the screen. Since the angles
// need to be in radians the values are divided by a large number
// to keep from very fast rotations
rotation_up   = (_root._xmouse - center.x) / 5000.0;
rotation_side = (_root._ymouse - center.y) / 5000.0;
```

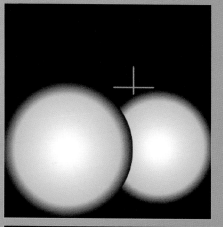

The file behaves completely differently now. As a possible game you could have the points in space act as mines that are attracted to you, and you have to dodge them.

File8

`file8.fla` moves away from placing the points in space randomly to show that you can give any structure to the points. The file is an exact copy of `file3.fla` except in the `for` loop of the intialization code the points are not given a random position. Instead they are placed in around the origin in a circle in the x/z-plane. Once initialized, you can rotate and spin the circle of points any way you want.

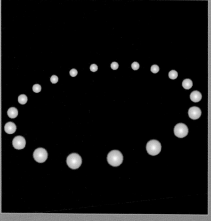

```
// radius of the circle of points
radius = 150.0;
// attach all the points to the stage and set their position around a
circle
for (var j = 0; j < num_points; j++)
{
    // attach an instance of the point to the stage
    _root.attachMovie ("point", "point" + j, j);
    // assign the point a random position
    point_positions[j] = new Vector3D ((radius * Math.cos (2 * Math.PI * j /
    num_points)), 0.0, (radius * Math.sin (2 * Math.PI * j / num_points)));
}
```

File9

We will now explore some solid objects in Flash. To do this we need to include the `Mesh.as` file for now on in our files. The file will simply be a cube, and camera as the viewing system. The code used for the camera in `file6.fla` is the same for the camera in this file. The box mesh is created in the initialization section of the code with the following:

```
#include "Vector3D.as"
#include "Camera3D.as"
#include "Mesh.as"
#include "Extra_Key_Properties.as"
// distance from the origin to any face of the box
dim = 30.0;
// mesh that represents the box
box = new Mesh (_root);
```

You must know exactly how your mesh is going to look before you start adding vertices. Here is a picture to show the order I added the vertices to the box mesh. For experimentation, try picking a vertex and changing its position slightly by adding or subtracting a small value to its current position to see how you can form new meshes.

```
// add the vertices of the box to the mesh object
box.create_vertex_triplet ( dim,  dim,  dim); // right top back  corner
box.create_vertex_triplet ( dim,  dim, -dim); // right top front corner
box.create_vertex_triplet ( dim, -dim,  dim); // right bottom back corner
box.create_vertex_triplet ( dim, -dim, -dim); // right bottom front corner
box.create_vertex_triplet (-dim,  dim,  dim); // left  top back  corner
box.create_vertex_triplet (-dim,  dim, -dim); // left  top front corner
box.create_vertex_triplet (-dim, -dim,  dim); // left  bottom back  corner
box.create_vertex_triplet (-dim, -dim, -dim); // left  bottom front corner
```

To create a face in the mesh, you must pick out the indices to the vertices that you want to create and pass them as an array. The red face showing is the first face created. Take note that the order of the indices matters. If the order for the first face had been changed to 0, 2, 1, 3 the face would be made of two crossed triangles.

```
// add faces to the mesh
box.create_face ( [ 0, 1, 3, 2 ], 0xFF0000, 100.0); // left face
box.create_face ( [ 4, 5, 7, 6 ], 0xFF0000, 100.0); // right face
box.create_face ( [ 1, 5, 7, 3 ], 0x00FF00, 100.0); // front face
box.create_face ( [ 0, 4, 6, 2 ], 0x00FF00, 100.0); // back face
box.create_face ( [ 1, 5, 4, 0 ], 0x0000FF, 100.0); // top face
box.create_face ( [ 3, 7, 6, 2 ], 0x0000FF, 100.0); // bottom face
```

The `onEnterFrame` function is much simpler in this file than any other covered so far. It updates the camera's position and orientation first, calculates what the mesh looks like to the camera, and renders the mesh. This is all done in only a few lines, since most of the functionality is encapsulated in the `Mesh` and `Camera3D` classes.

```
// function that handles rendering the box
_root.onEnterFrame = function ()
{
    // move the camera
    cam.move_forward (translation_inc * (Key.isDown (Key.W) - Key.isDown (Key.S)));
    cam.move_sideways (translation_inc * (Key.isDown (Key.D) - Key.isDown (Key.A)));
    // calculate the rotation angles of the camera
    rotation_y    = rotation_inc * (Key.isDown (Key.RIGHT) - Key.isDown (Key.LEFT));
    rotation_side = rotation_inc * (Key.isDown (Key.DOWN ) - Key.isDown (Key.UP ));
    // rotate the camera
    cam.rotate_around_side (Math.sin (rotation_side), Math.cos (rotation_side));
    cam.rotate_y           (Math.sin (rotation_y), Math.cos (rotation_y));
    // perpare the vertices for a camera transformation
    box.transform_vertices ();
    // transform the vertices based on the camera's position and orientation
    box.camera_transformation (cam, perspective_depth);
    // render the box
    box.render (center.x, center.y, perspective_depth);
}
```

Take note that the `transform_vertices` method was called even though a transformation was not being performed on the box. Remember it is the method that must be called before either the `camera_trans-formation` or `render` methods can be called.

File10

The next iteration, `file10.fla`, does the same as the previous file with the addition that the box will now rotate about the xyz-axes. In the initialization section of the code a matrix is instantiated, and variables for hold the rotation angle of the box. In the `onEnterFrame` function the rotation angle is incremented and the rotation matrix is loaded first. Next, the rotations and translations are performed on the camera. Finally the box is rotated by the matrix, transformed by the camera, and rendered.

```
// function that handles rendering the box
_root.onEnterFrame = function ()
{
    // increment the rotation angle of the box about the xyz-axes
    rotation_angle += rotation_inc;
    // calculate the sine and cosine of the rotation angle
    sine   = Math.sin (rotation_angle);
    cosine = Math.cos (rotation_angle);
    // load the rotation matrix of the box about the xyz-axes
    rotation.load_rotation_xyz (sine, cosine, sine, cosine, sine, cosine);

    // same camera translations and rotations

    // rotate the box
    box.transform_vertices (rotation);
    // transform the vertices based on the camera's position and orientation
    box.camera_transformation (cam, perspective_depth);
    // render the box
    box.render (center.x, center.y, perspective_depth);
}
```

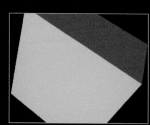

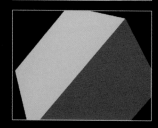
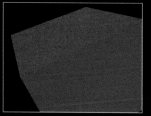

File11

file11.fla aims to bring together the recently used meshes with the static movie clips used in the earlier files. At the same time it shows how easy it is to add movement to any 3D environment. Since the positions of the points in space are always temporarily changed for rendering you can move them about however you want. This file uses the movie clip of the green circle from previous files, to represent a ball bouncing on a mesh of a flat surface. The whole environment is viewed with a camera with the same controls as before. In the initialization, variables are now created for the ball's position, velocity and acceleration as well as all the other variables always used. Here are the most recent additions:

```
#include "Vector3D.as"
#include "Camera3D.as"
#include "Mesh.as"
#include "Extra_Key_Properties.as"
#include "Extra_MovieClip_Methods.as"
// ...
// how much to translate and rotate the camera when a key is pressed
translation_inc = 5.0;
rotation_inc = Math.PI / 50.0;
// position of the ball in 3D space (give it some height for it to fall)
ball_position = new Vector3D (0.0, 150.0, 0.0);
// temporary point that holds the position of the ball after has been rotated
transformed_ball_pos = new Vector3D (0.0, 0.0, 0.0);
// acceleration due to gravity along the y-axis acting on the ball
acceleration = -0.5;
// velocity of the ball along the y-axis
velocity = 1.0;
// attach the point movie clip to represent the ball
_root.attachMovie ("point", "ball", 1);
// distance from the origin to any side of the plane
dim = 75.0;
// rotation angle of the camera about its side vector and global y-axis
rotation_side = 0.0;
rotation_y    = 0.0;
// ...
// mesh that represents the plane
plane = new Mesh (_root);
// add the vertices of the box to the mesh object
plane.create_vertex_triplet ( dim, 0.0,  dim);   // right back  corner
plane.create_vertex_triplet ( dim, 0.0, -dim);   // right front corner
plane.create_vertex_triplet (-dim, 0.0, -dim);   // left  front corner
plane.create_vertex_triplet (-dim, 0.0,  dim);   // left  back  corner
// add a face to the plane
plane.create_face ( [ 0, 1, 2, 3 ], 0xFF0000, 100.0);
```

The onEnterFrame function of this file is a little bit more complicated. Updating the camera's position and orientation is done first. After that the velocity of the ball is incremented due to acceleration, and then the ball's position is incremented due to velocity. Once you have the new position of the ball, there is a conditional statement to check if the ball has hit the flat surface. If the ball hit the surface then reset the ball's position so it is just on top of the surface, and reverse the ball's velocity so it goes flying back up into the air. After all this the code performs all the transformations on the objects and renders the environment.

```
// function that handles rendering the box
_root.onEnterFrame = function ()
{
  // same camera translations and rotations

  // increase the ball's velocity due to acceleration
  velocity += acceleration;
  // increase the ball's position due to velocity
  ball_position.y += velocity;
  // check if the ball has hit the plane
  if ((ball_position.y - origin_radius / 2.0) < 0.0)
  {
    // ball has hit the plane so reset its position and reverse its velocity
    ball_position.y = origin_radius / 2.0;
    velocity *= -1.0;
  }
  // transform the ball based on the camera's position and orientation
  transformed_ball_pos = cam.transform_point (ball_position, perspective_depth);
  // render the ball
  this.ball.render3D (transformed_ball_pos, center, origin_radius, origin_radius, perspective_depth);
  // prepare the mesh for the camera transformation
  plane.transform_vertices ();
  // transform the vertices based on the camera's position and orientation
  plane.camera_transformation (cam, perspective_depth);
  // render the box
  plane.render (center.x, center.y, perspective_depth);
}
```

File12

The iteration of the ball bouncing has the same situation, except this time the camera will always look at the ball file12.fla utilizes the very powerful method look_at_vector from the Camera3D class. Since the camera always looks at the ball the user cannot control the orientation of the camera. However, the camera's position along the x, y, z-axes is controlled with the arrow keys and the SHIFT and CONTROL keys. The only thing changed in the file is the onEnterFrame function. At the beginning of the function the camera is translated along the x, y, z-axes depending on which key is pressed. Towards the end of the code, before the camera transforms the ball's position, a call to the look_at_vector method is made to ensure the camera is looking at the ball. Everything else stays the same.

```
// function that handles rendering the box
_root.onEnterFrame = function ()
{
    // move the camera
    cam.translate_x (translation_inc * (Key.isDown (Key.RIGHT) - Key.isDown (Key.LEFT)));
    cam.translate_y (translation_inc * (Key.isDown (Key.SHIFT) - Key.isDown (Key.CONTROL)));
    cam.translate_z (translation_inc * (Key.isDown (Key.UP   ) - Key.isDown (Key.DOWN)));

// same calculations made for the ball's position

    // make the camera look at the ball
    cam.look_at_vector (ball_position);

    // same calculations for the transformations and rendering of the objects
}
```

File13

The next file and its iterations go back to the basics. They have been created mainly to show that you can create very nice effects with just a static movie clip. The base file is simply a field of points lined up along the z-axis. The points spaced evenly along the z-axis and distributed randomly in a small square area in the x, y-plane. A camera looking down the z-axis views the points. When you press the up and down keys the camera accelerates up and down the z-axis. At any given time you can only see ten points because as soon as a point goes behind the camera it is reset to some where in front of the camera, and distant objects have a low alpha. Therefore when one point goes behind you, it slowly fades itself back in front of you. This effect uses the last parameter of the render3D method in the MovieClip class. The last parameter controls how far an object must be for it to have zero for an alpha. It interpolates the objects alpha from 100 when the object is at z =0, and zero when the object's z-position is greater than or equal to the value passed.

The initialization of code of file13.fla is similar to past files, except this time we are assigning variables for the position, velocity and acceleration of the camera. A new variable called minimum_distance is introduced in this file. This will be the value passed as the alpha_plane parameter in the render3D method of the MovieClip class. It represents the minimum distance along the z-axis an object must be before it is rendered. It also represents the z-position of a movie clip when it has zero alpha; as the movie clip comes closer to the camera its alpha increases.

```
// number of points in the queue
num_points = 10;
// space along the z-axis between the points
space_z = 50.0;
// how much to accelerate the camera along the z-axis when a key is pressed
acceleration = 1.0;
// velocity of the camera along the z-axis
cam_velocity = 0.0;
// position of the camera along the z-axis
cam_z = -100.0;
// camera that will move through the queue of points
cam = new Camera3D (0.0, 0.0, cam_z);
// value that is multiplied with the camera's velocity everyframe to slow down the camera
velocity_reduction = 0.1;
// minimum distance along the z-axis point must be from the camera before it is rendered
minimum_distance = num_points * space_z;
// array of vectors that holds the positions of each point
point_positions = new Array (num_points);
// temporary points that holds the position of a point after it has been transformed
point_pos = new Vector3D (0.0, 0.0, 0.0);
// attach all the points to the stage and give them a random position
for (var j = 0; j < num_points; j++)
{
    // attach an instance of the point to the stage
    _root.attachMovie ("point", "point" + j, j);
    // assign the point a random position
    point_positions[j] = new Vector3D (Math.random () * 200.0 - 100.0,
                         Math.random () * 200.0 - 100.0, j * space_z);
}
```

The first thing the `onEnterFrame` function does is change the camera's velocity due to any acceleration the user is giving, change the camera's position due to velocity, and then finally update the camera's position. Once the camera is in place the code loops through the points for rendering. This part is slightly different from the previous files. The check for whether the point has gone behind the user is done before the camera transforms the point. The conditional is done by checking if the point's z-position goes less than the camera's. If the point goes behind the camera the code resets the point in front of the camera, and gives it another random position in the x, y-plane. If the point is not in front of the camera then it is transformed and rendered as usual.

```
// function that handles rendering the points
_root.onEnterFrame = function ()
{
    // change the camera's velocity due to acceleration depending on which keys
    // are pressed
    cam_velocity += acceleration * (Key.isDown (Key.UP) - Key.isDown (Key.DOWN));
    // change the camera's z-position due to velocity
    cam_z += cam_velocity;
    // reduce the camera's velocity so the camera will come to a stop if it is
    // not accelerating
    cam_velocity -= cam_velocity * velocity_reduction;
    // set the z-position of the camera
    cam.set_position_z (cam_z);
    // loop through all the points and apply the rotation matrix
    for (var j = 0; j < num_points; j++)
    {
      // check if the point has gone behind the user
      if (point_positions[j].z <= cam.cam_position.z)
      {
        // reset the point in front of the camera
        point_positions[j].z = cam.cam_position.z + minimum_distance;
        // give it a random x- and y-position
        point_positions[j].x = Math.random () * 200.0 - 100.0;
        point_positions[j].y = Math.random () * 200.0 - 100.0;
      }
      else
      {
        // find the position of the point relative to the camera
        point_pos = cam.transform_point (point_positions[j], perspective_depth);
        // render the point
        _root["point" + j].render3D (point_pos, center, origin_width, origin_height,
      ➥ perspective_depth, minimum_distance);
      }
    }
}
```

File14

The first iteration of the previous file adds a little more movement to the environment. In the new file `file14.fla` you can move the camera a small distance from the origin in the xy-plane by moving the mouse. To add this affect simply add the following lines before the `for` loop in the `onEnterFrame` function:

```
// set the x- and y-position of the camera depending on where the mouse is
cam.set_position_x ((_root._xmouse - center.x) / 5.0);
cam.set_position_y ((center.y - _root._ymouse) / 5.0);
```

Those two lines add more depth to the environment. Another small game could be made from this by making the points zoom in manually instead of having the user control it, and have the user dodge the mines.

File15

The final iteration, `file15.fla`, keeps the camera on the z-axis, but allows the user to look around at the points zooming by. Rotating the camera about its side vector and the y-axis based on the mouse movement creates this effect. The rotation angles for the camera are going to be calculated from the mouse's change in position. This means that if the mouse does not move the rotation angles are zero, and if the mouse moves then the rotation angles are calculated by subtracting the previous mouse position from the current. The rotation angles are calculated in the `onEnterFrame` function with the following:

```
// keep track of the old mouse position so we know how much to rotate the camera by
old_mouse_x = mouse_x;
old_mouse_y = mouse_y;
// new mouse position relative to the center of the screen
mouse_x = _root._xmouse - center.x;
mouse_y = _root._ymouse - center.y;
// rotate the camera based on how much the mouse moves between frames
angle_side = (mouse_y - old_mouse_y) / 500.0;
angle_y = (mouse_x - old_mouse_x) / 500.0;
```

The only other change in the code is that the calls to `set_position_x` and `set_position_y` from `file14.fla` are replaced with calls to methods that rotate the camera.

```
// rotate the camera
cam.rotate_around_side (Math.sin (angle_side), Math.cos (angle_side));
cam.rotate_y           (Math.sin (angle_y   ), Math.cos (angle_y   ));
```

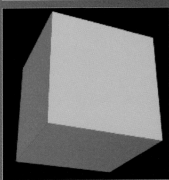

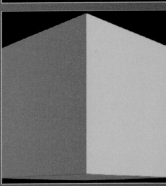

File16

The next file demonstrates that you do not always need to give the user control over the camera. `file16.fla` codes the movement of a camera around a box mesh. The camera moves around the box in a circle in the x, z-plane, and in a sine wave along the y-axis at the same time; somewhat resembling the movement of a roller coaster. This file used `file9.fla` as its basis. To control the new effect a few new variables had to be created. There is a variable for controlling the amplitude of the sine wave that the camera's y-position is based on, and a variable used as the parameter of the sine wave. A matrix was also created for the camera's rotation about the y-axis around the box.

```
// amplitude of the sine wave that the camera's y-position will be based on
cam_amplitude_y = 100.0;
// parameter and parameter increment in the sine wave function
parameter = 0.0;
parameter_inc = Math.PI / 200.0;
// how much the camera will rotate about the y-axis every frame
cam_rotation_angle = Math.PI / 500.0;
// rotation matrix about the y-axis that will be applied to the camera's
// position every frame
cam_position_matrix = new Matrix3x3 ();
cam_position_matrix.load_rotation_y (Math.sin (cam_rotation_angle),Math.cos
(cam_rotation_angle));
```

In the `onEnterFrame` function the parameter is incremented for the sine wave, the camera's y-position is set base off of the sine wave, and the camera is rotated around the box. Once the camera is in its final position a call to the `look_at_triplet` method is made to make the camera always look at the box. Finally, everything is transformed and rendered.

```
// function that handles rendering the box
_root.onEnterFrame = function ()
{
  // increment the sine wave parameter
  parameter += parameter_inc;
  // set the y-position of the camera based on a sine wave
  cam.set_position_y (cam_amplitude_y * Math.sin (parameter));
  // rotate the camera's position about the y-axis
  cam.transform_position (cam_position_matrix);
  // make the camera look at the origin (the box)
  cam.look_at_triplet (0.0, 0.0, 0.0);
  // perpare the vertices for a camera transformation
  box.transform_vertices ();
  // transform the vertices based on the camera's position and orientation
  // box.camera_transformation (cam, perspective_depth);render the box
  box.render (center.x, center.y, perspective_depth);
}
```

File17

`file17.fla` creates a large, complex polygon that looks like a slice of a terrain. The terrain slice can be rotated about the y-axis. The most complicated part of the script is in the initialization section where the terrain mesh is created. The mesh is created by initially creating one peak at the end of the terrain, and then every successive peak is randomly placed based on the previous peak. The code to create the terrain mesh looks like this:

```
// mesh that represents the box
terrain = new Mesh (_root);
// distance from the origin to the sides of the terrain
dim = 400.0;
// height of the previous peak
previous_peak = 100.0;
// set the position of the mesh so that it does not go off the top of the screen
terrain.set_position_triplet (0.0, -previous_peak/2.0, 0.0);
// number of peaks in the terrain
num_peaks = 20;
// add the two base vertices to the terrain, as well as the starting peak vertex
terrain.create_vertex_triplet ( dim, 0.0, 0.0);
terrain.create_vertex_triplet (-dim, 0.0, 0.0);
terrain.create_vertex_triplet (-dim, previous_peak, 0.0);
// loop through the remaining peaks and set their height randomly
for (var j = 1; j < num_peaks; j++)
{
    // x-position of the next peak
    var x = (j / num_peaks) * (2.0 * dim) - dim;
    // get the height of the next peak
    previous_peak += Math.random () * 50.0 - 25.0;
    // create a vertex in the mesh for the peak
    terrain.create_vertex_triplet (x, previous_peak, 0.0);
}
// create the array of indices for the terrain mesh
var terrain_indices = new Array (num_peaks);
for (var j = 0; j < num_peaks; j++)          terrain_indices[j] = j;
// create the face for the terrain mesh
terrain.create_face (terrain_indices, 0x0000FF, 100.0);
```

Once the terrain mesh is created the `onEnterFrame` function simply consists of the rotation angle calculation, a transformation of the mesh, and then rendering:

```
// function that handles rendering the box
_root.onEnterFrame = function ()
{
    // calculate the rotation angles of the terrain
    angle += rotation_inc * (Key.isDown (Key.RIGHT) - Key.isDown (Key.LEFT));
    // load the rotation matrix about the y-axis for the terrain
    rotation.load_rotation_y (Math.sin (angle), Math.cos (angle));
    // rotate the terrain
    terrain.transform_vertices (rotation);
    // render the box
    terrain.render (center.x, center.y, perspective_depth);
}
```

215

File18

The iteration of the previous file consists of putting each peak of the terrain on a separate sine curve giving the terrain an animated erosion look. Each peak is put on a separate sine wave so that they bob up and down along the y-axis. This is done by creating an array to hold the parameters of each peak, incrementing the parameters each frame, and displacing the peaks according to a sine wave. The onEnterFrame function performs most of this:

```
// function that handles rendering the box
_root.onEnterFrame = function ()
{
    // calculate the rotation angles of the terrain
    angle += rotation_inc * (Key.isDown (Key.RIGHT) - Key.isDown (Key.LEFT));
    // load the rotation matrix about the y-axis for the terrain
    rotation.load_rotation_y (Math.sin (angle), Math.cos (angle));
    // loop through vertices of the mesh, increment their parameters,
    // and positin them on a sine wave
    for (var j = 3; j < num_peaks; j++)
    {
        // increment the peaks' parameter for the sine wave
        peak_parameters[j] += parameter_inc;
        // set the y-position of the peak based on a sine curve
        terrain.set_vertex_y (j, (peak_amplitude * Math.sin
(peak_parameters[j]) +
peak_positions[j]));
    }
    // rotate the terrain
    terrain.transform_vertices (rotation);
    // render the box
    terrain.render (center.x, center.y, perspective_depth);
}
```

File19

The final file, `file19.fla`, uses nearly all of the functionality of each class to make a very complex 3D environment. The stage is split into two sides, and each side is an environment itself. The left side has a fixed camera high above the xy-plane looking down. At the origin is a large pyramid mesh, and off to the side is a small cube. The cube can accelerate and decelerate with the w and s keys, and can be steered with the arrow keys. The fixed camera always looks at the cube as it flies through the environment. The right side also has a camera and pyramid, except this time the camera is positioned in the cube from the left environment. The right side gives you a first-person look into what the cube sees as it fly through the environment, and the left side gives you an aerial view of the environment.

The initialization of this file is by far the largest of any file we have made. The first part initializes the properties of the box like its acceleration, velocity and position. We also have a rotation matrix for the box, because the box's orientation in the left environment must match the camera's orientation in the right environment. We construct such a rotation matrix by using the camera's method `return_rotation_matrix`.

```
// current position of the box-vehicle
box_pos = new Vector3D (400.0, 0.0, 0.0);
// current velocity of the box-vehicle in the direction it is facing
box_vel = 0.0;
// how much the box-vehicle accelerates depending on which key is pressed
acceleration = 5.0;
// rotation matrix that describes the box-vehicle's orientation
box_rotation = new Matrix3x3 ();
```

The next part initializes the two cameras used in the environments. The static camera is supposed to be high in the air for the aerial viewpoint.

```
// static camera that will look down on the environment
static_cam = new Camera3D (0.0, 1200.0, -1200.0);
// camera that will view the box-vehicle's perspective
box_cam = new Camera3D (box_pos.x, box_pos.y, box_pos.z);
```

After that the dimensions of the meshes are initialized, and then the meshes themselves. In order to keep the environments separate I created two empty movie clips right in the Flash authoring environment for holding each camera view. Setting all of the vertices and faces is rather long so it will be left out of these pages.

```
vehicle box
middle_dim = 200.0;
vehicle_dim = 15.0;
// meshes for the middle piece and vehicle box in the first environment
middle_piece1 = new Mesh (_root.environment1
// dimensions of the middle piece and small);
vehicle_box = new Mesh (_root.environment1);
```

The final part of the initialization is clipping each mesh to its viewport. The stage is 600 by 300, so the meshes should take up a 300 by 300 area. However, since the meshes are each contained in empty movie clips at the center of each half of the screen, the viewport must be held relative to the movie clip's origin.

```
// clip the meshes to the appropriate viewports
middle_piece1.clip_to_viewport (-150.0, -150.0, 150.0, 150.0);
vehicle_box.clip_to_viewport (-150.0, -150.0, 150.0, 150.0);
middle_piece2.clip_to_viewport (-150.0, -150.0, 150.0, 150.0);
```

The first part of the onEnterFrame function calculates the rotation angles of the vehicle's camera, and sets the camera's orientation.

```
// function that handles rendering the environments
_root.onEnterFrame = function ()
{
    // calculate the camera's rotation angles about its side vector and y-axis
    rotation_side = rotation_inc * (Key.isDown (Key.DOWN ) - Key.isDown (Key.UP));
    rotation_y   = rotation_inc * (Key.isDown (Key.RIGHT) - Key.isDown (Key.LEFT));
    // rotate the camera
    box_cam.rotate_around_side (Math.sin (rotation_side), Math.cos
    ➥ (rotation_side));
    box_cam.rotate_y (Math.sin (rotation_y), Math.cos (rotation_y));
```

Once the camera is in its final orientation we extract its rotation matrix so that it can be applied to the box in the left environment.

```
// set the rotation matrix for the vehicle mesh
box_rotation = box_cam.return_rotation_matrix ().transpose ();
```

Next, we move the camera depending on which keys are pressed. The velocity is increased due to acceleration, and the camera is moved in the direction it is facing due to its velocity. Then the mesh representing the vehicle is set to where the camera is, and some of the camera's velocity is taken away so it comes to a stop when the user is not accelerating.

```
// increase the vehicle's velocity due to acceleration
velocity += acceleration * (Key.isDown (Key.W) - Key.isDown (Key.S));
// move the vehicle camera due to its velocity
box_cam.move_forward (velocity);
// set the position of the vehicle mesh
vehicle_box.set_position_vector (box_cam.cam_position);
// take away some of the velocity so the camera comes to a stop
velocity -= velocity * 0.1;
```

The final calculation to make before the environments can be transformed and rendered is to make the camera in the left environment look at the vehicle. Once that is done all matrix or camera transformations are applied to each of the meshes, and then the meshes are rendered.

```
// make the camera look at the vehicle
static_cam.look_at_vector (box_cam.cam_position);
// prepare the meshes for the camera
// transformation
middle_piece1.transform_vertices ();
vehicle_box.transform_vertices (box_rotation);
middle_piece2.transform_vertices ();
// transform the meshes depending on the
// cameras' positions and orientations
middle_piece1.camera_transformation
➥(static_cam, perspective_depth);
vehicle_box.camera_transformation
➥(static_cam, perspective_depth);
middle_piece2.camera_transformation
➥(box_cam, perspective_depth);
// render the meshes
middle_piece1.render (0.0, 0.0, perspective_depth);
vehicle_box.render (0.0, 0.0, perspective_depth);
middle_piece2.render (0.0, 0.0, perspective_depth);
}
```

Conclusion

Flash MX's enhanced object-oriented programming language and native drawing methods make 3D effects quite an easy feat to accomplish. By building an object-oriented library of code to use universally in any file you can create very complex 3D environments in very few lines; not a single file made in this chapter was over 200 lines. The drawing API allows you to create solid 3D objects without a single graphic in the library. What more does Flash have to offer in the field of 3D? This is when Flash developers become as inventive and creative as the greatest mathematicians of all time. For over two thousand years, during the reign of Euclidean geometry, no branch of mathematics could rationalize the riddle: How can a person walk one mile south, turn and walk one mile east, turn and walk one mile north and end up in the same place he or she started? The advocates of non-Euclidean geometry could conclude that since we live on a spherical planet, the person started at the North Pole.

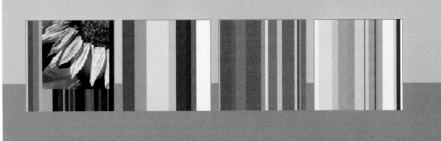

visual experiments with
dynamic content
danny franzreb

I would really love to tell you that when friends of ED asked me to contribute a chapter on my favourite new Flash MX feature and on how MX inspires me to break new grounds, everything came to my mind like *"BAM here it is"*. But in fact that wasn't the case for several reasons. First of all, Flash MX has lots of new features which I like to use and to explore on a daily basis; the tool has really grown up and become a powerful development environment. Second, my design process naturally works the other way around. Normally I don't look at the new features of a tool and start thinking about what I could do to design something that corresponds to these new features. Don't get me wrong, I love to play around with new programs and gadgets pushing them to their absolute limit, that's one of my preferred past time activities and Flash has been a major part of my life as developer for several years now. But I like to draw my inspiration from my environment; things I observe, people I meet, my family, friends or a wonderful piece of music that leaps through my ear the whole day.

From my point of view Flash MX is a big step forward regarding workflow, Macromedia's MX strategy enables us to focus on designing great applications instead of spending a huge part of our time on debugging and searching for workarounds. For me this new version of Flash means a more natural way of designing and added scripting control for nearly everything you can imagine you might want to control in Flash. Now you can think of a project and design it right away, that is what I call enhanced or dynamic creativity.

Ideas and inspirations

So what is my favorite Flash MX feature? To answer that question and to make you understand why I chose to do this specific experiment, I would like to talk about some projects that influenced me and I bet some of you too, over the years.

I remember buying my first book online and wondering how these guys where able to verify my father's credit card; later I became fascinated by just how they could tell me which books I'd previously bought. That got me into server-side scripting and databases a little bit. But since I am, as you are probably too, more attracted by visuals I'll try to come up with some other examples.

I also remember bumping around the web and checking some of my preferred locations including yugop.com. At that time Yugo Nakamura started those fingertrack-studies, which you can still check out on his web site. These experiments were able to record the movement of your cursor. On its own it isn't that exciting at all, everyone has seen millions of Flash-mousetrailers, but those studies where different. Not only because Yugo's unique style differs him from the average, but his extensive use of technology supports his design in a manner that makes you rub your eyes. Being able to communicate with the server utilizing a server-side scripting language and a database enabled him to save that data and to put it out on the screen again together with more fingertracks collected from that database. Varying these studies and letting you interact with other users in that way made them a truly exciting experience.

There are many other examples like that, where the communication between Flash and applications running on the server is used to generate some astonishing artwork. For instance the Carnivore project, a software application which listens to all internet traffic on a specific local network, was used by Praystation and some other web sites to create front-ends, which interpreted that data into compositions in visuals and sound.

So now, I guess you can imagine a little bit better why I am so excited about the extended ability of Flash MX to communicate with server-side applications. This is an essential part of the MX strategy. If Macromedia is right, we'll use the web in a slightly different way in the near future. Rather than browsing, we'll have "rich" applications running inside our browsers, some of which are already emerging on the web. Macromedia for instance did a nice little application for a hotel-chain to illustrate what they mean by "rich" – they rebuilt their booking service MX-Style. Before you needed to click through various HTML pages to book a room, that wasn't the best user experience and took you lots of time. Afterwards you could do the whole room booking much faster using one page within a Flash front-end. The front-end automatically loaded in pictures of the room you selected, updated the room-prices according to your selected features and guided you through the reservation process. That not only boosted the hotel's online reservations, but also made me want to book a room right away, forgetting that I didn't even know where the hotel is located.

Sounds good? For me it sounds like a brilliant way of adding value to a web site. But being the guy I am, I only add value to a web site in daytime. During the night another darker side of myself shows up, the "I-just-want-to-have-fun-with-stuff-that-isn't-useful-at-all-and-I-don't-even-care" side of my character. Isn't that the real reason why most of us started to develop with Flash, because it was more fun and because Flash has such a great creative community that motivates us all to push the limits further from day to day? Let's ignore that Flash is able to enhance the user experience on a web site, let's ignore that you can create great usable interface with Flash MX, let's even ignore the fact that Flash is one of the most widely spread plug-ins on the Internet. I would like to look at the communication between Flash and other applications as extending your creative skill set. Giving you another powerful ability to express yourself and if you like to, you can also use that ability to develop some great Jacob-friendly applications, proving that Flash isn't 99% bad at all. If not, don't get curious, I heard that bad boys always attract beautiful girls.

© http://rhizome.org/carnivore/

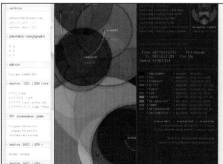

© www.praystation.com

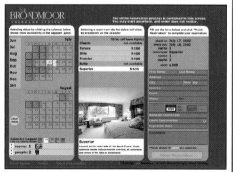

© http://reservations.broadmoor.com/

Perspectives

After talking you through all my initial thoughts and impressions. I would like to give you a little outline of what I plan to do within this chapter. I am going to introduce you to a new object in Flash called `loadVars` and I would also like to work with the `XML` object. Some of you might already know of the latter from Flash 5 but in MX it got a much better implementation. Both objects can be used to send and load data from external sources. I chose `loadVars` and `XML` for the experiment we're going to create, instead of some other cool new back-end features like Flash-remoting and server-side ActionScript, because a lot of you won't have the choice. Some will use PHP, some ASP, JSP, ColdFusion or even something completely different. So sometimes you will have to be very flexible in the way you load in data from an external source. That is where `loadVars` and `XML` jump in.

We are going to do an application that is able to load a JPG picture into the Flash movie and at the same time will load in some more information about that picture, outputting that information in another aspect. I was always fascinated by individuals that took a particular piece of art, for example a piece of music, and were able to transform that already existing artwork to something completely different. Things that are not even interesting at all in the beginning can be extremely exciting if you take a moment and try to look at them from a different perspective. So I want to break apart the picture we are loading in a little; since Flash can't do that our movie will ask another backend-application to run through that picture and to take a look at every single pixel of that picture. That application will count all the different colors of our pixel-image and tell us through variables or XML how often each color occurs in our particular image. After that we will use the information we gathered to do a simple interpretation using the new drawing methods of the `movieClip` object. But our main focus will be how we get the data into our movie and prepare it for processing by our drawing engine. Therefore we need to have a look at that back-end application at first.

ColorCounter

The application I was talking about is called **ColorCounter**; we developed it exclusively for this chapter of the book. It is a program that runs under Windows, but we also did an online version based on ASP.NET for those who are working behind a Mac or don't want to install our software. Let me talk about the PC version first. You'll be able to download it from the book site or my web site (www.franzreb.com); there you will also find a link to the online version. Both can be used as long and as extensively as you want, there are no restrictions regarding the license. Before you use the software on your system I would like you to know that this is a very experimental piece of software and that you are using it on you own risk. Not that we didn't test it, we did and it worked well on every system we tried it on, but you never know. Just in case that it isn't going to work or will crush your system, make sure that you have done a back-up of all your data. We've added a README file to the download to be able to update the software, so please read that file to get to know if we did any major changes to the application. Installation is pretty easy, just download the file and execute it. Note that the .NET Framework has to be installed on your machine, please refer to the README file for further information and instructions.

For the movie we'll build in this chapter, you don't actually need ColorCounter, all files including the text, XML, JPG and GIF Files are downloadable from www.friendsofED.com. ColorCounter is just a goodie to enhance your creative possibilities in case you want to create your own files after reading this chapter.

Refer to `read_me.html` and `ColorCounter.exe`

If you open ColorCounter, three different buttons will be presented to you. The first, Open Picture, is used to browse your local hard drive and to select the image you would like to process. Currently ColorCounter supports GIF, JPG, PNG, BMP and WMF. Although the program is able to process image formats with more than 256 colors I wouldn't recommend that. First, we don't need that many color values for the FLA we're going to create and second, doing all the necessary calculations for these color-values will take lots of processing power. My recommendation would be to use GIF graphics with 32 to 128 colors to generate satisfying results.

Open Picture	Generate XML	Generate Vars

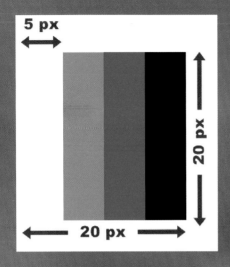
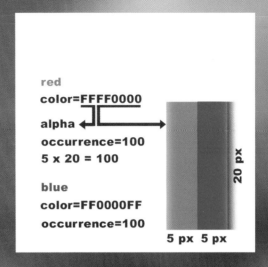

After you have chosen a graphic from your hard drive you can output and save the different color-values as variables in a text-file or as XML. We will write two appropriate SWFs to read in those files in some seconds.

Let's do a little example, to understand how ColorCounter processes an image. I've got a GIF graphic which is 20 pixels wide and 20 pixels high. The first color of that file is white, in a hex value that would be FFFFFF. That white area inside our GIF is 5 pixels wide and 20 pixels high. After that I've got a red area (FF0000), blue area (0000FF) and a black area (000000), all 5 pixels wide and 20 pixels high.

Since ColorCounter runs through that file from the upper-left to the lower-right, ColorCounter will at first find the white area and count that FFFFFF occurred 100 times (5 *20) in that image. Then 100 times red, blue and black.

The output for the Vars text file would look like this:

```
&color0=FFFFFFFF&occurrence0=100&color1=FFFF0000&occurrence1=100&color2=FF0000FF&occur-
rence2=100&color3=FF000000&occurrence3=100&values=4
```

The first two F characters in each color value represent the transparency of that particular color. In our case FF means that the color has no transparency. The last variable values tells us how many different color values have been found in the graphic.

The XML-output looks pretty similar:

```
<?xml
version="1.0"?><colortable><color><value>FFFFFFFF</value><occurrence>100</occurrence></color><col
or><value>FFFF0000</value><occurrence>100</occurrence></color><color><value>FF0000FF</value><occu
rrence>100</occurrence></color><color><value>FF000000</value><occurrence>100</occurrence></color>
</colortable>
```

If you haven't worked with XML yet, don't worry. I'll do a short introduction to XML later in the chapter.

The online version of ColorCounter works very similarly, like I said it is an application based on the .NET Framework that runs on our TAOBOT-Server and is accessible through my web site www.franzreb.com. The only reason we've limited the maximum colors and size of an image file you can process is so our web server won't be fully crippled calculating the color-values of a 16-million color image.

Refer to the **gifImages** folder within the downloads for this chapter, and you'll see the lovely pictures of flowers that we're about to use.

Now, if you would like to generate the variables and the XML data we are going to use for yourself, you need to open the files `flower1.gif` to `flower5.gif` one after the other in ColorCounter. Generate a `Vars` file and save it as `flower1.txt`, save the XML file as `flower1.xml`, and so on. Please make sure that all your files for the project are located within the same folder on your local hard drive.

LoadVars object

Before Flash MX we had to use `getURL`, `loadVariables` or `loadVariablesNum` to transfer data between a server-side script – such as ASP, ColdFusion, Perl, PHP, JSP or even a text file – and a Flash movie. These methods weren't really straightforward ways to do that – you had to use loops and a variable to determine if all the data had been loaded in correctly. With the introduction of the `loadVars` object in Flash MX, communicating with a server-side script has become much easier and it also is another step towards object-orientated programming.

Hopefully you won't mind, but I won't list all the methods and properties of the `loadVars` object, basically because you can read about them in the ActionScript documentation if it takes your fancy. I'd rather start right away with our application. Time to get stuck in, so make sure you have the source files for the chapter handy, and let's get started...

Building basics

Open up `dynamicFlowersVars00.fla`, you will see three layers. One is used for the ActionScript, one for the buttons and one for the background. Within the background layer you find the drawBackground movie clip which we are going to use as a reference to draw our data. The buttons layer is set up with five buttons in it, named from `flower1` to `flower5`. Technically we could have used an empty timeline and created our layout directly with ActionScript in Flash MX. But having at least some visual reference on the screen is a more pleasant working experience for me.

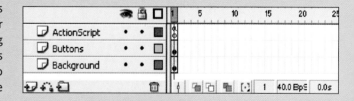

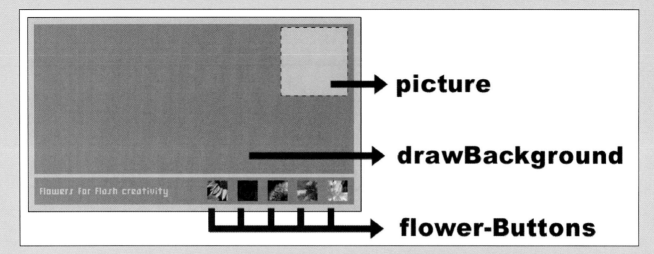

picture

drawBackground

flower-Buttons

From now on throughout the chapter, every single line of ActionScript will be written into frame one of the ActionScript layer.

At the beginning we'll set the rendering quality of our Flash file to LOW so graphics are not anti-aliased and bitmaps are not smoothed; this will provide us with additional processing power for future calculations. In terms of the visual output we won't recognize any major difference because our graphics are placed on full pixels, so they wouldn't be anti-aliased at all. If a graphic is placed between two full pixels, Flash doesn't know to which of the two pixels the edge of that graphic belongs to. Therefore the movie isn't able to draw the graphic clearly to the screen and anti-aliases it in high-quality; this is the default rendering quality for a Flash movie.

```
this._quality ="LOW";
```

Now we initialize a new loadVars object called myVars, which will act as our connection to the outside world.

```
myVars = new loadVars();
```

After the loadVars object has finished loading some external data, it needs to know how to process it. So we assign a function called processData to the onLoad event-handler of myVars, this event is fired when the external data has been loaded in completely. We will have a detailed look at the processData function later.

```
myVars.onLoad = processData;
```

We need to create three arrays; two are used to store our external data and one for some calculations regarding the visualization of that data. As we already know, ColorCounter gives us information about the colors of an image and the occurrences of each color. We store that info in the colorValues and colorOccurrences arrays. Our drawing engine will do a pretty simple visualization of these values. We want to draw rectangles on the drawBackground movie clip, each one as high as drawBackground and with the width that a particular color-occurrence shares compared to all color-occurrences of the image – a representative percentage based on the amount of each in the image. So we have to determine the horizontal starting point of each rectangle, which we will store in the startingPoints array.

```
colorValues = new Array();

colorOccurrences = new Array();

startingPoints = new Array ();
```

The rectangles will be drawn one after another from left to right and I want to play a short sound when a new color is processed. Therefore we initialize a new sound object mySound and attach to it a sound from the library also exported as mySound.

```
mySound = new Sound();

mySound.attachSound("mySound");
```

227

A new, empty movie clip called draw will do the drawing of the color-data. We'll set the _x and _y properties of draw to the corresponding values of the drawBackground movie clip, so it will start to draw in the upper left corner of drawBackground. Note that drawBackground's registration point is also located at its upper left corner.

```
this.createEmptyMovieClip("draw",1);

draw._x = drawBackground._x;
draw._y = drawBackground._y;
```

I would also like to present an original image of the data we will draw. For that purpose we create another empty movie clip, picture, at the upper right of our file and an empty movie clip inside picture called pictureHolder. We will use picture to do a preloader while the image is loading and pictureHolder as a container for the actual JPG image. Loading external JPGs into a movie clip is another new feature in Flash MX.

```
this.createEmptyMovieClip("picture",2);

picture._x=380;
picture._y=15;

picture.createEmptyMovieClip("pictureHolder",1);
```

We've got five button objects on stage named flower1 to flower5 and we're able to assign an onRelease event-handler to each button using a for loop, saving us some boring writing work. If one of the buttons is released, it should call a function and pass the button's name to it. That will enable us to access data in correspondence to that name.

```
for(i=1;i<=5;i++){
   this["flower"+i].onRelease = function(){

   drawData(this._name);
   }
}
```

Check your file at this point against dynamicFlowersVars01.fla.

Rectangles
Next up, we add some functions starting with drawRectangle:

```
drawRectangle = function(mc, xStart, xEnd, yStart, yEnd, theColor){
   mc.beginFill(theColor,100);
   mc.lineTo(xEnd,yStart);
   mc.lineTo(xEnd,yEnd);
   mc.lineTo(xStart,yEnd);
   mc.lineTo(xStart,yStart);
   mc.endFill();
}
```

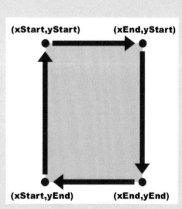

`drawRectangle` is used to draw the color rectangles on drawBackground. We pass some arguments to that function, where `mc` is the movie clip that is going to draw our rectangle using the new drawing methods in Flash MX and `theColor` represents the color-value of the rectangle we are drawing. I think `xStart`, `xEnd`, `yStart` and `yEnd` are pretty self explanatory – the x and y start and end co-ordinates. Inside the function, we start by telling our `mc` the color that we like to use as fill color for our rectangle and its alpha value (100); we don't need a `lineStyle` here. Then we begin drawing the rectangle – since our movie clip is positioned at the upper left corner of the rectangle, the first line will be drawn from there to the upper right corner. We are going on clockwise till we end up again in the upper left corner to close our rectangle.

We've seen that the variables we are going to receive will have an alpha value in front of the color value represented by `FF`. For our basic experiment we don't need that value, Flash will accept something like `0x336699` as a fill color. To achieve that we need to slice that string starting with the third letter of the received color-value and add `0x` in front of it. Keep in mind that the first index of a string is 0 not 1.

```
function trimColor(theColor){
    return "0x"+theColor.slice(2);
}
```

Getting an image

If you refer to `dynamicFlowersVars02.fla` you should see an FLA very similar to that we've created. The next function is called when a button is released; take a look at it first:

```
function drawData(btn){

    delete draw.onEnterFrame;
    draw.clear();

    picture.pictureHolder.loadMovie(btn+".jpg");
    picture.onEnterFrame = function(){

        if(this.pictureHolder.getBytesLoaded()>0){

            this.onEnterFrame = function(){

                var alreadyLoaded = this.pictureHolder.getBytesLoaded();
                var toLoad = this.pictureHolder.getBytesTotal();

                if(alreadyLoaded<toLoad){

                    var loadPercentage = (alreadyLoaded/toLoad)*100;

                    drawRectangle(this, 0, loadPercentage, 0, 100, 0xFFFFFF);
                }else{
                    myVars.load(btn+".txt");
                    this.clear();
                    delete this.onEnterFrame;
                }
            }
        }
    }
}
```

The argument `btn` passed to this function, is the name of the button that called the function `onRelease`. At first we delete the `onEnterFrame`-handler of `draw` and remove all drawn vectors, in case the `drawMovieClip` has been employed before to draw another image.

```
delete draw.onEnterFrame;
draw.clear();
```

Now we use `btn` as a reference to dynamically load a larger JPG into pictureHolder.

```
picture.pictureHolder.loadMovie(btn+".jpg");
```

Next we're going to figure out if the JPG started loading and assign a preloader to the movie clip picture. You might wonder why we use the `onEnterFrame` handler instead of `onData` to check whether the JPG started loading. Naturally `onData` is executed when a movie clip starts to receive some data, so that would be perfect for us. But if you load a JPG into a movie clip, you overwrite the previously assigned event handlers. A function assigned to `onData` wouldn't be executed any more, so we need a little workaround. After we used `loadMovie` we assign an `onEnterFrame` event to picture, this will check if the bytes loaded by pictureHolder are greater than zero. If that turns to `true` we know that the JPG has started loading and we are able to assign the real preloader to the `onEnterFrame`-event. We need to determine if the JPG has already started to load because we get values of 0 and -1 for `getBytesLoaded()` and `getBytesTotal()`. This would cause our preloader to evaluate the `if` statement that checks whether `alreadyLoaded` is still less than `toLoad` as `false` during the first few runs and delete our preloader before any bytes of the JPG are actually loaded.

```
picture.onEnterFrame = function(){

    if(this.pictureHolder.getBytesLoaded()>0){

    this.onEnterFrame = function(){
            …
    }
  }
}
```

Our preloader starts by storing the bytes of the JPG that have already been loaded and the total size in bytes of that JPG, because we are going to need these values twice.

```
var alreadyLoaded =  this.pictureHolder.getBytesLoaded();
var toLoad = this.pictureHolder.getBytesTotal();
```

We test if we still need our preloader by comparing these two values. If we still need it, we are able to determine the loading percentage by dividing `alreadyLoaded` through `toLoad` and multiplying the result by 100. Since the area of the JPG image is 100 x 100 pixel, we can use the value of `loadPercentage` without further modification for the width of our preloader bar. The movie clip picture will draw a white (`0xFFFFFF`) preloader bar that commences at its registration point, and which is `loadPercentage` pixels wide and 100 pixels high.

```
var loadPercentage = (alreadyLoaded/toLoad)*100;

drawRectangle(this, 0, loadPercentage, 0, 100, 0xFFFFFF);
```

If the image has finished loading, we begin to load our external data. Therefore we again use `btn` as a reference to load the matching text file with color variables related to the released button. We also clean up the picture because we don't need the `onEnterFrame`-handler that managed our preloader any more.

```
else{
myVars.load(btn+".txt");
   this.clear();
   delete this.onEnterFrame;
}
```

Refer to `dynamicFlowersVars_03.fla` to see our version of the file thus far.

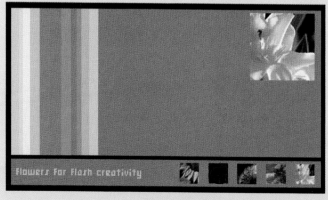

Processing data

The next event that is going to happen is the onLoad event of the myVars object. This will call the processData function that we previously assigned to it and pass an argument to it verifying whether loading was successful. processData is the core function, where all the parsing and drawing action takes place:

```
function processData(success){
  if(success){
    colorValues.splice(0,colorValues.length);
    colorOccurrences.splice(0,colorOccurrences.length);
    var allTogether = 0;
    for(var i=0;i<this.values;i++){
      colorValues[i]=trimColor(this["color"+i]);
      colorOccurrences[i]=Number(this["occurrence"+i]);
      allTogether+=colorOccurrences[i];
    }

    startingPoints.splice(0,startingPoints.length);
    for(var i=0;i<colorValues.length;i++){
      var point = (colorOccurrences[i]/allTogether)*drawBackground._width;
      startingPoints[i+1]=point+startingPoints[i];
    }

    actualPoint=0;
    count = 0;
    soundPlayed = false;

    draw.onEnterFrame = function(){
      if(count<colorValues.length){
        if(Math.ceil(actualPoint)<startingPoints[count+1]){
          actualPoint+=(startingPoints[count+1]-actualPoint)/2;
          drawRectangle(draw, startingPoints[count], actualPoint, 0,
drawBackground._height, colorValues[count]);

          if(soundPlayed == false){
            mySound.start(0,1);
            soundPlayed = true;
          }
        }else{

          drawRectangle(draw, startingPoints[count], startingPoints[count+1], 0,
          drawBackground._height, colorValues[count]);
          draw.moveTo(startingPoints[count+1],0);

        actualPoint=startingPoints[count+1];
        count++;
        soundPlayed = false;
        }
              }else{
                delete this.onEnterFrame;
```

```
                    }
                  }
               }else{
                  trace("Connection failed");
               }

      }
```

First we check the variable `success` - which is passed to `processData` as an argument, to verify that loading was successful.

```
  if(success){
  …
  }else{
  trace("Connection failed");
  }
```

Then we remove all previous values from the `colorValues` and `colorOccurrences` arrays. If all images we process have the same number of colors, for example 64, we wouldn't need to do this, because we could just overwrite previous values. But in case we are processing images with a different number of colors, we would get unexpected results processing a picture with less colors than the one before.

```
  colorValues.splice(0,colorValues.length);
  colorOccurrences.splice(0,colorOccurrences.length);
```

We will need a variable `allTogether` where we add up all color occurrences for feature calculations. If all works out correctly, this should be the same value as the image's width multiplied by its height, essentially because adding up all color occurrences would be the same as counting every single pixel of the image.

```
  var allTogether = 0;
```

Now, before we process the loaded variables, I would like to ask you to look at the sample text file again, to understand how variables are passed to Flash.

```
  &color0=FFFFFFFF&occurrence0=100&color1=FFFF0000&occurrence1=100&color2=FF0000
➡FF&occurrence2=100&color3=FF000000&occurrence3=100&values=4
```

With the `loadVars` object in Flash MX, variables loaded from a server-side script or in our case a text file, must always be sent as a string of `variable=value` pairs separated by ampersands. After the variables are received by the `loadVars` object, you can access them as a property of this object. In our example, if `myVars` is the `loadVars` object that receives the data and I want to know the value of the variable `color1`, I could access it by `myVars.color1`. Here the returned value would be `FFFF0000`.

Back to `processData`; remember that the function is executed directly after all external variables have been loaded and that we have already tested if loading was successful. So at this point we know that we are able to use the variable `values` indicating the number of colors we found in the image. We run a loop according to that number to store all variables in the corresponding arrays. Inside that loop we access the variables by the use of `this.["variable name"]`, we use the `trimColor` function to do small modifications to the single color values like I mentioned earlier in the chapter. The `occurrence` variables are passed to Flash as strings, so we use `Number` to do a typecast. `AllTogether` holds the added color occurrences.

```
for(var i=0;i<this.values;i++){
colorValues[i]=trimColor(this["color"+i]);
    colorOccurrences[i]=Number(this["occurrence"+i]);
    allTogether+=colorOccurrences[i];
}
```

Calculating the width of a rectangle for a single color value is pretty much the same as calculating the load percentage for a preloader bar. We know the occurrence of that single color; dividing that through the overall occurrences and multiplying the result by the width of `drawBackground` will return us the share it has in the width of `drawBackground`. Now we only need to add that to the previous starting point to get the current one.

```
for(var i=0;i<colorValues.length;i++){
    var point = (colorOccurrences[i]/allTogether)*drawBackground._width;
    startingPoints[i+1]=point+startingPoints[i];
}
```

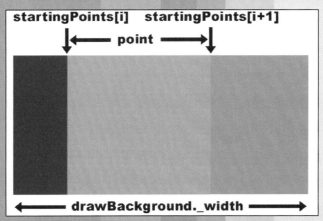

Although `startingPoints[0]` is undefined and we should have defined it manually as 0 before the loop, we don't need to do this. Flash, unlike languages such as Java, interprets that value automatically as 0 for us. Also note that we have one more value in the `startingPoints` array than the amount of color values received. The last value of `startingPoints` will actually act as our end point and should be always equal to `drawBackground._width`.

`actualPoint` keeps track of the current horizontal position of our drawn rectangle. Then we need a variable to determine which color-value of the array we are drawing, `count` will do that for us. Since we also want to play a sound when we start to draw a new color, we need to know if the sound for that color has been played yet.

```
actualPoint=0;
count = 0;
soundPlayed = false;
```

Now we are able to start our drawing engine by assigning an `onEnterFrame`-event to the draw movie clip. First we verify that there are still some color values in our `colorValues` array that we didn't draw on drawBackground yet, otherwise we wouldn't need `onEnterFrame` any more and could delete it. Afterwards we round up `actualPoint` to the next full pixel and check if that value is still smaller than the starting point of the next rectangle we would like to draw. If that is the case, we increase `actualPoint` by half the difference between itself and the next starting point. Then we draw a rectangle from the starting point of that color to `actualPoint`, with the height of drawBackground and the currently active color value. We will also play a sound if it was the first loop for that color value. In case that `Math.ceil(actualPoint)` isn't smaller than the next starting point, we know that the full area of the colors corresponding rectangle has nearly been drawn. So we draw a rectangle matching the full, calculated area of the active color's occurrence. The horizontal range between its own starting-point and the next starting-point represents that. Since we have drawn the full rectangle for our current color now, we can move our "drawing pencil" to the starting point of the next color value, increase count by one and set `soundPlayed` to `false` again. This will loop until we have drawn all colors to the stage and stop afterwards by deleting its own `onEnterFrame`-handler.

```
draw.onEnterFrame = function(){

    if(count<colorValues.length){
    if(Math.ceil(actualPoint)<startingPoints[count+1]){

        actualPoint+=(startingPoints[count+1]-actualPoint)/2;
        drawRectangle(draw, startingPoints[count], actualPoint, 0,
        ➥ drawBackground._height, colorValues[count]);

        if(soundPlayed == false){
            mySound.start(0,1);
            soundPlayed = true;
        }
    }else{

        drawRectangle(draw, startingPoints[count], startingPoints[count+1], 0,
        ➥ drawBackground._height, colorValues[count]);

        draw.moveTo(startingPoints[count+1],0);
        actualPoint=startingPoints[count+1];
        count++;
        soundPlayed = false;
    }
    }else{
        delete this.onEnterFrame;
    }
}
```

Export the Flash movie and take a look at what we have created (it should function identically to dynamicFlowersVars_final.fla). I find it interesting how the image has been transformed to something completely different. We have now managed the `loadVars` object, so lets move on to XML.

Drawing conclusions from XML

The file that we'll create within this section is in the source files as `dynamicFlowersXML.fla`. You can either take a look at this now or check at the end that your file is the same. As I've already mentioned, I will do a short introduction to XML first before we use the built in `XML` object of Flash MX, which is actually up to 20 times faster than it was in Flash 5 because now it is written in C++ instead of ActionScript. Since whole books are written on the topic of basic XML, this introduction will be far away from being a complete reference. But we need some knowledge of XML to be able to access its data from within a Flash movie.

XML means **eXtensible Markup Language**, and it is used to describe and structure data. One of the ideas behind XML is to separate the data from its visual presentation. Flash for example and a screen-reader could both access the same XML document and output it in two wholly different ways. A very basic XML application, to store some info related to my chapter of the book, could look like this:

```
<creativityinFlashDesign>
        <chapter number="5">
                <name>Back-end weirdness</name>
                <author>Danny Franzreb</author>
        </chapter>
</creativityInFlashDesign>
```

Like in HTML, XML elements like `<creativityInFlashDesign>` have angled brackets around their names. Unlike HTML, you can name these elements whatever you want, they never overlap, are case sensitive and every element must be closed. Elements can have attributes that describe that particular element further, values of attributes are surrounded by quotation marks. All that stuff together is organized as an XML-tree structure, where everything is represented as a node. If `<creativityInFlashDesign>` is the first element in our node-tree, `<chapter>` would be a child node of `<creativityInFlashDesign>` and `<name>` would be a child node of `<chapter>`. `<author>` would be a sibling to `<chapter>` because they are on the same level of the tree. That concept is very similar to the movie clip structure of Flash.

The XML-output generated by ColorCounter will look like this:

```
<?xml version="1.0"?>

<colortable>
 <color>
   <value>FFFFFFFF</value>
   <occurrence>100</occurrence>
 </color>
 <color>
   <value>FFFF0000</value>
   <occurrence>100</occurrence>
 </color>
 ...
 ...
 ...
</colortable>
```

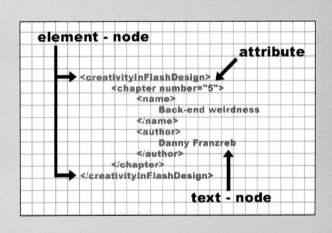

Although it is not a must, every XML file should start with its declaration **<?xml version="1.0"?>**. Then you've got one and only one node on the first level, here <colortable>. After that we structured our data into color nodes which contain <value> and <occurrence> nodes. These nodes contain our actual information about the image.

You might wonder why ColorCounter outputs the nodes all glued together. This is because the Flash parser interprets all characters that appear blank within an XML file, for example a carriage return, as a node. If you don't want to get confused by that you have two choices – you can set the ignoreWhite property of the XML object in Flash to true or you can output XML that has no white space. Ignoring white space would mean extra parsing time, so we choose to generate XML files without white space. If you open such a file in Internet Explorer, you can see that Explorer is able to identify it as XML and automatically adds some structure to it.

Now let's have a look at the changes we need to apply to our dynamicFlowersVars_final.fla to enable it to read in XML data instead of plain variables. Since the two objects act very similalyr, we don't need to change as much as you might think. First we create a new XML object instead of loadVars then we assign the same processData function to the onLoad event of our XML object.

```
myXML = new XML();
myXML.onLoad = processData;
```

We also need to change one line within the drawData function. Substitute myVars.load(btn+".txt") with:

```
myXML.load(btn+".xml");
```

```
<?xml version="1.0" ?>
- <colortable>
  - <color>
      <value>FFCB6F18</value>
      <occurrence>300</occurrence>
    </color>
  - <color>
      <value>FFB06C1D</value>
      <occurrence>133</occurrence>
    </color>
  - <color>
      <value>FFBC6D1C</value>
      <occurrence>210</occurrence>
    </color>
  - <color>
      <value>FFAC631F</value>
      <occurrence>300</occurrence>
    </color>
  - <color>
      <value>FFE3990C</value>
      <occurrence>237</occurrence>
    </color>
  - <color>
      <value>FFFED606</value>
      <occurrence>440</occurrence>
    </color>
  - <color>
      <value>FFF5BC04</value>
      <occurrence>139</occurrence>
    </color>
  - <color>
      <value>FFA1591F</value>
      <occurrence>208</occurrence>
    </color>
```

XML in Internet Explorer

237

Nearly everything else stays exactly the same, we just need to rewrite our first loop inside processData a little. We know that the first child node of our XML is colorTable, so we start from there and loop through all child nodes of colorTable. Each child of colorTable is always a <color> element, its first child node is a <value> element, the variable currentNode will store a reference to that element for us. When currentNode is a <value> element, the first child will be a text node. To access its value, we use the nodeValue property of the XML object. currentNode still holds a reference to a <value> element to get to the <occurrence> element on the same level; we use nextSibling and add firstChild.nodeValue to access the <occurrence> element's value. That's all, we changed an application that was able to process variables within a few lines of code to an application that is able to process XML data.

```
colorTable = this.firstChild;

for(var i=0;i<colorTable.childNodes.length;i++){

    currentNode = colorTable.childNodes[i].firstChild;

    colorValues[i]=trimColor(currentNode.firstChild.nodeValue);

    colorOccurrences[i]=Number(currentNode.nextSibling.firstChild.nodeValue);

    allTogether+=colorOccurrences[i];
}
```

Maybe you are able to use ColorCounter combined with some other techniques of the book to build interesting variations of this file. Or you could write your own movies, an image-browser based on that code would be an interesting application. I created an example that utilizes some 3D functions together with the undocumented microphone feature of Flash MX. You are able to download a well-commented version of that file from my web site. Whether you choose the loadVars or XML object to communicate with external sources, is up to you. XML is definitely first choice for structured and very complex data — I prefer it anyway.

Now we've finished our experiment and gained some basic knowledge on communicating with external sources. I myself am not the kind of guy that loves sitting in front of pure code for hours; I'm much more attracted by the visual stimulation of great graphic design. But combining that with great coding is what creates really outstanding results. Learning languages like PHP or ColdFusion to communicate with the server and other applications is the natural progression for you and me as designers. Not because you are able to sell your skillset better to a client, but because you are able to enhance your creative potential and have much more fun.

video fx in Flash MX

jim armstrong

My path into Flash was different from most, as a 3D animator specializing in digital video, I became interested in Flash as a means to produce animated textures for 3D Studio MAX. Having a low-cost vector paint application that could export to QuickTime format enabled a wide range of visual effects in video that would have been difficult to create directly in 3DS MAX. The fact that Flash could be used to create animations for both web and broadcast-video delivery was very exciting, although my primary use of Flash was FX for video.

So why am I so excited about Flash MX? Could it be the new interface? The drawing API? Components? Those are all great features, but my primary excitement relates to my core business interest — digital video for the Web and CD. Let me give you some background, then I'll show you what I mean with some real examples.

In recent years, there has been a groundswell of client interest in online, interactive video. The combination of manageable file size and interactive control is the real creative challenge for online multimedia. The biggest drawback to Flash in this area has been embedding video for web and CD applications. In the past, integrating video in Flash was a cumbersome process, especially taking optimization into account. For many videos, it was necessary to resort to software such as Discreet's Cleaner and the Sorenson-2/3 codecs to obtain reasonable file sizes. Those QuickTime videos had to be displayed in a pop-up window. Yes, you could overlay a Flash track onto the video, but in the days of QuickTime 4, you could only overlay a Flash 3 track. Not exactly what my clients wanted for truly interactive video!

What was missing from my dream environment was the ability to incorporate compressed digital video directly into the Flash environment without having to resort to external applications. This would allow all the interactive features of Flash to be applied in one seamless presentation.

Finally! The dream is now reality. With Flash MX, we can directly integrate digital video into Flash movies with compression! No more pop-up windows and all the interactive features of MX ActionScript are at our disposal. Not only does Flash MX contain a true video codec, a new speech codec is provided that is optimized for voiceovers. Now we can seamlessly integrate sophisticated bitmap animations with vector animation and interactivity. True, nonlinear, interactive multimedia — with file sizes suitable for Web- and CD-based delivery. A browser plug-in with a history of new versions becoming very pervasive very fast. I think I can sum this situation up with three words ... yes, Yes, YES!

In this chapter, I will first talk about the process of dealing with video in 'the old days'. Through three examples, I hope to illustrate the transition to working with digital video in Flash MX. These examples also illustrate how I am applying this technology to current projects. Each example represents a project that I would have been unable to consider before the release of Flash MX. I hope these examples illustrate how far you can push digital video in Flash MX.

I should also mention that digital video is not a 'paint by the numbers' field. There is a certain 'art' to obtaining good results with compressed video. By deconstructing examples and discussing the thought process behind the example, I hope you obtain some useful production hints that reduce your learning curve. Flash MX provides efficient video compression and the ability to composite vector motion graphics with raster animation. The final animation can be exported to SWF, taking advantage of the best of both worlds! I hope that the examples in this chapter illustrate this point and change the way you think about motion graphics in Flash.

Simulated video in Flash 5

One of the best ways to look at video in Flash MX is to compare with video in previous versions of Flash. How did we deal with Flash video before MX? Although it was possible to import digital video in Flash 5, these movies could only be exported to another video format. QuickTime was the most common choice. For animated textures in 3DS MAX, I rarely obtained a workable video with the AVI format. In order to embed video in a Flash 5 presentation for SWF export, the video was 'simulated' as a linear sequence of bitmap images. Sound was imported, then composited with the image sequence in separate layers. The only control over video file size was JPG compression of the separate bitmap images on export.

Shortly before writing this chapter, I completed a Flash 5 presentation containing an embedded video (with sound). For those who may be new to working with video in both Flash 5 and MX, a brief deconstruction of the process follows. This will give you some idea of my past workflow to compare against the Flash MX process.

In this project, the client provided a captured video clip of 90 seconds duration at 320x240x30fps, with stereo sound. The client wanted this video clip incorporated into the end of a Flash quiz game. The idea was that after working through the quiz game, students could see a video on the subject of the game. This particular game dealt with the martial art of Capoeira (okay, you're interested now, try www.capoeiraarts.com for some information about the martial art). The clip was a narrated excerpt from a documentary titled *Bahia: Africa in the Americas*. In addition to illustrating the process difference between Flash MX and Flash 5 video, this clip is a really good codec test because of its length and the numerous fast changing martial arts sequences.

I was faced with a video file of 410MB. Needless to say, the source material needed to be reduced in both size and frame rate before importing into Flash. It's an easy step to reduce the frame rate from 30fps to 15fps, but 205MB of video is still way too large. Halving the window size in both dimensions only reduces file size by a factor of four, so it was necessary to reduce the length of the video clip that was to be incorporated into Flash.

The video was imported into Adobe Premiere and the client finally accepted a 'critical' section of 30 seconds of video to be included in the Flash movie. This target was well short of the original desire to incorporate almost all of the 90-second captured video clip. The audio and video for this segment were rendered to separate WAV and AVI files, with the video downsized to 128x96, 15fps. The AVI file was imported into Adobe After Effects for additional processing. The purpose of this processing was primarily for optimization, application of filters and manual blurring largely based on experience. In general, two or more passes through the entire process may be required to generate the best results. Three passes were required for this particular project. It was very time consuming.

A level of JPEG compression was chosen based on the type of action in the video segment. The final composition in After Effects was rendered to a JPEG sequence. This JPEG sequence was imported to Flash and into a graphic symbol.

The WAV file for the corresponding sound was imported into Flash. The sound file was placed on a layer just above the graphic symbol containing the simulated video sequence. Sound was set to Stream. On export, the audio was exported as mono, in MP3 format. Since the JPEG sequence was already optimally compressed out of After Effects, the JPEG Quality level on export from Flash 5 was set to 100. The final video played in Flash with little discernible loss in image quality. Since the sound was a voiceover with light background music, MP3 compression worked well for the audio. File size for the embedded video and audio was just under 1MB.

Regardless of approach, you can see that working with video in Flash 5 required *both* Flash 5 *and* at least one or two other tools, plus a lot of time, plus a lot of effort, plus a lot of experimentation. A rather large learning curve was necessary to eventually minimize the amount of experimentation for each project.

Now, let's see how this process compares to video in Flash MX.

Digital video in Flash MX

For this project, the video was embedded into a quiz game. The Flash game is part of an exhibit sponsored by the Texas Council for the Humanities. Children view and study an online exhibit. After working through the exhibit material, students play a quiz game. The game both reinforces exhibit concepts and tests understanding of the material. Based on experiments, we determined that approximately 750KB of video could be loaded in the background during game play on an average dialup connection during peak evening hours. With some additional preloading and taking advantage of progressive download, we decided to extend the limit to 1MB of video (including audio).

This size limit forced numerous compromises. The most serious compromise was reducing window size from 320x240 to 128x96. The second major compromise was reducing the video clip from 90 seconds to 30 seconds. The client did not care for the small window size, but it was better than no video at all. The final optimization effort produced a video (with high-quality audio for the narration) at a size of 989KB.

In reality, most students study these online exhibits during school hours on school equipment with broadband connections. Many students have access to home computers with broadband connections. Some students answer questions very fast, so given the minimum time to cycle through all questions, we estimated that somewhere between 2.0 and 2.5MB of video could be easily downloaded in the background on a average, high-speed connection. Actual experiments during high-traffic hours in the evening pegged the number at about 2.3MB.

When Flash MX was released, this video was my very first test of the software. Given a very conservative ceiling of 2.3MB, I wanted to determine the largest window size that allowed playback of the full 90-second clip. Video quality had to be as good as the hand-optimized, simulated sequence from Flash 5. I thought this would be a good test as the video is a very high-action clip.

The video was embedded into the main timeline of a new Flash document. Video import settings were fine-tuned on the basis of a few experiments. The final settings I decided upon are illustrated in diagram 1.

Since this is a high-motion clip, image content varies significantly from frame to frame. This is the reason for the high frequency (low interval) of keyframes.

The video was captured at 30fps, but played in a Flash movie at 15fps. The Synchronization option was used to reduce the effective video playback rate to 15fps. With the settings illustrated in diagram 1, Flash MX drops every other frame of video on import. You can always check the playback rate in the Output Properties section of the dialog window.

In case you're a bit new to video compression, let's stop and discuss the Keyframe Interval and Quality settings. Video codecs apply two types of compression, 'spatial' and 'temporal.' Spatial compression refers to compression within a single frame of video, most often performed with JPG compression. Higher Quality settings apply less compression and so larger file sizes result from the higher-quality images.

Temporal compression works by assigning a sequence of 'keyframes' during the video sequence. These keyframes form a 'reference' for the state of the video sequence at a certain point in time. Subsequent video frames are encoded based on the difference between the current frame and the keyframe. Only the image data that differs from the keyframe is stored. If you have a video with limited motion such as a talking head, substantial temporal compression can be applied with little loss in quality.

The Keyframe Interval setting is the number of frames between keyframes. The lower the Keyframe Interval, the greater the number of keyframes generated in the compressed video. For high-motion clips, there is little common image data between frames. In these cases, the best setting will be a low number. So, why is the number in this example 4 and not 3 or 5? This is an example of the 'art and experimentation' aspect of digital video compression. A Keyframe Interval of 4 seemed to provide the best trade-off between file size and quality at the current level of spatial compression. There will always be some level of experimentation to determine the 'best' compression settings.

It is tempting to think that a Keyframe Interval of 1 and a Quality setting of 100 would reproduce the original video in its uncompressed form, but you may notice slight compression artifacts even with quality settings at absolute maximum.

You may also be wondering what is that plug for 'expanded video capabilities' and Sorenson Spark Pro? We'll get to that later in the chapter.

Audio

You may have noticed that there are no compression controls for the audio. Flash MX uses the Global Audio Settings (from the Publish Settings dialog) to compress the audio track from the embedded video. You may adjust these settings to affect the quality of audio playback, as in Flash 5.

One of the cool new features of Flash MX is a speech audio codec. The speech codec is ideal for video presentations whose audio tracks are narration. Speech can be selected from the Sound Settings dialog. For those who have worked with audio in Flash, this is a familiar process with a new compression option. A sample rate of 11KHz is generally suited for audio tracks containing only speech. A rate of 22KHz may be needed for a combination of narration with background music. For this experiment, I used 11KHz.

Output

After importing the video, it was exported to SWF format. The Compress Movie option was not used, although it makes no difference in the file size. For a high-action clip, the quality was quite good. I was pleased that the window size could be pushed up to 192x144 from the previous size of 128x96. What really blew me away were the results from the new speech codec. The audio sounded almost as good as the original source clip. I created a new movie in which only the video was imported. When comparing file sizes, the audio was a relatively tiny percentage of the overall file size. Yet, it sounded better than what I thought was high-quality MP3 exported from Flash 5! Flash MX is forcing me to rethink my definitions of good quality in terms of compressed audio and video.

How long did it take? I'm glad you asked. I spent an entire afternoon working on the Flash 5 simulated video sequence. While I was really pleased with the results, I was working under a fixed-cost bid. Every hour I spent on the video reduced my effective hourly rate and served as an opportunity cost for other projects. Working on a 1.5GHz P4 system, with three passes to fine-tune compression options, creating the initial SWF containing only the video took less than ten minutes. With a preloader and progress bar, a self-contained demonstration movie was created, requiring 2.35MB of file size and about twenty minutes worth of effort. It is applications like this where the software pays for itself in one project!

The good news is that the decompressor in the Flash 6 player is very lightweight. What it means to you is that compressing a lot of video can take a lot of time – probably more time than you might expect. System resources are the limiting factor in terms of how much video can be compressed. The system on which I run Flash MX is a 1.5GHz P4, with 512MB RAM, 2x9GB Ultra-Wide SCSI drives, and an nVidia Quadro 2 Pro board. I have experienced no difficulty compressing several minutes worth of video, with file sizes exceeding 1GB. Of course, I always break for a cup of tea during this process.

Well, that should give you some idea of the workflow differences in dealing with Flash 5 and Flash MX video. Now let's look at what you really wanted to see – sexy effects. The next example is a sophisticated 3D animation.

As I am a CG animator, most of my video work is animations created in third-party software packages. Regardless of how you create your videos, the workflow and thinking process behind embedding them in Flash MX is the same.

This example illustrates some of the more advanced effects and animations that are now reasonable to consider with the video features of Flash MX. In these next two examples, we will look at how to combine raster animation with Flash's native vector animation. The strategic combination of vector animation with the new video features of Flash MX enables effects that would not have been possible or practical in the Flash 5 environment.

Video and visual effects in Flash MX

It's one thing to import and compress digital video in Flash MX for educational and instructional purposes. The next question is, "can we use Flash MX to add effects to videos?" The answer is yes. In fact, there are many instances where you would want to combine the vector animation capability of Flash with video sequences from camcorders or other programs to create an animation.

In this second example, I'll to expand on a 3DS MAX/Flash animation I created some time ago. The animation was originally created as a codec test. It contains a high degree of motion, subtle glows and gradients, lighting effects, video-in-video, and rapid text animations. This combination of elements provides a substantial challenge for video codecs.

In its original implementation, the animation was designed to mimic some of the motion graphics that might be seen in an opening animation for a network or cable news program. The original video was a six-second animation with no sound at 640x480x30fps. When Flash MX was released, I immediately wanted to see if I could add some additional FX to the animation, then produce a downsized result that would be suitable for a web-based intro.

So what do I mean by intro? Many of my clients are interested in using video to provide narrated introductions to products and services. It is reasonable for a web site to offer a link to animated content. When I talk about an 'intro', I am referring to an introduction or opening sequence to an online video, not the often-abused 'Flash intro' to a web site. I'm not proposing forcing your visitors to wait through several megabytes of video before they can view site content.

This animation is a hypothetical introduction to a hypothetical news program, titled 'Around the World in 60 Seconds.'

Not seen on the screen shot are some additional motion graphics at the beginning of the video and a group of animated arrows that move horizontally across the screen. One group of arrows moves across the top of the screen while the other group moves across the bottom.

The background animation with the binary digits was created in Flash, then rendered to QuickTime format. This QuickTime video was imported into 3DS MAX and used as an animated background. The globe animation was rendered on top of the background video. The animation that streams around the rings is a combination of video clips and Flash-generated animation.

This is an interesting process that may be of interest to those who also use 3D software in conjunction with Flash. The Flash animations are brought into 3DS MAX as black-and-white QuickTime movies. This animated texture is used as an opacity map. A Mix material is created from the same video to mix in some color. The complete animated texture with coloring and opacity map is mapped to the ring geometry. The rendered MAX animation (QuickTime video) is imported into Flash. The vector arrow and text animations are composited on top of the video. The final animation is rendered to QuickTime from Flash. That's sort of a one-paragraph description of how I use 3DS MAX and Flash to create visual FX for video. If you are interested in a more detailed tutorial, I covered this process in an article for the 3D Café VIP Lounge (www.3dcafe.com/asp/platinumdefault.asp).

As produced, the uncompressed file size for the video is 158MB. For an online animation, the frame rate could be dropped to 15fps. The window size could also be reduced to 320x240. These changes would still leave a video of just under 20MB in size (uncompressed). Given the difficulty this animation presents in terms of compression, starting from a 20MB base with the goal of *adding* even more motion graphics *and* producing a web-based (broadband) version is quite challenging. I prefer to think of it as fun!

The original animation was constructed as a composite of animations created both in 3DS MAX and Flash. When working with video in the Flash environment, it is helpful to divide the project into individual animations that are best accomplished in either raster or vector mode. A perfect example is text animation. Text in video often compresses poorly because of Gibbs effects. Gibbs effects are compression artifacts most often evident by jagged lines around areas of high contrast. Gibbs effects tend to occur around outlines, due to incorrectly-colored pixels. Experienced videophiles often refer to this effect as 'mosquito noise.' Now you have a new phrase to impress friends and family at parties!

Vector text in Flash MX, layered on top of video, will render to SWF without those compression effects. So, the approach to creating this animation in Flash MX is to limit raster animation to sequences that are best accomplished in a video format. Remaining animation will be composited on top of the video in Flash's native vector format.

Remember the topic of temporal compression from the previous example? Best results are obtained from temporal compression when there is minimal motion in the video. Smooth, gradual transitions in motion sequences are preferred. Abrupt changes in the video require more keyframes to produce a quality result. From a production standpoint, you can often obtain better results from compression by arranging smooth, gradual transitions in effects (cross-fades for video editors).

A good production hint for obtaining better results from spatial compression is to avoid large areas of high color contrast. This will reduce those nasty Gibbs effects. In some cases, you can 'hide' compression artifacts against a darker background.

I wanted to start with a white background, masking part of the opening frame. Then, I wanted the video background to gradually change from white to a darker color, but not the bright blue from the previous example. In Flash, the background color is controlled by a rectangle in the lowest layer. This background symbol was altered to tween from white at frame 1 to #003366 at frame 30.

The new Flash movie was exported to QuickTime, then imported into 3DS MAX. The globe animation was rendered onto the video. Many other 3D software packages provide the capability to use a video as the rendering background, so this process is not exclusive to 3DS MAX.

The binary digit animation is no longer present. This is the new video asset that will be imported into Flash MX.

For fun, suppose this animation is for the local news program. Suppose the station's logo is the number 5 with two rings around the number. I wanted to use an animated version of this logo to open the Flash animation. The logo animation masks a static frame at the beginning of the video. Another instance of the animation logo overlays the mask layer, but with opacity set to a very low value. Then, the logo animation cuts away, leading into the opening of the video. The final frame of the logo animation is converted to a symbol in Flash, then layered on top of the video animation. That sounds like an interesting opening for the animation.

To create a lightweight vector logo animation, the logo and rings were modeled and animated with 3DS MAX, then rendered to SWF format. This can be accomplished with any of the vector renderers currently on the market. It's an easy animation to accomplish with standalone packages such as Swift 3D (www.erain.com) and Plasma (www.discreet.com). The final frame of the logo animation is illustrated here:

Although the video plays at 30fps, the Flash movie will run at 15fps. The logo animation was designed to play over 18 frames. I thought 320x240 was a bit small for the window size. I really wanted to be aggressive with this test, just to see how far I could push MX and the Flash 6 player. 480x360x15fps seemed like a good starting point.

Since the embedded video will dwarf the vector animation in terms of file size, the next step in the animation is importing and compressing the video.

The problem with a 480x360 window at 15fps is that the uncompressed video would be about 45MB. Since crisp vector graphics are to overlay the video, it is necessary to obtain a very high-quality result from the compression. I still wanted something that could at least play over a broadband connection with only a modest preloader. Starting from a base of 45MB with a video that simply would not compress well in the first place made for an interesting challenge. Like I said before … it's a fun challenge.

The first step was to go through the same compression process as the previous example. I was able to achieve a reasonably good result at a file size of 1.7MB. This result was obtained from a Quality setting of 90 and a Keyframe Interval of 3. That's not bad at all considering the nature of the motion graphics in the video. As before, some experimentation was involved to arrive at the final settings.

Squeeze me

This is probably a good point to demonstrate what can be accomplished with the Sorenson Spark Pro codec that is available for Flash MX through Sorenson Media. The standard version of the Spark codec ships with Flash MX. The professional version is an add-on that is purchased as part of the Sorenson Squeeze product for Flash MX. Squeeze contains the Professional version of the Spark codec as well as numerous additional options to fine-tune compression, such as two-pass variable bitrate (2xVBR) encoding.

Videos compressed with Squeeze can be exported in Flash MX's native video format (FLV), then directly imported into an MX document. For this particular project, Squeeze was very helpful as I was able to take advantage of the added video filters to fine-tune brightness and contrast. With some experimentation, I was able to obtain a result that was equivalent quality to the standard Spark result, but at a file size of 1.1MB. It took about ten minutes of work to reduce the file size by 600K, with no reduction in quality. For more information on Squeeze, visit www.sorenson.com/sparkpro.html.

With good results from the video, it's time to work on the animated logo. The static frame that will be masked by the vector animation is illustrated here. The frame was imported into a graphic symbol in Flash. You may notice that the globe appears 'brighter' than other screen shots.

It is beyond the scope of this book to discuss, but the 3DS MAX materials are designed to 'react' to the background environment. The brighter the background, the more the globe appears to glow. This is one of the reasons for starting with a white background in the Flash animation.

The vector logo animation was imported to a separate graphic symbol.

The static frame from the video and two instances of the logo animation were placed on the timeline as illustrated in diagram 6. One instance of the logo animation masks the static bitmap image. The second logo instance is scaled up five percent with opacity adjusted to 20%.

When the animation is played, it appears as if the logo is a 3D textured animation with a ghost. After 18 frames, this animation hard cuts into the video. Although a hard cut sounds 'bad' from a compression standpoint, the animation will cut into a white background that gradually progresses to the darker color.

The white background provides nice contrast, but looks a little plain for a high-tech opening. The next step is to spruce up the background a bit.

Diagram 7 illustrates the animated logo overlaid on a static background. The video is also overlaid on this same background. The video symbol was set to 65% opacity. This tends to hide some of the compression artifacts and gives the video that 'softer' look often seen on television. Adjusting brightness/contrast and opacity are a couple tricks you can employ to hide some of the compression artifacts when working with large or difficult-to-compress videos.

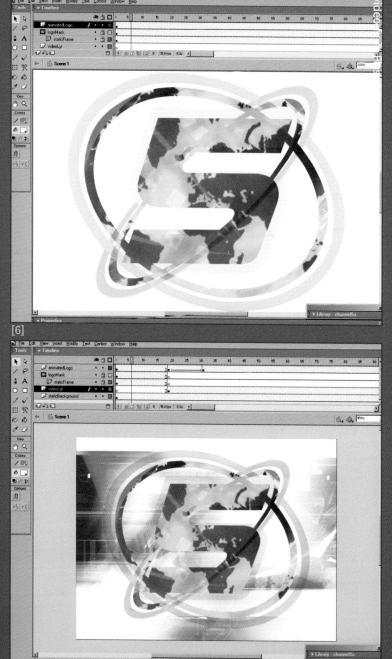

[6]

[7]

The background was a stock image from Eyewire (www.eyewire.com). You can also create customized images of this nature in Photoshop.

Here's a single frame of the video with adjusted opacity, overlaid on top of the background. This screen shot is close to the end of the tween from white to the darker background. Notice how the globe does not appear to 'glow' as much as in previous screen shots.

After looking at the logo overlaid on the video, it was clear that the logo distracted too much from the animation. The distraction will only be amplified once additional motion graphics and text animation are added.

It is probably better to have the logo present in a title layer, above the primary animation. I always like to illustrate the thinking process during a project. That is often more instructive than a 'point-by-point' tutorial. Part of the process is eliminating elements that don't fit well into the animation.

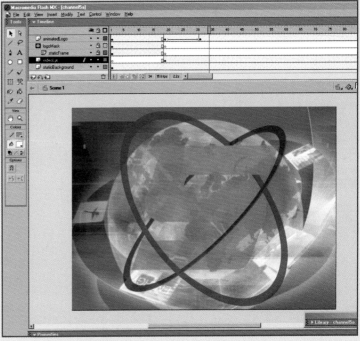

Of course, our News program probably already has a standard logo and title graphic.

The globe outline was rendered to SWF format in outline mode from 3DS MAX, then imported as a graphic symbol in Flash MX. Again, I want to emphasize that you do not have to use 3DS MAX to create this effect. This type of outline render is easily created from standalone packages such as Swift 3D or Plasma, using freely available models.

The timeline was adjusted to have the 'Channel 5 News' title display above the video while the animated logo in the introduction fades to zero opacity.

The large version of the logo grabs attention at the beginning of the animation. The smaller version at the top of the animation maintains visibility of the logo for branding purposes. Clients like branding!

After the opening, I wanted the text 'AROUND THE WORLD' to fly in letter by letter. We know what that took in the days of Flash 5. With Flash MX, the process of breaking text apart and distributing to layers is just too easy.

The numbers 0-60 flash by one frame at a time to fill out the 'Around the World in 60 Seconds' theme. With some additional motion graphics and a fast fade to white at the end, the intro is pretty much complete.

Below are images illustrating some of the added vector animation. Compositing the vector animation on top of the video produces a very crisp result free of compression artifacts. You can apply your imagination to come up with numerous variations of this example using either CG animations or your camcorder.

When exported to SWF, the final intro animation was 8 seconds in length at 1.28MB. The Compress movie option was checked on export. File size was 1.35MB without this option. This file size includes some background music. This SWF is available for download from www.friendsofED.com.

I compressed the original six-second QuickTime video with Cleaner and the Sorenson-2 codec. File size for a comparable-quality movie was 980K for a 240x180 window. The big problem with the QuickTime video was compression artifacts with the text animation and other motion graphics on top of the 3D animation.

With Flash MX (and Sorenson Squeeze), the animation was extended to 8 seconds with more motion graphics, audio, *and* a window size of 480x360. This illustrates the power of combining compressed video with vector motion graphics in Flash MX.

How ace are buildings?

The next example is a continuation of this theme. The application is different as the example is taken from the field of architectural visualization. In previous examples, embedded video was played without delay. This example illustrates how some light ActionScript can be employed to control video playback. The video will be halted on occasion to emphasize certain points with background narration. This type of presentation is easily accomplished by importing the video into a movie clip symbol.

Basic ActionScript can be used to control video playback, simple functions such as `stop`, `play` work with video as well as any other movie clips. Although I used CG animations for this example, the process illustrated in this deconstruction applies to a wide variety of animations, including those you may record on your own.

Available to download from www.friendsofED.com is an FLA by Kristian Besley from our book Macromedia Flash MX Video (ISBN: 1-903450-85-3). It is a simple video controller, and demonstrates amiably just how simple video control is with ActionScript in Flash MX.

A few months before the release of Flash MX, I was asked to participate in a proposal. The goal of the project was to illustrate how video and Shockwave 3D could be used for fly-throughs and interactive online visualization of multi-purpose buildings. The current rage in real estate is multi-purpose buildings. These buildings are constructed to cater to tenants, businesses requiring office space, and retailers. In a typical setting, the first one or two floors are devoted to retail. The middle section of the building is office space. The upper section of the building is living space. The business proposal was a combination of online multimedia, integrated with e-commerce. The goal is to illustrate the property relative to its surroundings, then allow the viewer to interact with the particular type of space that interests them. In the multimedia area, viewers could see a video fly-through to visualize the building and its surrounding location. This could be done in a pre- or post-construction environment. In the former case, interactive multimedia could be used to present the building concept to investors. In the latter case, the goal is to attract tenants.

An interactive Shockwave 3D presentation would allow visitors to preview the specific type of living, office, or retail space that suited their interest. My business partner wanted a video to illustrate how the technology would work at a very high level. The original presentation had a mix of text animation, 3D motion graphics, background music, and narration. The initial version was provided on CD at 640x480. After Flash MX was released, I wanted to re-create the animation, separating motion graphics that were best done in raster as video elements. This is an extension of the idea discussed in the previous example, with the goal of creating a broadband presentation that could be viewed online.

The presentation is divided into four sections — preloading animation, video fly-through, Shockwave 3D simulation, and benefits summary. The preloader is designed for an average DSL connection. It consists of some simple text animation that describes the goals of the presentation. The preloader hides the load time while providing some useful information to the viewer. It's a step up from a 'loading' bar

The video fly-through sequence is a 3DS MAX animation of a city scene. The animation illustrates the location of a particular building relative to the surroundings. I wanted to emphasize the ability to reproduce realistic textures and even view the interior of the building. These features are emphasized both in narration and supporting vector animation overlaid onto the video.

The following screen shots illustrate several key points in the fly-through, including a couple of the stop-motion frames.

First is one of the stop-motion frames. This frame appears less than a second into the fly-through. The camera freezes as the narration discusses isolation of the building of interest relative to the surroundings. In Flash MX, this is accomplished by overlaying a wireframe animation on top of the video frame.

Wireframe animations were created with a beta version of Discreet's Plasma. The rendered SWF file was imported into Flash MX for hand optimization and additional animation.

The camera has moved between the two buildings to the right and is just starting a bank to the left. With this camera path, the building of interest is viewed both from the side and the front.

Here we get the first glimpse of the building of interest from a front view. The camera moves closer until the entry into the building is framed. That is the next stop frame of the Flash movie, at which point another wireframe vector animation is overlaid onto the static video frame. We do not pay any additional file size for stopping the video at any point in time. The vector animation is very lightweight, so this approach is effective in terms of impact, yet more efficient than a pure video format in terms of file size.

A notable feature of the texturing is the grime and streaking on the building glass. This is consistent with what we might expect to see in a downtown area. There are no cars and no people in this video. That's for another time and another animation.

One of the building doors opens, then the camera moves into the interior. The material for the door glass employs both raytraced reflections and refractions.

The reflections are easy to see. The amount of refraction is too much for a still image, but just right to draw attention to the effect during an animation. One of the advantages of refraction is that it naturally 'breaks up' the image, hiding some of the compression artifacts. During a fly-through, it may be more difficult to tell the difference between a refractive effect and a compression effect.

After the fly-through animation, the presentation proceeds to the second stage which is interactive CG. Shockwave 3D is proposed in this section. The goal of the video is to simulate how the interactive process might work in an online environment. This begins with an illustration of how realistic textures are added to a low-polygon model of the building. The combination of low-polygon geometry and highly compressed geometry and textures allows building detail to be customized to a variety of bandwidth scenarios.

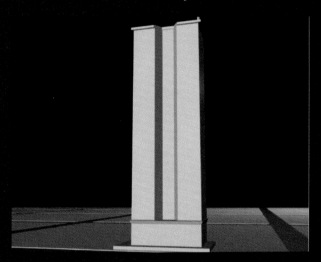

This shows the low-polygon model of the building in isolation. There is no texturing at this stage.

Here texturing has been applied to the building geometry. In the video fly-through section, we saw additional objects such as doors and a chandelier. Since the doors, floor/ceiling tile, chandelier and other interior items are separate 3D objects, they are not shown in this illustration.

Suite and to the point

Of course, the whole purpose of Shockwave 3D is to add interactivity, so the next part of the animation simulates an interactive visualization. There isn't much benefit from showing the building exterior unless you can interactively view the part of the interior that is of interest. Let's suppose our viewer is a real high roller, who is interested in the penthouse suite.

In the next part of the animation, the entertainment area of the penthouse suite is animated with another camera fly-through. The Flash animation is augmented with simulated navigation controls, illustrating how a viewer might navigate through the room.

The entertainment area is very lavish with a pool, hot tub, bar, and wall-mounted sound system and television. Since this animation was created in a CG environment, we have control over many items that will affect compression. Simple colors are used as opposed to detailed wall patterns (only one wall has a pattern). Ideally, I would have liked to use soft shadows to reduce the contrast in areas where shadows were present. Time constraints did not allow this addition, so I compensated by downsizing the video. Instead of a 320x240 window, the video was rendered at 240x180.

Raytraced reflections and refractions were used for the water material. As before, the refraction 'breaks up' the pool water, helping hide some of the compression artifacts.

After simulating navigation through the room, the ability of Shockwave 3D to heavily compress geometry and textures, then render in real-time is illustrated by showing the difference between a wireframe and textured version of the scene.

The image was rendered to a PNG file with alpha channel so that it could be overlaid on any background. In fact, this symbol is used twice in Flash – once in the animation and once in the preloader.

Based on the storyboard, narration was recorded and a background music track was chosen. To complete the assets for the animation, a vector 3D animation was created for the low-polygon 3D building. Two vector wireframe renders were created to overlay onto the stop-frames in the first video. These renders were broken apart, then hand-optimized in Flash. Both wireframe renders were converted to animations. These animated symbols are placed on top of the video layer while the video is halted in ActionScript. After the animation and corresponding narration is finished, the wireframe animations are deleted from the timeline and ActionScript is used to restart the video sequence.

Along with the static frames (PNG files), this completes all the assets for the Flash movie. The two embedded videos were 35MB (320x240) and 11MB (240x180) in size. The videos were used at their native size and frame rate in the Flash movie, so there are no file size gains from additional downsizing the video.

Who lives in a house like this?

The next step is to incorporate all the assets into the Flash movie. Other than the embedded video, this is nothing different than what you have probably done in the past – there's not a great deal of ActionScripting - the following screen shots illustrate some key points during the animation. You could watch the presentation while reading this – it's available for download as `aretectual.swf` from www.friendsofed.com.

The first shot is from the preloader animation, the presentation is simple and clean with a relaxed flow to the motion graphics. The preloader animation sets the stage for the presentation, conveys some useful information, and hides the download time for a DSL or higher connection.

Notice how the PNG file containing the wireframe render illustrated above is re-used in Flash MX.

After the opening, the presentation proceeds to the city fly-through animation. You can see the wireframe overlay to identify the building of interest in this animation. The wireframe appears top-to-bottom with a simple mask.

Sometimes, you will be able to reduce file size from a wireframe vector render by applying curve optimization in Flash.

Halting, then restarting the video is accomplished with some very basic ActionScript.

The wireframe overlay at this stage is a more sophisticated animation, illustrating the types of texturing that can be applied to the building. The wireframe animation is more economical to create in Flash's native vector mode. It would be very difficult to compress in a video format.

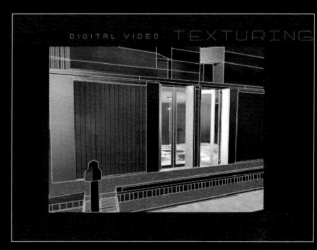

We now fly-through into the building interior. This is very similar to the static image presented earlier in the chapter. Now, it's integrated into Flash MX as video. The building video is displayed with compression applied in Flash MX. The break-up you see in the building interior on the left side is from refraction through the door glass. It is not a compression artifact. In fact, it is pretty difficult to see any compression artifacts at this stage.

You can see that a high level of quality is used in the animation.

The next stage of the animation simulates how Shockwave 3D would be applied to this project, you can see part of the animation illustrating how the building is sectioned into retail, office, and living space.

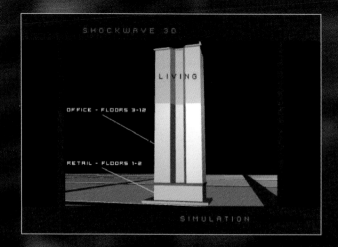

The next sequence, shows a simulation of the viewer selecting the penthouse suite. These animations are easily accomplished directly in Flash.

In a previous screen shot, you saw a large, static image of the opening animation for the penthouse suite simulated navigation. This is the actual video incorporated into Flash MX, along with simulated navigation controls.

Most of the compression artifacts along the walls are at the outlines from the spotlights. They are less evident at the 240x180 window size.

The camera circles around to show the back part of the room. The navigation controls and surrounding graphics are kept simple so as not to distract from the room visualization. Besides the video, the only motion in this sequence is the simulated navigation controls. They change in coordination with the camera angle. You may be able to see that the textured wall compresses much worse than the plain wall. I wanted to illustrate the difference in this example. This is a big advantage of creating animations in a 3D software package – the ability to control many of the factors that contribute to good video compression.

Finally, a cross-fade is used between a wireframe and fully textured frame to illustrate how Shockwave 3D renders highly compressed geometry and textures in real-time. This final animation sets the stage for the presentation summary. The summary section is nothing more than simple text animation.

The cross-fade is performed as a tween in Flash, not done in video. Only use video when it is absolutely necessary.

What have we learnt?

Well, that's a nice walk-through of the presentation, but the big question is file size. In the past, I would have only considered this type of animation to be suitable for a CD-based presentation. Working with simulated video sequences in Flash 5 would have been a complete headache, given the nature of the texturing and motion graphics in these videos. Flash MX will completely change any prior concept you have of working with sophisticated raster animation in the Flash environment.

As with the previous example, the motion graphics and texturing present substantial compression challenges. The challenge is complicated by the stop-frames. Since video playback is halted twice during the presentation, the video must be very high quality. Crisp vector animations overlay the video, so the quality of the two must be comparable. This is not a good omen for small file sizes.

For this example, I wanted to illustrate what was possible with the standard Spark codec that ships with Flash MX. Each video took four attempts to obtain a good balance between file size and quality. The entire animation (not counting preloading) is over ninety seconds at 480x360x15fps. Sound was exported as stereo MP3, 64 kbps. Recall that the sound includes both background music and narration. Total file size was 3.4MB.

In my view, this was a pretty astounding result, especially for a 90-second, video-intense animation. As I mentioned earlier, there was no file size benefit from downsizing the videos after importing into Flash MX. Each video was embedded in Flash at its native size and frame rate. The entire movie contained over 60MB of assets in raw form (images and sound). Every one of the bitmap assets was very difficult to compress given the quality restrictions.

To further give you an idea of the magnitude of this result, the initial city fly-through animation was compressed with Cleaner/Sorenson-3. The result was just over 3MB for a high-quality version and 2.4MB for a medium-quality version that was not quite as good as the compressed version in the Flash movie. This was only a 13-second animation at 320x240. To extend the animation to over ninety seconds, at a larger window size, with another video, and sound, yet maintain comparable file size was a very significant result. If anything, this example should be a testament to the power of combining vector and raster animation in Flash MX.

Closing

The video capabilities of Flash MX have opened up a complete new range of applications for my business — things I would never have dreamed of doing in Flash 5. Although we all have our own opinions, mine is that video is the top new feature in Flash MX. But then, what did you expect me to say? The ability to composite vector and raster animation in the same environment, then output to SWF format opens up many new capabilities that are not possible when working with a pure video format. The ability to add interactivity to animations with embedded video gives Flash MX a substantial advantage over competing video environments. When combined with the generally fast acceptance of new versions of the plugin, I really believe Flash MX will stimulate the creation of a new generation of interactive applications in online education and instruction.

I hope you enjoyed these three examples of what I'm doing with Flash MX. Whether you are a CG animator or videographer, the same workflow and thinking process applies to embedded video in Flash MX. I hope these examples engage your creative imagination and I look forward to what readers of this book will create with Flash MX.